Many books about the Song of Songs approach its message too broadly, ultimately proving to be unhelpful or resulting in confusion. *Song of Songs for Singles*, however, leads the reader to view the Song of Songs through the lens of seeing God's design for the daughters of Jerusalem. God's gentle provision and care give hope to the next generation of believers who walk in the way of the Lord. In a broken world, this book shines brightly as it plainly speaks of sex and intimacy as God intended. Tim and Angela tastefully encourage the older generation to invest in the younger, shaping their minds and affections in accordance with God's Word. With courage and wit, the authors address the dangerous perspectives of sex in our day, and they call the believer to find hope, identity, beauty, and life in Christ alone.

—Sam Choi
Pastor, Prior Lake Baptist Church, Prior Lake, Minnesota

An ancient Jewish sage claimed, "No one under the age of 30 should read the Song of Songs." Gratefully, Tim and Angela do not follow his poor advice. The reason they do not follow this unwise counsel is because they recognize what is often missed—that the wisdom of the Song of Songs is not only written to married couples who are encouraged to enjoy marriage intimacy now but also to singles who can look forward to experiencing intimacy within their marriage. Tim and Angela provide a desperately needed resource for believing singles in today's Christian world. As a single follower of Jesus, if you want to learn to navigate sexuality wisely, this book is a good starting place.

—Mark McGinniss
Assistant Seminary Dean,
Professor of Old Testament Literature, Language and Exegesis,
Baptist Bible Seminary, Clarks Summit, Pennsylvania

Sex is a topic many talk about but rarely from a biblical perspective. Tim and Angela address issues many singles wonder about and discuss but from a thoroughly biblical worldview. I have often thought that if the church does not teach the next generation about sex, young people will look for answers from somewhere else. Song of Songs for Singles will be a tremendous help and encouragement to all who read it. By walking the reader through the Song of Solomon and making practical application of it, Tim and Angela help equip the next generation to glorify God through their relationships.

—Dr. Jim Tillotson
President, Faith Baptist Bible College & Theological Seminary

Judaism and Christianity have been guilty of misconstruing the Song of Songs for centuries. By forbidding it from being read until an appropriate age or mystifying and spiritualizing its message, scholars have left Bible readers wondering how the book applies to the believer's life. Rooted in sound exegesis, Song of Songs for Singles unpacks the Song of Songs in a sound and practical manner. In a day and age when so many Christians lack biblical knowledge and wisdom regarding sex and intimacy, this book provides guidance that is both desperately needed and extremely helpful.

—Dr. Patrick Odle
President, Baptist Mid-Missions

Song of Songs
for singles

AND MARRIED PEOPLE TOO

LESSONS ON LOVE
FROM KING SOLOMON

FAITH
PUBLICATIONS

ISBN: 978-1-960820-00-6 (paperback)
ISBN: 978-1-960820-01-3 (digital)

Library of Congress Control Number: 2023907186

While the stories in this book are true, some of the names and identifying information have been changed to protect the privacy of the individuals.

First printing edition 2023

Faith Publications
1900 NW 4th St.
Ankeny, IA. 50023
faith.edu/publications

www.songofsongsforsingles.com

Song of Songs for Singles
and Married People Too:
Lessons on Love from King Solomon

Front cover image and book design by Lance Young with Higher Rock Creative Studio

Interior design by Lance Young with Higher Rock Creative Studio

THIS BOOK IS DEDICATED TO

our children—Josiah, Zachariah, Daniel, Judah, and Aliza.

We love you and wrote this book for you, praying that you will love successfully.

TABLE OF CONTENTS

Preface   9

Acknowledgments   13

Introduction   15

CH. 1
The Song of Solomon Is a Song (of All Songs) *(1:1–4)*   29

CH. 2
Ignorance Is Bliss; Knowledge Is Power *(1:1–4)*   47

CH. 3
Is Beauty in the Eye of the Beholder? *(1:5–11)*   57

CH. 4
Do Not Disturb *(2:7; 3:5; 8:4)*   79

CH. 5
Awakening The Senses *(1:12—2:7)*   97

CH. 6
Finding Your Happily Ever After *(2:8–17)*   109

CH. 7
Love Made Me Do It *(3:1–5)*   125

CH. 8
I Now Pronounce You Husband and Wife! (Now What?) *(3:6—5:1)*   141

CH. 9
Falling Out of Love Is Just Another Excuse *(5:2—6:3)*   157

CH. 10
Love and War: It's All Fair, Right? *(6:4—7:10)*   171

CH. 11
You Can Recreate the Garden of Eden *(7:11—8:4)*   189

CH. 12
Beginning Love Correctly, Part 1 *(8:5–10)* **203**

CH. 13
Beginning Love Correctly, Part 2 *(8:11–14)* **227**

CH. 14
Are Things Different Now? **239**

Appendix: The Song of Songs **257**

Scripture Index **267**

PREFACE

I (Tim) grew up in New York, while Angela was raised primarily in Iowa. God graciously allowed both of us to grow up in Christian homes. We placed our faith in Jesus at young ages and were baptized shortly thereafter. Neither of us dated in high school. We were regularly encouraged to live pure lives for the glory of God. Nevertheless, both of us were engaged to someone else in college. Years after those engagements ended, we met each other and were married in less than a year. God has now blessed us with five children—four sons and one daughter. Our journey is a good journey, but it has had some bumps. We were technically virgins on our wedding day, but we had struggled to uphold God's standard of purity.

My most memorable moments in the Song of Songs were as a youth writing some of the verses on letters and anonymously mailing them to the girls at church camp. The Song was a joke to me; I treated it as profane literature rather than the Word of God. As I matured, I desired to study the Song but never had an opportunity. Later, that opening arose during my doctoral program, when I learned that one of my professors, Mark McGinniss, had written his dissertation on the Song of Songs. He suggested I write a paper on an Old Testament theology of sexual arousal from the Song of Songs for one of my classes, and thus began my study of the Song. As I studied the Song and talked to Angela about it, God equipped us to address the sexual dysfunction in our relationship. We knew there were problems in our relationship, but we didn't know what exactly was wrong or how to fix it. Fixing the dysfunction took several years. Sin was destroying the intimacy that God desired for us to enjoy—sin that had started before we knew each other. Sin that was ignored, buried, and never confessed. Sin that continued into our marriage. We were deceived by the world's lies and, therefore, failed to enjoy intimacy the way God designed it. While studying the Song of Songs, we recognized and confessed sin. Our repentance led to forgiveness and healing in our relationship.

During this study, I first learned about the adjuration refrain: "Do not stir up; do not even awaken love, until it pleases" (Song 2:7; 3:5; 8:4). As I reflected upon this exhortation, the sexual dysfunction in our marriage, unconfessed sin, and the world's lies, I became convinced that singles needed to hear the message of the Song of Songs. I began talking to friends and pastors about it. As I explained our premarital struggle for purity, I quickly learned our struggle was far too common. As I discussed our sexual dysfunction, I learned that this struggle is also common. Angela and I have, therefore, become even more convinced that the church needs to teach singles about the Song of Songs.

As we began speaking and teaching the Song, we found the resounding sentiment surprisingly positive. Many believers have ignorantly feasted on the world's instruction concerning intimacy but have been left starving. Relationally famished believers crave God's instruction concerning relationships, marriage, and intimacy. We pray that the next generation has more mature memories of the Song of Songs than sending anonymous letters to girls at church camp.

INTENDED AUDIENCE

All ages can learn something from the Song. When our daughter was four years old, I was watching a movie with her and began reflecting upon the idea of romance that our culture was teaching her through that movie. I began thinking, "How young is too young? If the world is teaching my daughter what love is like when she is four, shouldn't

I be teaching her what the Bible says when she is four?" As a result, I decided to do a four-part series on "friends" from the Song of Songs for our K–6 children's ministry which I lead. I read the adjuration refrain to the children each night. All ages—even the very young—can learn something from the Song of Songs.

While the Song has a message for all audiences, our book is not written for children but for high schoolers and above. While the Song is primarily directed to single, marriageable ladies, it contains a message for young men as well. As we wrote *Song of Songs for Singles*, we imagined what we would approve of our young teenage son reading. Writing from this perspective has obvious disadvantages. For example, we will not answer some questions because to do so could unintentionally awaken the sleeping desires of the innocent. Those desires need to sleep (Song 2:7; 3:5; 8:4).

If you are older or already sexually experienced, you may be reading along and be thinking, "Yeah, but what about such-and-such?" The Word of God has answers for all of your questions, but we will not answer them here. Our book presents a picture of what intimacy is supposed to be more than it is a digression into the mess. The Song of Songs teaches the truth concerning intimacy so that you will be able to identify its counterfeits. Too often we Christians spend so much time examining the counterfeit that we forget what the genuine looks like. Just as a bank teller learns to discern counterfeit currency by studying the genuine, so also will the Song cultivate your affections for the genuine, thus preparing you to identify the counterfeit. Perhaps you have transgressed God's boundaries concerning intimacy. The Song encourages you to pursue purity going forward and gives guidance on how to successfully maintain purity.

We are glad you are reading this book, and we do believe you can truly benefit from it. Some will think we are being too descriptive. Others will wish we were more descriptive. As we will argue in chapter two, we do not believe the problem is too little information but, rather, too much. Talk to your parents or mentor if you want more information. It may be appropriate for you to get more. But trust your parents/mentors! If they say you do not need any more information right now, believe them and trust their judgment. When you are tempted to find more information through other sources, say no! This temptation is your flesh. Mortify the flesh (Col 3:5). Kill that desire. Set your mind on things above (3:2) and exhibit the virtues of the new man (3:12).

ACKNOWLEDGMENTS

Many people assisted us in the publication of this book. First, Mark McGinniss introduced us to the Song of Songs, sharpened our interpretation of the Song, and encouraged us to write on the Song. Many colleagues, pastors, friends, and family also sharpened our thinking and encouraged our hearts. Andy Stearns and Charlie Carter, my (Tim's) colleagues on the Thinklings podcast, were a sounding board on and off the air for the last several years. I tell my children that Doug Brown is my Gandalf. My wise colleague, mentor, and friend who tempers, directs, and encourages me. Everybody needs a Gandalf in their life, and I am grateful for him. Several people donated funds to make this publication possible. Thank you for your generosity. Thank you to the administration of Faith Baptist Bible College & Theological Seminary, who supported our publishing efforts. Finally, we thank the college students who have pushed us to think about how the biblical teaching of the Song of Songs confronts the modern believer in Jesus the Messiah.

INTRODUCTION

SONG OF SONGS FOR SINGLES

Song of Songs teaches wisdom concerning intimacy. This small book of the Bible was not an afterthought but one of the sixty-six divinely inspired books that God intentionally placed in the Bible. It is one of the most overlooked, misunderstood, abused, misinterpreted, and ignored books of the Bible. Because Song of Songs concerns intimacy, it is often argued that the Song is for married couples only. I (Tim) was talking to a friend and mentioned writing this book, *Song of Songs for Singles*. The friend chuckled and said, "That should be an easy book to write! All you need is a nice cover and a bunch of blank pages." His joke reflects the sentiment of most people. Singles should not read the Song, and the Song does not apply to them. Nothing could be further from the truth. Song of Songs teaches everyone wisdom concerning intimacy.

Some singles themselves have concluded that the Song of Songs is irrelevant to them. One college student remarked, "That is one of those books that I always skip over because I don't know what to do with it." Eric Demeter writes, "[Singles] need holistic teaching on how to develop a healthy Christian sexual ethic [set of moral principles] based on Scripture."[1] Demeter is correct, but he, along with most authors of Christian dating books, writes with an apparent ignorance of the Song of Songs. These authors argue for a specific ethic based more upon experience, statistics, and anecdotal (based on reports or observations) wisdom than the Word of God. God gave the Song to teach a sexual

---

1   Eric Demeter, *How Should a Christian Date? It's Not as Complicated as You Think* (Chicago: Moody, 2021), 136–37.

ethic, and singles need to study it so they know what God says concerning relationships, love, marriage, and intimacy.

READING THE SONG OF SONGS

The Song is wisdom literature, which means it is better studied than merely read. After studying a passage, you can find value just reading it. But simply reading through the text will likely leave you scratching your head. Wise men of old wrote in riddles to encourage thinking. The Proverbs of Solomon were written to help a person "understand a proverb and an enigma, the words of the wise and their riddles" (Prov 1:6). Sages wrote in a way that made the reader think. One young man sat in my office, where we began a study of Song 2:8–17. After studying it for a bit, the young man said, "I didn't understand any of this just reading it. It makes sense now." You will need to think about the Song. Angela and I pray this book will guide you.

The Song teaches not only a young, naïve reader but also an older, experienced reader by using veiled figures of speech that both reveal truth and conceal truth. A young, naïve audience will not understand the true meaning of some of the figures of speech, while an older, more experienced audience can be exhorted and instructed by them.

The Song can shape the reader's affections by describing Edenic (unspoiled, idyllic) love through two characters—the ideal husband and the ideal wife. Young men should seek to marry a woman like the "Song of Songs wife." Young women should seek to marry a man like the "Song of Songs husband." Unfortunately, we don't live in the Garden of Eden anymore. You are not a sinless Adam/Eve, and you will not marry a sinless Eve/Adam. You live in a real world with real sin and real hurt. The Song presents the ideal, but it also teaches the reader how to live in the real; that is, in a broken, sin-filled world.

The Song of Songs addresses singles—particularly women. Throughout the Song, Solomon instructs the "daughters of Jerusalem" (Song 1:5; 2:7; 3:5, 10; 5:8, 16; 8:4), who are single females. The end of Song 1:3 states, "Therefore the virgins love you." These women are of marriageable age, but still unmarried (cf. Gen 24:43; Isa 7:14). They are sexually pure, inexperienced, and waiting to be married. These virgins are the "daughters of Jerusalem," who appear throughout the Song. These virgins love the husband of the Song of Songs because he is the type of guy they should want to marry. He represents a godly, ideal man. If the Song is truly a book that only married people should read, why do single, marriageable girls find such a prominent place in the book? Why does the female lover regularly exhort the daughters of Jerusalem (Song 2:7; 3:5, 10; 5:8, 16; 8:4)? Why do the virgins love the husband of the Song (1:3)? The church has failed Christian singles, particularly young women, by telling them not to read or study this biblical book and has thus denied them biblical instruction concerning friendship, love, marriage, and intimacy.

ROLE OF PARENTS AND CHURCH LEADERS

God has blessed us with five children. Like most parents, we want the very best for our children. We pray they grow in the fear of the Lord,

 DIGGING DEEPER

The idea that Song of Songs is *primarily* written to single young ladies is not a new interpretation. Sparks explains, "The Song of Songs originated as a wisdom composition, as a collection of love songs edited to teach young Jewish women propriety in matters of love and sex," Kenton Sparks, "The Song of Songs: Wisdom for Young Jewish Women," *CBQ* 70, no. 2 (April 2008): 278. O'Donnell similarly states, "The primary target audience is the unmarried, specifically single young women, 'the daughters of Jerusalem,'" Douglas Sean O'Donnell, *The Song of Solomon: An Invitation to Intimacy*, Preaching the Word (Wheaton IL: Crossway Books, 2012), 23.

mature, marry, and enjoy intimacy as a gift from God (Eccl 3:13). If God calls any of them to a life of singleness, we pray they wholly devote their lives to the ministry of the Lord and glorify Him with their calling (1 Cor 7:32). Singles who devote their lives in service to God recognize their unique calling to serve the Lord (7:32–35). No matter what God has planned for our children, they can learn what God teaches concerning intimacy from the Song of Songs.

Parents are the primary instructors in a youth's life (Deut 6:6–9; Prov 1:8). If you are a parent, we encourage you to read this book and teach the Song of Songs to your children. While you could give this book to your child to read alone, as a parent, you cannot be replaced. Your child needs you. In fact, Song 8:2 presents the mother teaching her daughter about intimacy. Nevertheless, some parents are hesitant. Teaching about intimacy can be awkward, embarrassing, and uncomfortable for both parents and children. Furthermore, many Christian parents have themselves failed sexually and, therefore, feel disqualified to instruct their children.

The issues concerning intimacy are too multifaceted and varied to be addressed in a single book. *Song of Songs for Singles* can give you confidence in what the Word of God teaches concerning intimacy regardless of any mistakes in your past. Let the Word of God teach your child; you are simply God's instrument for instruction. Let God use your mistakes for His glory. We believers serve a merciful God who is ready to forgive. Humble yourself, repent of your sin, be cleansed, and walk in newness of life. If you need help, Jesus equipped His church with pastors who can guide you by the Word of God. Commit to attend a Bible preaching church. After dealing with your own sin, you will be better equipped to guide your child into Christian maturity. This book is not enough. Your son/daughter needs you. If you do not teach your child about intimacy, someone else will, and it is likely that someone else is already teaching your child.

Our fallen world has created countless broken homes where young people mature without godly parents to guide them in the way of truth. However, God ordained not only the family but also the church to help guide people into Christian maturity. If you are single, get involved in a church that preaches the Bible, and find a mentor. Seek a godly Christian of the same gender who can guide you through the journey of life. Contrary to popular belief, your love life is other people's business (more on this later). The people close to you will be affected by the decisions you make. Humble yourself and draw close to both your physical family (if possible) and your church family. Submit to the biblical authorities God has placed in your life, because this book cannot replace personal counsel from those authorities. We pray our book serves as a supplement to guide you in making wise decisions based upon the Word of God.

> Your love life is other people's business.

SEX IS A BIG DEAL

Sex is a big deal. You've probably heard this message on multiple occasions, but it bears repeating because it is true. If you mess up sexually, you could contract a sexually transmitted disease, get someone pregnant (or get pregnant), burden yourself with shame and guilt, destroy your walk with the Lord, destroy the other person's walk with the Lord, hurt the ones who love you, heap financial burdens on yourself and/or others, create destructive habits, and a host of other maladies. Sex really is a big deal.

Sex is also a big deal because it is a very powerful desire. The biblical book of Proverbs warns young men how the desires for money and sex can destroy them. Multiple times the wise father admonishes his son to avoid immorality (Prov 2:16–19; 5:1–20; 6:20–35; 7:5–27; 9:13–18). The sage (wise man) explains that the one who walks on the path of immorality walks on a path that leads to death (2:19–20). Immorality is more than an intimate encounter; it represents a definition of life, and the end of that path is death (9:18). You see, sex really is a big deal.

SEX ISN'T A BIG DEAL

Sex is a big deal, but how big of a deal is it really? It certainly feels like a big deal! The world claims that sex is a really big deal, in fact, the epitome (embodiment) of happiness. The desires within you probably communicate the same message. The world argues that you are a sexual being, and if you haven't had sex yet, you haven't even lived. To the world, sex is a REALLY big deal. But it is not just the world that promotes this message: it is the world and the flesh and the devil. They communicate that sex equals happiness and that if you haven't experienced it, you cannot be happy.

This equation of happiness with sexuality has caused many of the world's ills. If sex makes a person happy, then the sooner someone enjoys it, the better. As a result, the world has encouraged children to discover themselves sexually. The Song teaches, however, that a person should not prematurely awaken love (Song 2:7; 3:5; 8:4). People of the world claim that if sex makes someone happy, that person should enjoy it as much as possible and with whomever he/she desires. Of course, they say, sexual expression must only be fulfilled between consenting individuals. But, as they see it, if the experience is consensual, it is normal and good. As a result, sexual expression that is selfish, contrary to nature, and dangerous has been not only deemed good but also celebrated, leaving broken and confused people in its wake.

Furthermore, the world wants to silence people who say that sexual desire should be repressed. After all, they are infringing on others' happiness. How dare they! This includes the purity movement of the last generation. Many pastors and speakers encouraged young people to refrain from sex until marriage. Now that these young people are adults, many of them are angry. They think these pastors and speakers ruined some of the best years of their lives that they could have spent in sexual expression and, thus, happiness.

The world's view that sex equals happiness is a myth, but a popular one. Enlightenment philosophers argued that the goal of human existence is to be happy. Sigmund Freud then applied this goal to sex.[2] The myth seemed rather believable; after all, God made sex enjoyable (Song 5:1). We don't intend to diminish the reality of your feelings or experiences. Sex may be a very important thing to you. It certainly feels like a really big deal. Your feelings and desires are real, but are they true? If sex makes us humans happy, our sexualized world should be in a constant state of euphoria. But very few people are happy. The world has taken something good and enjoyable that God created and twisted it.

Freud's research has been debunked multiple times over. Sex is certainly not the source of happiness; it will never satisfy; it is a lousy god. Purity pastors and speakers encouraged young people to wait until they were married, then they could have all the sex they wanted, and it would be great! I applaud them for their emphasis on self-denial before marriage, but what about self-denial after marriage? Many young

---

2   Carl R. Trueman, *The Rise and Triumph of the Modern Self: Cultural Amnesia, Expressive Individualism, and the Road to Sexual Revolution* (Wheaton, IL: Crossway, 2020), 203–6.

people who waited for marriage became disillusioned and unhappy because marital sex did not satisfy them the way they thought it would. Marital sex is certainly not the source of happiness; it will never satisfy; it is a lousy god.

Sex really isn't a big deal. Jesus lived a celibate life. Paul, similarly, lived a celibate life (1 Cor 7:7), and Paul even encouraged others to remain celibate so they could attend to the things of the Lord (7:32). Contrary to the world's message, a person can live a fulfilled and happy life as a celibate individual who is devoted to "the things of the Lord."

Sex really isn't a big deal. The family, however, is a big deal. God ordered the world a certain way, and the family is an important part of that order. Ancient cultures recognized the importance of the family and created laws to protect the family. The Old Testament Law similarly valued the family and regulated sex in a way that would protect the family (Deut 5:6–21; 22:13–30; 24:1–5; 25:5–12). Some of these laws seem odd to us today, but they were instituted because God valued the family more than He valued a person's sexual inclinations. In His day, Jesus taught the Pharisees the permanence of marriage, particularly in relationship to sexuality (Matt 19:1–12). Jesus' instruction on this issue led the disciples to conclude, "It is better not to marry." But Jesus' high standard for marriage remained consistent with Old Testament teaching concerning marriage and divorce that protected the family.

Finally, sex really isn't a big deal. But a person's relationship with God is a big deal. Ecclesiastes 7:20 teaches that there is not a righteous man on earth who does good and does not sin. That includes you. You are a sinner, and your sin makes God angry (Isa 13:9). One day God "will punish the world for its evil," and He will do that by making "mankind more rare than fine gold" (13:11–12). As sinners, you and I justly deserve God's wrath. The prophet Isaiah, a godly man, cried out before the presence of God, "Woe is me! Because I am destroyed! For I am a man of unclean lips, . . . and my eyes have seen the King, the Lord of armies" (6:5). Even this godly man in the presence of the perfect God deserved to die. Similarly, you and I deserve death.

The wrath of God is a concept lost on modern sensibilities. We don't like thinking about an angry God, much less one that is all-powerful, all-knowing, and all-present. Nonetheless, the God who created this world (Isa 40:26–28) and sustains your life (42:5) is the God who cannot learn anything because He already knows everything (40:13–14), and that includes everything about you: "You know my sitting down and my rising up; you understand my thought from afar" (Ps 139:2). And this God who knows everything about you, who created the world and sustains your life, is angry with you because of your sin. And you are concerned about . . . sex? You see, sex really isn't a big deal.

Two categories of people exist in this world, the ones who have everlasting life, and the ones who will not see life because "the wrath of God abides" on them (John 3:36). If you have never confessed your sin to God and believed in His plan of salvation, then the wrath of God abides on you. The most important decision you need to make is not whom you will marry, but whom you will believe. Jesus bled on the cross so you can be reconciled to God and have peace with Him (Rom 3:24–25). The Holy Spirit indwells the one who believes in Jesus for salvation, and He empowers that believer to walk in the Spirit and not fulfill the lust of the flesh (Rom 8:1–11). This redeemed and Spirit-indwelled believer is dead to self, but alive to God (i.e., a living sacrifice, Rom 12:1).

Belief is the foundation of the Christian life. Belief is the foundation of a Christian sexual ethic too. Further, belief in Jesus is a wholehearted thing. You cannot experiment or try it. You must be "all-in." James wrote, "Do you not know that friendship with the world is hostility toward God"

(Jas 4:4). Solomon similarly wrote, "The fear of the Lord is the beginning of wisdom" (Prov 1:7). The Song of Songs teaches a sexual ethic rooted in the fear of the Lord. This fear of the Lord kind of sexual ethic rejects the world's sexual ethic. When the world, the flesh, and the devil tempt the Christian with real desires and feelings, the fear of the Lord instructs the believer to believe in the truth of God's Word. Without belief, people find the sexual ethic in the Song foolish, for "the unspiritual man [unbeliever] does not receive the things from the Spirit of God, because they are foolishness to him" (1 Cor 2:14). Furthermore, if you as a Christian do not believe your life is a living sacrifice, then the Song of Songs will not make a lot of sense to you. As you begin this study, I encourage you to believe. Cast your sexuality before the Lord and say, "God, whatever you say I should do, that is what I will do." Recognize that your life is a living sacrifice and do not live for your pleasure, but for God's glory. Sex will never make you happy; it really isn't a big deal.

STRUCTURE OF THIS BOOK

Solomon wrote Song of Songs as a sage. Wise men like Solomon spoke in enigmas (something hard to understand) and riddles. Because of the Song of Songs' enigmatic character, interpretations abound. Therefore, we begin by discussing how to read and interpret the Song. Many people shy away from the intimate content. They "sanctify" the book by making it an allegory of God's love for Israel or Jesus' love for the church. In this chapter we defend a regular biblical hermeneutic (principle of interpretation) of the Song of Songs and analyze the major characters of the Song (Solomon, Shulamite, etc.).

The second chapter discusses some keys to a thriving relationship. Song 1:2–4 shapes the affections of singles by presenting an intimate relationship that every couple would want. Rather than telling young ladies to "not marry a bad guy," the Song presents a beautiful intimate relationship, which a young lady can enjoy if she marries a good guy. Many marital intimacy issues stem from a wife's failure to trust her husband. Sometimes she doesn't trust him because he is a jerk! It will be easier for a young woman to enjoy intimacy the way God designed it if she marries a trustworthy man. So chapter two discusses how to identify a good reputation and how to examine your own spiritual state. This chapter also discusses the maxim "knowledge is power." The Song can shape young men's affections by presenting a woman whom every young man would want to marry and by teaching them the value of a good reputation and the power of knowledge. Not all knowledge is good knowledge, so the Song teaches young men what they do and do not want to know.

Women, on the other hand, regularly struggle with image insecurities. The Song corrects both female and male readers' understanding of human beauty. Every single adult should prioritize internal beauty, but too often the conversation stops there. In chapter three, we analyze Song 1:5–11 and develop what the Bible teaches about human beauty. The Song teaches singles how to enjoy beauty as a gift from a good God.

Three times the Song of Songs wife speaks directly to young women (and indirectly to all readers), encouraging them to "not awaken love." Chapter four examines this refrain and guides singles concerning not just the physical side of a relationship but also the emotional side. Too often, Christian leaders have only encouraged singles to not have sex before marriage. The Song of Songs instructs the reader not only to remain pure before marriage but also to not even awaken love.

In chapter five, we step back to Song 1:12—2:6 and talk about how married lovers awaken love. Intimacy according to the way God made the world employs all the senses, and the most powerful sense is hearing. The couple flirt back and forth, awakening love. While many within the Christian community find flirtatious speech innocent, the Song teaches that it awakens love.

Song 1:1—2:7 presents a rather ideal love, but Song 2:8—3:5 teaches a real love. Every married couple will have to work through issues in this world, and the central couple of the Song is no different. In chapter six, singles learn from the lovers that marriage does not mean couples have sex whenever they want. Situations and sin come between a husband and wife, destroying intimacy. This chapter teaches singles the importance of marrying a believer and knowing how to deal with sin.

It is easy to love the one who loves us in return, but what about when someone has sinned against us? What if the one who should love us has offended or betrayed us? Song 3:1—4 teaches an assertive, Christ-like kind of love through the Song of Songs wife, who provides a striking representation of biblical love that fights for love even when a spouse is struggling.

Song 3:6—5:1 describes a wedding and honeymoon! In chapter eight we discuss the bride's focus on the wedding day and the groom's anticipation of the wedding night. The Song provides guidance to newlyweds on how to begin love correctly.

Song 5:2—6:3 discusses a common issue within marriage, sexual incompatibility. Intimacy for men and women is different. In chapter nine, we discuss the nature of true biblical love regarding sexual incompatibility.

Chapter ten analyzes Song 5:2–7:10 and warns brides of the temptation to weaponize intimacy in the marriage relationship. The wife's selfish act in Song 5:3 has an ancient root in the Garden of Eden. In Song 6, the couple is at war. The Song of Songs wife teaches young brides how to fight for the exclusive love that God designed in creation.

The Song of Songs wife recreates the Garden of Eden in Song 7:11–8:3. She is not a timid or hesitant lover, but bold and assertive. Chapter eleven discusses how to recreate the Garden of Eden through the various places, times, and fruits of love.

The world corrupts a person's affections, but the Song transforms those affections through the renewal of that person's mind (Rom 12:1–2). Specifically, Song 8:5–14 cultivates a believer's affections for God's design for intimacy. Chapters twelve and thirteen explain why not awakening love is so important and teach singles what to look for in a spouse. The Song ends with the young man searching for the Song of Songs female lover. The believer who truly wants to marry well will likely find the Song of Songs lover. Usually, couples do not experience intimacy according to the order of creation (the way God designed intimacy to work) because they want the wrong things. The Song concludes by shaping the reader's affections for God's design for intimacy.

Obviously, you and I don't live in the days of the Old Testament. Jesus and Paul chose lives of celibacy, and Paul encouraged the Corinthians to follow his example. Are things different now? In chapter fourteen we discuss the instruction from the New Testament and offer some final thoughts on how a Christian can love successfully.

DISCUSSION QUESTIONS:

1. Why should we study the Song?

2. How should we study the Song?

3. Who are the two primary characters who teach truth in the Song?

4. Who is the primary audience of the Song, and how do we know that?

5. Why don't most parents teach their children about intimacy (therefore abdicating the role to someone else)?

6. Why is your "love life" everyone's business?

7. How old do you have to be to learn about the Song?

8. Why is sex a big deal? Why is it not a big deal?

9. What is the foundation of the Christian life and sexual ethic?

10. How does the fear of the Lord relate to your sexuality?

CH. 1 | THE SONG OF SOLOMON IS A SONG (OF ALL SONGS)
(1:1–4)

The Song of Songs, like all of Scripture, should be read, studied, and lived. We titled this book *Song of Songs for Singles*, not *Sex and Singles*, because we want to draw you into the Song of Songs. As a result, sometimes this book may read more like a commentary than a book on Christian living. The lessons we have learned and taught come directly from the Song, and we want to direct your attention to God's Word as well. As you read and study this puzzling little book of the Bible for yourself, we pray that our book will help you do just that.

The *primary* audience of Solomon's Song of Songs is single virgins. It should not surprise anyone that God-fearing singles still want to know what God has to say about love, marriage, and intimacy. I (Angela) attended a college chapel where Tim spoke on the Song of Songs. Afterward, God dropped a unique opportunity into my lap. A young lady came up to me and asked if I'd be willing to lead a Song of Songs Bible study with her and a couple of other newly engaged young ladies. I was thrilled and thankful for this opportunity but a bit terrified as well. It was as if someone had handed me all the ingredients to make a complex and decadent dessert that I'd never made before. I can cook and bake, but my wheelhouse is down-home, everyday, comfort-food baking!

I knew God had given me an incredible opportunity, so in faith I took it. Tim would help me strengthen my understanding of the Song, then I would teach it to the young ladies. As my "daughters of Jerusalem," they were hungry to hear what God had to say about their upcoming lives as wives. It was a privilege to walk them through the Song and to be a part of their preparation for married life.

Word spread around our small campus that I had led this study, and the next year another handful of engaged ladies asked if I would be willing to lead them through the same study. Godly young Christian ladies want to know how to be good wives, but many are never instructed how to love their husbands. They possess a hunger for truth, but they've been overlooked, often because the church does not want to endure an awkward conversation, and/or it mistakenly assumes that the young women will figure it out for themselves. Being a Titus 2 woman doesn't just mean that older women teach these young ladies only how to submit to their husbands and be good mothers, as well as guide them concerning general wife/mom topics. Young ladies need to learn how to love their husbands well (Titus 2:4). A significant component of teaching "loving one's husband" is guidance concerning a wife's intimacy with her husband—that is, how to be a good lover. These girls want to know how to love their soon-to-be husbands, and it is parents' and older women's biblical responsibility to teach them.

Proverbs regularly addresses "my son," indicating that the book is *primarily* written to young men (Prov 1:8, 10, 15; 2:1; 3:1, 11, 21). Song of Songs, on the other hand, regularly addresses the "daughters of Jerusalem," indicating that it is *primarily* written to young ladies (Song 1:5; 2:7; 3:5; 5:8, 16; 8:4). In the Song of Songs, the wife speaks over half of the time and regularly gives advice to the daughters of Jerusalem.

In Proverbs, the father speaks as the sage instructing the young man. In Song of Songs, the wife speaks as the sage carrying on the instruction she received from her mother. Both books, of course, contain information helpful for all, but the primary audience of Song of Songs is single ladies. Because the primary audience is single women, our applications are generally directed more toward single women.

CORRELATION BETWEEN PROVERBS AND SONG OF SONGS		
	PROVERBS	SONG OF SONGS
Speaker	Father/Sage	Mother (appears 7 times); Father is absent
Addressee	"My son"	"Daughters of Jerusalem"

Don't worry, young men, there are some good points here for you as well. In fact, the Song ends with an exhortation directed to you (Song 8:11–14). Specifically, Song 8:13 mentions young men: "The one who dwells in the gardens, companions are listening for your voice. Let me hear it!" The companions in this verse are young men who want to hear the voice of a "Song of Songs" kind of wife. They want to marry a Song of Songs kind of girl. So Song 8:11–14 teaches them how to find her. Nevertheless, Song of Songs is primarily a married woman teaching an unmarried woman. The word *mother* occurs seven times in the Song (1:6; 3:4, 11; 6:9; 8:1–2, 5), but the father never appears.

Second Timothy 3:16–17 explains that *all* Scripture is profitable to make a person mature. Song of Songs *is* part of inspired Scripture. Instruction concerning relationships, sexual desire, the body, beauty, and a host of other topics is part of Christian maturity. The Song of Songs matures not only the married but also the soon-to-be married, the currently single, and those called to singleness.

We encourage you to read the Song of Songs. Read it multiple times. Read it in different translations (see Tim's translation in the Appendix). Read it just like you read any other book of the Bible. Don't blush, giggle, or roll your eyes. This book is God's revelation to you concerning love, relationships, and intimacy. Read it prayerfully, thankfully, and reverently.

Read it with a soft heart, letting the Holy Spirit work through the Song to renew your mind (Rom 12:2).

INTERPRETING THE SONG OF SONGS

As you read the Song of Songs, you will need to interpret it. Then, you need to apply it. In fact, you should read any part of the Bible the same way. For example, whether you read Psalm 1 or Song of Songs 1, you should observe, interpret, and apply.

Many people believe the Song of Songs should be interpreted differently than the rest of the Bible. They struggle with the sexuality in the Song. For example, the first verse reads, "Let him kiss me with the kisses of his mouth, for your caresses are better than wine" (Song 1:2). The Song of Songs wife desires her husband's kisses because she enjoys being intimate with him. Wow! What a way to begin a book, much less a book in the Bible! Remember that this is God's Word, and you should read it prayerfully, thankfully, and reverently. Do not be embarrassed by or skeptical about it; don't trivialize it either. Take every thought captive to the obedience of Jesus (2 Cor 10:5).

In Song 1:4, the wife states, "Draw me after you, let us run! The king has brought me into his chambers." Her words "Let us run!" indicate she wants to be intimate with him now. It is easy to understand how some Christians might have problems with this overt sexuality.

Is there something sinful about a wife earnestly desiring her husband's affection? Song of Songs answers that question. In fact, Song 1:2–4 introduces and summarizes the way intimacy should be. The real sin issue occurs when a married Christian couple does not desire each other in a Song of Songs kind of way. Frankly, Christian couples often don't even know that God designed intimacy as Song 1:2–4 describes it. They don't know God's design for intimacy because nobody has taught them. This is one reason singles should read and study the Song. God gave you the Song of Songs so you know how intimacy is supposed to be even before you love someone.

Unfortunately, this overt sexuality has caused some interpreters to allegorize (symbolize) the Song of Songs. Jewish rabbis believed the Song of Songs allegorically described God's love for Israel, and the early church fathers believed it described Jesus' love for the church. Jewish rabbis believed that Song 1:2—"Let him kiss me with the kisses of his mouth"—referred to God's giving Moses the Law "face to face as a man who kisses his friend because of the great love with which He loves us." The rabbis and early church fathers allegorized the Song of Songs, stripping it of its intimate instruction and creating an interpretation that the author never intended. Yes, God loves Israel; and, yes, Jesus loves the church. These truths, however, are not taught in the Song of Songs. Paul uses Jesus' sacrificial love for the church as an analogy for how a husband should sacrificially love his wife (Eph 5:28–33), but Paul is not creating a way of interpreting the Song of Songs. Meanwhile, Jesus continues to be an example of how a husband should love his wife in the marriage bed and outside the marriage bed—selflessly and sacrificially.

THINKING THROUGH THE SONG OF SONGS

Since Song of Songs was written by God for you, reading and studying it can help you not only discuss intimacy with maturity but also think about it maturely. In other words, the mature Christian (2 Tim 3:17) should be able to read, study, and discuss Song 1:2–4 reverently and seriously. Perhaps God put the Song of Songs in the Bible to help young people mature in this way.

When you read the Song of Songs, you will see some words that you may not be used to seeing in the Bible. These words refer to female anatomy, which you were probably taught not to talk about or discuss. When parents and teachers instructed you not to say certain words, it wasn't so you would never say them, but so you would speak of them only in the correct way. Our young children know they are not supposed to say certain words. As they grow and mature, they learn to speak these words appropriately. Since God made our bodies and made the female body, the words that He uses to describe the body are words we should similarly use, but reverently and holistically, not crassly or jokingly.

Another "intimate" passage of Scripture illustrates how to *think* about the Song (remember to think reverently and holistically about it).

SONG
1

¹³*A sachet of myrrh*[A1] *is my lover to me,*[B1]
   he spends the night between my breasts[C1]
¹⁴*A cluster of henna blossoms*[A2] *is my lover to me,*[B2]
   in the vineyards of En Gedi.[C2]

Song 1:13–14 explains one of the common metaphors in the Song of Songs—the vineyard. Like many other writers in the Bible, Solomon used parallelism, which is repeated similarities introduced for effect. The translation above illustrates the parallelism using a system of letters and numbers (A1, B1, C1; A2, B2, C2). So "a sachet of myrrh" in verse 13 is repeated, though slightly differently, in verse 14 as "a cluster of henna blossoms." The phrase "is my lover to me" in verse 13 is repeated in verse 14. Similarly, "between my breasts" in verse 13 corresponds to "the vineyards of En Gedi" in verse 14.

Identifying the parallelism in this passage helps us understand and interpret the text. The speaker's breasts are the vineyards of En Gedi, where the Song of Songs husband enjoys his wife's intimate fruits. And the word *vineyard* functions as a metaphor for all the intimate pleasures that the Song of Songs wife offers her husband. To learn the lessons from the Song, you will have to *think correctly*. And if all you can do is feel embarrassed or act silly when you read certain words, you will not understand the truths God is trying to teach you.

The Song of Songs also helps singles learn how to discipline their minds. The Old Testament commanded the people of Israel to *love* the Lord their God with every part of their being (Deut 6:4–5). Jesus taught that this is the greatest commandment (Matt 22:37–40). Genuine Christianity is not only external but also internal (Matt 5:27–28). For example, extramarital sex is an external sin, but *desire* for extramarital sex is an internal sin. If you don't *want* to have extramarital sex, you won't *do* it. Therefore, you need to train your affections, or desires, and the Song can help you do that. As we work through the Song, if your mind wanders and you start thinking of someone or something sinful, call it what it is—sin. Confess the sin, then discipline yourself to think correctly about intimacy. In this way, the Song will help you grow in wisdom and discipline concerning intimacy.

Your mind may have been polluted by sexual sin, and you may seriously struggle reading and working through this topic with a pure mind. We want to encourage you to not give up. Decrease your consumption of worldly media and increase your consumption of God's Word. When you sin, confess it. Confess it every time. Read and pray though 1 John 1:9, Psalm 51, and Romans 13:12–14. Do not treat sin lightly! External sin begins as internal sinful desires (Jas 1:13–15). The number of times you have sinned in your heart doesn't matter. The number of times you have lusted doesn't matter. Each time was a sin, and you need to call it sin; confess it and walk in newness of life. One of the beautiful truths of the Christian life is the ability to be forgiven for your sin.

Just a quick word of caution—if you lusted after a specific individual, your sin was a sin of the heart. Confess it to God in your heart and leave that poor person alone. You do not need to confess your lustful thoughts to that person. Your confession would likely do more harm than good. Study Galatians 5 and consider what it means to "walk in the Spirit, then you will not fulfill the lust of the flesh" (Gal 5:16). Purify your mind and take every thought captive to the obedience of Jesus. As you read, interpret, and apply the Song of Songs to your life, meditate on purity.

THE CHARACTERS IN THE SONG OF SONGS

While some believe the Song of Songs is an allegory of Jesus and the church, others believe it is a story about two or three people like a Christian romance novel. Some believe Solomon is the man, and Shulamite is the woman. Solomon meets a country girl, finds her attractive, then courts and marries her (Song 3:6–11). The rest of the Song describes marital challenges and pleasures.

Another story is that Shulamite has a shepherd lover. Solomon, in this story, is the villain who attempts to woo Shulamite away from her shepherd lover. In the end, Shulamite rebuffs Solomon (Song 8:11–12) and runs off with her shepherd lover (8:13–14).

Additional variations of this dramatic interpretation of the Song exist, but these two views are the most common. Who are these characters in the Song? Is Solomon the hero or the villain? Let's analyze some of these characters to determine how to read the Song of Songs.

But first, the Song of Songs is a song, not a drama. It does not tell a story but presents characters that should be emulated or avoided. The only real-life character is Solomon, and he is not the hero. Rather, Solomon writes the Song to teach others the true nature of love. Solomon had a thousand women. He did not experience intimacy the way God designed it, so he teaches readers how he erred and how they can love correctly.

Daughters of Jerusalem

The daughters of Jerusalem are not real people but any single and marriageable virgin who is innocent concerning love. The "daughters" appear seven times in the Song (1:5; 2:7; 3:5, 10; 5:8, 16; 8:4). The Song of Songs wife exhorts the daughters of Jerusalem to purity three times (Song 2:7; 3:5; 8:4). She also asks them to search for her husband when she has lost him (Song 5:8, 16). It may seem odd to us that the wife asks single unmarried women to find her husband, but the Song is not a drama. The single unmarried virgins of Song 1:3 love the husband of the Song, and the daughters of Jerusalem are trying to find this kind of husband, so it is fitting that the wife exhorts the daughters of Jerusalem to look for her kind of husband.

The daughters of Jerusalem speak twice (Song 5:9; 6:1), both times setting the female lover up to speak about her husband. Since the daughters of Jerusalem are not real, the wife uses them as a literary, collective character to exult in her husband and to teach real-life virgins about love. Elsewhere, the daughters of Jerusalem have something to do with Solomon's royal carriage (3:10), though the meaning is hotly debated. In sum, the daughters of Jerusalem represent a single and marriageable virgin who is naïve concerning love.

Male Lover

The male lover in the Song takes several forms. Sometimes he is a king (Song 1:4, 12); other times he is a shepherd (1:7–8). The wife even describes him as a gazelle (2:8–9, 17; 8:14)—a metaphor that fails to interest a modern audience but that the ancients, no doubt, found compelling. He is a man of a man—a hunk (5:10–16). This guy has a good reputation that the single virgins find attractive (1:3). However, the male lover is married to the female lover; they are husband and wife and united by a covenant (8:5–6). Although Solomon describes a wedding, the male lover is not a participant in that wedding. It is Solomon's wedding, and, as the author, he distances the ideal couple from his wedding.

The male lover is a main character in the Song. Like the daughters of Jerusalem, he is a representative figure rather than a real person. He is the ideal man whom every husband should emulate and whom every single girl wants to marry. He is not a historical individual (like Solomon) but a literary creation. As a literary creation, he can be both a king and a shepherd. He could be the poorest, most insignificant individual in the land (shepherd) or the richest, most significant (king). Because he is an ideal man, any man can seek to emulate him and seek to enjoy the pleasures of intimacy as he enjoys them. And as an ideal man, he can be married to the excellent wife, while, as an ideal, he is loved and sought for by unmarried women. As a husband, he overcomes obstacles in the marriage relationship instead of seeking ungodly options (Song 2:8–15). By overcoming these obstacles, he takes care of his wife, tending to her like a vineyard owner tends to his vineyard (Song 2:15). He desires his wife but never forces himself on her (5:2–5). While he provides an example for married men, as an ideal character, he sets the bar high. He defines the bounds for sexual intimacy (that it is an exclusive, covenantal, monogamous, heterosexual relationship) and exemplifies intimacy according to the order of creation, or wisdom, in which God delights (5:1).

Female Lover

Like the male lover, the female lover takes many forms. She is dark in skin (Song 1:5–6) yet fair as the moon (6:10). At times she's a vineyard keeper (1:6), a shepherdess (1:7–8), or a queen (1:12–14). As she compares the male lover to a gazelle, he likens her to a mare (1:9). This metaphor offends modern audiences but, no doubt, flattered an ancient woman. The Song of Songs woman is also incomparably beautiful (Song 4:1–7; 6:4–9; 7:1–6). Her appearance is intoxicating (4:10; 7:9–10). And she is lovesick for her man (2:5). Outside the covenant of marriage, she is a locked garden (5:12) and an impenetrable fortress (8:10), but within the covenant of marriage, she desires her husband (1:2–4) and is sexually assertive (3:1–4) and creative (7:11–13).

The female lover is a main character in the Song. She is the ideal woman whom every woman should emulate and whom every man should seek to marry. Like the daughters of Jerusalem, she is not a historical individual but a literary creation. The Song of Songs wife is what each wife should seek to attain sexually: she desires her husband (Song 1:2–4; 3:1–4), freely offers herself to him (5:16; 6:2), and is exclusively his (4:12–5:1; 6:2–3; 8:10–12). The Song of Songs woman is an ideal character; she, too, sets the bar high. She defines the bounds for sexual intimacy (as an exclusive, covenantal, monogamous, heterosexual relationship) and exemplifies intimacy according to the order of creation, or wisdom, in which God delights (5:1).

Shulamite

Shulamite appears one time in the Song of Songs (Song 6:13). From this one occurrence, some conclude that she is a historical character. Attempts to find a historical Shulamite have proven elusive. Some have connected her with Abishag the *Shunamite* (1 Kings 1:3). This association, however, is unlikely. The difference between the *n* and *l*, while seemingly insignificant to English readers, is significant in Hebrew.

Shulamite is a feminine form of *Solomon.* Even in English, the similarity is clear. The added *t* at the end makes the word feminine in Hebrew. Here Solomon creates a literary individual, Mrs. Solomon. And because Solomon's name means "peace," he is Mr. Peace, and she is the Mrs. Peace he is looking for. The literary creation here is beautiful, because to enjoy intimacy the way God intended, a couple needs *peace*.

For a husband and wife to enjoy intimacy according to the order of creation, they must learn how to live at peace with one another. The Song teaches the reader how to live at peace. In fact, the second half of the Song rotates on the axis of peace—its absence, desire, and creation. The Song employs army/military metaphors to represent the absence of peace. In Song 8:8–10, the woman describes herself as a fortress. Various suitors seek to conquer her and enter the fortress. The male lover succeeds, not through conquest, but through a peace treaty (marriage). The woman concludes Song 8:10 by stating, "Then I became in his eyes as one who found peace!" When two "countries" enter into a peace treaty (marriage covenant), the gates of one country open, and the other country is willingly permitted into the fortress. Mrs. Peace is a fortified wall, a boarded-up door (Song 8:9). She is *not* intimately at peace with others. She is at peace with only one person, and that peace was created by a covenant. The *time* for peace is marriage! If you are single, you do not have this kind of peace (that is, sexual peace) with anyone! Peace comes after the covenant.

Solomon

The name *Solomon* appears seven times in the Song of Songs (1:1, 5; 3:7, 9, 11; 8:11–12). It seems a little too ironic that the mother, daughters of Jerusalem, and Solomon all occur seven times in the Song. Solomon is the author (1:1). He has beautiful curtains (1:5), a fancy carriage and wedding (3:7, 9, 11), and a big expensive vineyard that is different from another vineyard (8:11–12). You would expect him to be the hero, the "Mr. Peace" of the Song, and the one who truly enjoys intimacy according to the order of creation (the way God designed intimacy). But he is not the hero. He is a Mr. Peace, who is still looking for Mrs. Peace. Solomon, the most powerful, richest, and wisest man of his time was rejected by Mrs. Peace, the ideal female lover and wife (8:12).

The final reference to Solomon is the reason many people do not believe Solomon is the hero of the Song. Song 8:11 describes Solomon's vineyard, but then the woman says, "My vineyard, which is mine is before me; the thousand to you, Solomon" (8:12). She is distinguishing between Solomon's vineyard and her vineyard. Then in Song 8:14, she runs off with her lover.

Solomon also does not make a fitting hero of the Song. First Kings 11:1–3 explains that Solomon, having seven hundred wives and three hundred concubines, loved many foreign women. He abandoned the Lord and worshiped other gods, so the Lord abandoned him and created hardship during the latter years of his life (1 Kgs 11:9–25). In the Song of Songs, the vineyard is a metaphor for the wife's sexual delights (remember Song 1:13–14). When Solomon the author says that Solomon the king had a vineyard at Baal Hamon, he is referring to the sexual delights of his enormous harem. *Baal Hamon* means "Master (Husband) of Many." Solomon was literally the husband of many. He had so many women that he could not care for his vineyard (harem) himself but had to appoint others to take care of the vineyard for him (Song 8:11). The Song of Songs male lover, by contrast, takes care of his own vineyard (2:15). The woman in Song 8:12 excludes her vineyard from Solomon's and then runs off with the male lover, leaving Solomon with his harem but without the Song of Songs female lover.

Solomon is the wealthiest individual with the best and most extravagant of everything. His beautiful curtains (Song 1:5), extravagant carriage (3:7–10), and joyous wedding (3:11) communicate that extravagance. He has everything! Even the beautiful bride. It seems as though he figured out how to truly enjoy intimacy according to the order of creation. Or did he? The Song of Songs male and female lovers seem disconnected from Solomon's wedding (3:11). Solomon married many times, almost as if he was looking for something, or maybe someone.

Because the woman does the majority of the speaking, some believe the Song of Songs was written to Solomon rather than by Solomon. The Hebrew permits this interpretation, but it is not the natural or historical reading of the text. In his wisdom later in life, Solomon wrote Ecclesiastes and Song of Songs by the inspiration of the Holy Spirit. Learning from his sins, he wrote Ecclesiastes to encourage contentment and wrote the Song of Songs to teach—particularly young people—about intimacy. In his earlier attempt to enjoy sex to the fullest, Solomon had married many and the best (Song 8:11). In his wealth and abundance, he had denied himself nothing (Eccl 2:10). No doubt, this applied to women and sex as well (Eccl 2:8). But Solomon learned that true joy is found in contentment (2:24; 3:13; 5:19), and that contentment extends to the marriage bed (9:9). Solomon writes his best song to shape the affections of young men to desire a Song of Songs kind of wife and not a "harem girl" kind of wife.

Solomon as a character functions as a type—a type of a man that a godly man doesn't want to be. The world says a man wants to be a Solomon—rich, powerful, with any woman he desires (Eccl 2:1–11). Solomon lived that life. He married woman after woman, looking for that one that would satisfy. All the while, the female lover of the Song of Songs was just watching from the sidelines (Song 3:11).

While Solomon was gathering and collecting wealth and women (Eccl 2:1–11, 24–26; Song 8:11), he was all the time looking for but never finding the excellent wife (Prov 31:10–31), that is, the female lover of the Song of Songs (Song 8:12). Young man, you have the opportunity to enjoy something Solomon only wrote about—a woman who actually loves you. Can you find her? What are you looking for? A beautiful harem girl (8:11) or a common vineyard keeper (1:6)? Solomon teaches that the most likely reason you will *not* find the Song of Songs woman is you (Eccl 7:29).

CONCLUSION

The Song of Songs is a song, not a story. It is a composition, not a narrative. As a song, the characters in the Song are literary creations, not historical characters. The husband and the wife represent ideal characters whom every husband and wife should seek to emulate. Their sacrificial, selfless love may seem difficult to emulate, but that love is what every husband and wife should seek to model. Just as Jesus provides an impossible, sacrificial example for the believer to model in holiness, so do the characters in the Song of Songs provide impossible, sacrificial examples for a husband and wife to model in sexual selflessness. And just as the believer should always pursue sanctification and holiness, knowing that the struggle with the flesh will not end in this life, so also should a husband and wife always pursue sexual selflessness, knowing that their struggle with the flesh here on earth will never end.

As the two Song of Songs characters model God's parameters for intimacy, the reader learns that God's parameters include an exclusive, covenantal, monogamous, and heterosexual relationship. Analyzing the Song instructs the believing single about God's order of creation concerning love, marriage, and intimacy.

DISCUSSION QUESTIONS:

1. Who are the primary audiences of Song of Songs and Proverbs, and who are their respective teachers?

2. Historically, why have many believed the Song should be interpreted differently than the rest of the Bible?

3. Why should singles study the Song?

4. Generally, how has the Song been interpreted, particularly by the Jewish rabbis and early church fathers?

5. How does Jesus' love for the church correspond to a husband's love for his wife?

6. How does reading and thinking correctly about the Song of Songs help a believer mature?

7. How can you fight the potential struggles encountered while reading the Song?

8. Why did Solomon write the Song of Songs?

9. What are the characters in the Song, and whom do they represent?

10. Discuss the meaning of the word *Shulamite*.

CH. 2 | IGNORANCE IS BLISS; KNOWLEDGE IS POWER
(1:1–4)

Song of Songs begins, not with timidity or caution, but with a wife who declares, "Let him kiss me with the kisses of his mouth." The wife then gives two reasons why she desires her husband's affection, directing the second reason specifically to single young women: "therefore the virgins love you" (Song 1:3). The Song both educates the reader that learning to love well begins when that person is single, and teaches two keys to a thriving intimate relationship. You may be thinking, "Oh! I figure out these two keys and then I am good to go." Well, it is more complicated than that. Before we look at the two keys to a thriving intimate relationship, we need to understand how the Song is wisdom literature.

SONG OF SONGS AS WISDOM LITERATURE

Wisdom literature describes the way things are supposed to be, the way God ordered the world. If you are going to build a house, you first must create a blueprint. The blueprint represents the house's design plan. Wisdom is the design plan, or order, of creation. God created the blueprint, or wisdom, before He made the world (Prov 8:22–24). This blueprint includes the physical world (science) and the metaphysical world (human flourishing). You want to live according to God's blueprint/wisdom because that is "the good life." We use the terms "order of creation" and "wisdom" synonymously in this book because wisdom is the way God made the world.

Sin, however, messes up the order of creation, creating countless problems. For example, Proverbs 10:4 states, "He who has a slack hand becomes poor, but the hand of the diligent makes rich" (NKJV). This proverb describes a general truth. Lazy people are poor, and diligent people are rich. Sometimes, however, we observe situations where lazy people are rich and diligent people are poor. Ecclesiastes 9:11 laments, "The race is not to the swift, nor the battle to the strong, nor bread to the wise, nor riches to the understanding, nor favor to the knowledgeable; because time and chance happen to them all." Life is not a mathematical formula. Proverbs 10:4 describes how life should function, but Ecclesiastes explains that it doesn't always work that way. In fact, no one is guaranteed anything. "Time and chance" happen to everybody. Disasters destroy, the selfish steal, people perish, everything is a mess so that no one really knows much of anything (Eccl 6:12; 8:17; 11:5–6). Ecclesiastes explains how a person should live even when life is so puzzling: "Fear God and keep His commandments, for this is man's all" (12:13). So, when things don't work the way you would expect, you must fear God and trust Him. God is sovereign and in control of whatever situation you are going through, and He is using that situation to teach you to fear Him (3:10–15). When wisdom literature teaches, "This is how things work," it is really saying, "This is how things usually work."

The Song of Songs is wisdom literature as well. This means that we are going to work through some areas where things are supposed to work a certain way. But you are guaranteed nothing. You could be a great person, marry a good person, but then your spouse abandons you. Relationships are not supposed to work that way, but sometimes, unfortunately, they do. God has given each person the freedom to make his/her own decisions. You need to fear the Lord and trust Him through the good and the bad. Honor the Lord regardless of others' sin.

Most of the time, however, wisdom works according to God's design. One spouse is a jerk because the other spouse is a jerk! If one spouse, however, chooses to love the other sacrificially and selflessly, expecting nothing in return, then it often brings couples together. A person is guaranteed nothing, but usually wisdom works this way. The same principle applies to singles. Young man, the Song explains how you are more likely to find a wife like the female lover in the Song. Young lady, the Song explains how you are more likely to find a husband like the male lover in the Song. The Song doesn't guarantee you anything. But if you fear the Lord and keep his commandments, you have a higher probability of having a marriage that aligns with the order of creation.

KNOW YOUR SPOUSE

SONG 1 | *²Let him kiss me with the kisses of his mouth, for your love [caresses] is better than wine.*

The female lover states explicitly that she wants her husband to kiss her because his "love" is better than wine. The word love here is actually a plural in Hebrew—loves. She is not describing the abstract idea of love, as in "I love my children." She has chosen an intimate word, saying that his "loves" are better than wine. This woman finds her husband's touches and caresses intoxicating. The NET Bible is a little closer to the idea: "Oh, how I wish you would kiss me passionately! For your lovemaking is more delightful than wine." This woman is married, delights in her husband's caresses, and desires his intimate caresses again.

The principle for married men is that they need to know how to caress their wives in a way that pleases them. The Song exhorts husbands to serve their wives sexually. Single, you are probably thinking, "This isn't relevant to me!" Angela and I want to draw an indirect application to you from this passage. The world, the flesh, and the devil all tempt a single person with lies like, "You will be a better lover if you know this now." If you really think you need to know something right now, go talk to a person of the same gender who loves and cares for you—a parent, pastor, or mentor. Usually, you don't need to "know" whatever it is that you think you need to know. This desire to know is likely your flesh, and you need to kill it (Col 3:5). I fell for this lie many times during my single years. In the name of curiosity and knowledge, I learned some truth but also many more lies that created problems after I married. Be ignorant! Love your ignorance. When others who possess sexual knowledge mock your naivety, don't be ashamed. Whatever knowledge other singles supposedly possess is littered with lies. The time to know comes with the one whom you are to know—your spouse.

Knowledge is not always power. Sometimes knowledge is destructive. It was knowledge that plunged the world into sin, and it is knowledge that can destroy the intimacy that God wants you to enjoy with your future spouse. Complete ignorance is not the answer either. The knowledge you need, however, is not the world's reverberating noises that echo in your ears. The amount of knowledge and timing of education should be guided by parents, a premarital counselor, or a pastor. In Song 8:2, for example, the mother teaches the daughter about intimacy. Your knowledge acquisition, however, should primarily come after marriage. Crooked and perverted knowledge corrupts innocence. After Adam and Eve ate from the tree of the knowledge of good and evil, "they knew that they were naked" (Gen 3:7). They were naked in the garden the entire time. It was not until they had sinned that they possessed this knowledge. Sometimes knowledge corrupts and destroys. Sexual knowledge can corrupt and destroy as well.

When I was single, I thought caressing my future wife would be easy. My mind was tainted by pornography, which had some truth but many more lies! The male lover in the Song does not know how to touch a woman; he knows how to touch his wife. God designed women, so some similarities exist among them, but differences exist as well. Learning how another woman likes to be touched will not prepare you to be a good lover for your future wife. Furthermore, depending on the source of your knowledge, you may really be learning some perverted guy's fantasy. You do not want this knowledge. When you marry, you bring these thoughts, desires, and expectations into the marriage bed with your real wife. When she doesn't like certain things, you begin wondering what is wrong with her, because you "know" so-and-so liked it. Again, in the Song, the male lover doesn't know how to touch a woman; he knows how to touch his wife. Until you marry, be ignorant. Your future wife will appreciate it. After you marry, let her teach you. This is the way of wisdom. This is the order of creation. This is the way God designed it, and it is good.

HAVE A GOOD REPUTATION

SONG
1

> [3]*The scent of your oils is good;*
> *oil poured forth is your name,*
> *therefore virgins love you.*

A casual reading of Song 1:3 seems like the female lover is talking about her husband's aroma. Just as wine is intoxicating (1:2), so also is a good smell (1:3). The second sentence, however, explains, "oil poured forth is your name." It is definitely a good idea to smell good, but what the wife finds intoxicating is her husband's name, or reputation. Since aromas are delightful, she uses the image of a good-smelling man as an analogy for his reputation. She desirously craves him in part because of his good name.

Your spouse will know the real you. He/She will see you at your best and worst. You can put on a façade in public, but when it comes to your private life, your spouse will not be fooled.

The morally and spiritually bankrupt man cannot be trusted. He uses a woman for his own selfish, physical pleasures. He may act like a servant at times, but his motivation is to receive something in return. His wife becomes one object and tool to satiate his insatiable lust. Young lady, you do not want to marry this kind of man.

The Song of Songs wife is not concerned that her husband will hurt her, use her, abuse her, or leave her. He has a good reputation. He will love her sacrificially. Christian intimacy books repeatedly emphasize that a wife must trust her husband to enjoy intimacy freely the way God designed it. The Song teaches that intimacy with a man of ill repute is like being intimate with someone who has BO and furry teeth.

A man with a good reputation is first and foremost trustworthy. The person who lies should be dumped. You must be able to trust your spouse. Young man, if you have a propensity to lie, get help. You are unmarriageable material until you are willing to tell the truth, even when telling the truth will hurt you. Young lady, the man who is more concerned with bolstering or preserving his fragile reputation instead of bolstering and preserving the Lord's reputation is not worth your time. He is arrogant and consumed with himself, and he needs to be humbled. Dump him. It could be the best thing that ever happened to him (and you).

A man with a good reputation serves his wife. He puts her needs—physical, financial, and sexual—above his own. The Apostle Paul commanded husbands to love their wives in this way: "Husbands, love your wives, just as Christ also loved the church and gave Himself for her" (Eph 5:25 NKJV). A Christian husband should love his wife to the point where he would be willing to die for her. While many men may say they would die for their wives, their everyday treatment of them brings their sincerity into question. If a man is unwilling to serve his wife financially or sexually, would he truly be willing to die for her? Trustworthiness, however, is only the beginning. The man with a good reputation loves and serves others.

ROLE MODELS

The Bible not only tells you what kind of a guy to be (or to marry) but also provides a role model for you to follow. Boaz was the man with a "good name." Boaz married Ruth at great personal expense. According to Jewish law, another man was supposed to marry Ruth because he was the closer relative.

In the days of the Old Testament, if a man died, his brother was supposed to marry his wife and have a son with her to continue his family name. Now that may sound really weird to us, but that was what God required of His people in His law (Deut 25:5–10). You can be grateful that we no longer live under this requirement of the law! (Many of the Old Testament people didn't like this law either.) Ruth's husband, Mahlon, died. This closer male relative had a responsibility according to Deuteronomic law to marry Ruth, have a child with her, and perpetuate Mahlon's name. At first he was willing to marry Ruth because he saw an opportunity to increase his wealth. But when Boaz informed him that he must father a child through Ruth "to perpetuate the name of the dead through his inheritance" (Ruth 4:5), the man said no, "lest I ruin my own inheritance" (4:6). That man was selfish. He was concerned about his own wealth; he was not concerned with doing what was right according to God's Law.

Boaz said to that man, "Come aside, friend, sit down here" (Ruth 4:1 NKJV). In Hebrew, the word for "friend" is a rhyme, *Peloni Almoni*, which was not the man's actual name; a modern equivalent would be "John Doe." That man is the unnamed one. His name was deliberately omitted from the account of Boaz and Ruth because he was selfish; he had a bad reputation. He refused to submit to God's Law, marry Ruth, and raise a son for his dead relative. Young man, this is the kind of man you don't want to be. Young woman, this is the kind of man you don't want to marry.

If you marry a person with a bad reputation, you will heap sorrow and grief upon yourself. Remember the imagery of the Song of Songs? A Boaz kind of guy is "oil poured forth," but a "John Doe" kind of guy is like being close, sexually close, with someone who literally stinks. And, through marriage, you have covenanted to live with this stinky person for the rest of your life. If you're a lady, you want to be a Ruth, and you want to marry a Boaz.

RESOLUTION

SONG
1

> [4]*Draw me after you, let us run!*
> *The king has brought me into his chambers.*
> *Let us be glad and rejoice in you!*
> *Let us exult in your caresses more than wine.*
> *Rightly do they love you.*

In Song 1:4, the couple unites, and the section ends. Some Bible translations incorrectly create a dialogue between the wife and the daughters of Jerusalem in this verse. The wife, however, speaks all of verse 4, earnestly desiring and exulting in their union. She communicates her earnest desire through the exhortation "let us hurry!" The "us" is the couple—husband and wife. In the ancient Near Eastern world, love poetry was sometimes written with first-person plural pronouns (we, us, ours, ourselves) to communicate the union of lovers.

So the union of husband and wife, the two becoming one, is reflected in the pronouns we and us. By exulting in the couple's union, the Song celebrates intimacy enjoyed at the right time according to the way God designed it. This is a good design. Young woman, young man, desire intimacy God's way and heed the instruction from the Song of Songs.

 DIGGING DEEPER

The words "Let us be glad and rejoice with you! Let us exult in your caresses more than wine" are usually attributed to the daughters of Jerusalem instead of the Song of Songs wife (see NKJV and ESV translations). Shalom Paul, however, argues convincingly that "in ancient Near Eastern and biblical love poetry is the employment of the first-person plural in ecstatic amatory discourse . . . which I would like to designate the 'plural of ecstasy,' replaces the otherwise expected first-person singular in rapturous utterances of the female lover," Shalom Paul, "The 'Plural of Ecstasy' in Mesopotamian and Biblical Love Poetry," in *Solving Riddles and Untying Knots*, ed. Ziony Zevit, Seymour Gitin, and Michael Sokoloff (Winona Lake, IN: Eisenbrauns, 1995), 585–86.

DISCUSSION QUESTIONS:

1. What does the term *order of creation* mean?

2. Explain how the Song is wisdom literature.

3. How and when can knowledge be destructive?

4. Why is a husband's reputation so important to his wife?

5. What biblical role model seems directly connected to the Song?

6. What kind of a man should young ladies look for in a future husband?

7. Read Ruth 4 and note the presence and absence of names. Discuss the meaning of a good name.

CH. 3 | IS BEAUTY IN THE EYE OF THE BEHOLDER?
(1:5–11)

God loves beauty. He made everything beautiful (Gen 1:31), does everything beautifully (Eccl 3:11), and will make everything beautiful again (Isa 60). As fallen humans, we have sought after beauty, idolized it, and coveted it, but very few have actually enjoyed it as God intended. This chapter defines beauty and presents principles on how to enjoy beauty biblically.

Caleb was stuck. He really liked Jill, but nothing about her physical appearance was really stunning. She was just an average looking young lady. She had a great personality and a lot of friends. Many times he had seen her getting her hands dirty, working hard, and loving people well. He loved these characteristics of her, but she wasn't a knockout, and he wasn't attracted to her. Of course, character is important, but how could he spend the rest of his life with someone he wasn't attracted to? As a result, he really wondered if Jill was the girl he should marry. After all, wouldn't Jill want to marry a guy who found her attractive?

Jenny was discouraged. She was a godly Christian girl, but men never expressed interest in her. Her friends were getting swooped up by guys, but she was just there waiting in the background. She realized deep down even good guys were looking for a knockout. She knew she would never measure up to that standard. Can/should she adorn herself? How far should she go to get their attention?

Beauty, particularly human beauty, is a sensitive topic. Because our culture wants everyone to feel good, we tell people they are beautiful.

But we know that some people are at a different place than "beautiful" on the beauty spectrum. Nobody is ugly. Some people, however, are more objectively beautiful than others. God's Word supports these statements. Those who accept them can be liberated from the world's idolatrous worship of beauty.

> Because our culture wants everyone to feel good, we tell people they are beautiful. But we know that some people are at a different place than "beautiful" on the beauty spectrum.

INTERNAL BEAUTY

Internal beauty is of paramount importance, making it more important than external beauty. In the New English Translation Bible (NET), 1 Peter 3:3–4 reads, "Let your beauty not be external—the braiding of hair and wearing of gold jewelry or fine clothes—but the inner person of the heart, the lasting beauty of a gentle and tranquil spirit, which is precious in God's sight." The NET translation reflects a common confusion concerning beauty by using the word *beauty* metaphorically. Physical beauty concerns physical symmetry and order. First Peter 3:3–4 does not even use the word *beauty* but instead uses the term *outward form*. Peter contrasts the external *ordering* of the body and the internal *ordering* of the heart. So Peter is prioritizing the internal ordering of a person's desires over the external ordering of his/her appearance.

The Hebrews did not speak of beauty metaphorically as we do today. When a person today tells someone he/she is "beautiful on the inside," the person uses the word *beautiful* metaphorically, saying simply that the other person's character is ordered well. Our character is important to God. It is more important than a person's external looks.

This chapter primarily concerns external beauty. Many contemporary authors seem to not want to hurt anyone's feelings, so they emphasize internal character. Character is more important than beauty; we agree! But the church needs to wrestle with the topic of external beauty rather than skirting the issue and offering platitudes to young people, hoping to make them feel good about themselves. They aren't naïve, and they don't feel better about themselves. Deep down, Christians would much rather know what God has to say about beauty and how they can be content with where God has placed them on the beauty spectrum than to hear platitudes. Those who accept God's instruction concerning external beauty have found contentment and freedom to live in the skin that God has placed them in.

Interestingly, the Bible talks more about beautiful women than about handsome men. So this chapter focuses on female beauty. Young lady, stick with us through this chapter. Some parts may be difficult to hear, but we pray you are encouraged and can think more biblically about beauty.

CHARACTERISTICS OF BEAUTY

If even the Bible describes some people as more attractive than others, then shouldn't we be able to define beauty? This section examines beauty from a biblical perspective and explains what makes some people more beautiful.

Objective vs. Subjective

The first time I taught through the Song of Songs, I misunderstood beauty and failed to lead the class to understand its true definition. "Beauty is in the eye of the beholder," though an old proverb, is common in these postmodern times. It teaches that beauty is defined by the one doing the looking. Beauty, in this view, is subjective, meaning that all people can define beauty however they perceive it individually. What one person considers beautiful may not be what another person considers beautiful. Presumably, biblical evidence for this view comes from Song 1:5 and 6:10, where 1:5 describes the woman as dark-skinned and 6:10 describes her as light-skinned. Some men find dark skin more attractive than fair skin—beauty, therefore, seems to be in the eye of the beholder.

However, the idea that beauty is in the eye of the beholder confuses a person's taste from what is objectively beautiful. Of the five senses (taste, sight, touch, hearing, and smell), the most subjective sense is taste. Why one of us abhors olives and the other loves them defies rational objective thought. Other criteria like symmetry, order, color, and variety are universal signs of beauty that transcend cultures. These characteristics of beauty are even found in the Bible.

Tastes, on the other hand, are subjective. Eye color, hair color, skin color—you probably have your favorites. But tastes can change. Usually, you have specific tastes for some reason (for example, media influence, your peers' taste). The American "ideal" woman was a pencil-thin, blue-eyed blonde. How many men preferred a blue-eyed blonde, pencil-thin woman simply because our culture presented this "ideal" beauty?

> Beauty is objective, but tastes are subjective.
> Can you learn to like something different?

Obviously, there is nothing wrong with being a blue-eyed blonde. But this definition of beauty is actually not a definition of beauty but a specific taste that has been cultivated among the populace. So I have to ask, "Can you *learn* to *like* something different?"

The "beauty is in the eye of the beholder" view is philosophically based upon an unbiblical postmodern worldview. Western culture emphasizes equality, so to say someone is more beautiful than someone else sounds unfair or unjust. Everyone has beauty, but that beauty is more pronounced in a few. For example, a one-hundred-year-old woman is still beautiful, but her beauty differs from when she was eighteen. Her beauty has faded. Every person is made in the image of God and possesses beauty. Sinful choices, the curse, and effects of the fall of mankind, however, have marred beauty at various levels. People who are blessed with extraordinary beauty are young and rare.

Biblical Beauties

The Old Testament has a few words and expressions that describe beautiful people. Sarah is described as beautiful (Gen 12:11) and later as *very* beautiful (Gen 12:14). Rachel was beautiful "in form and appearance" (Gen 29:17). So Sarah was beautiful, but Rachel was the real knockout. When the text states that she was beautiful in form (shape), it likely means that she had curves (hips and breasts). Interestingly, our culture does not value at least one of those things anymore. We'll just leave that there. These words, however, are two of the words the Old Testament uses to describe beauty.

Genesis 29:17 creates a comparison when it states, "Leah's eyes were weak, but Rachel was beautiful in form and appearance." Our cultural view of justice and fairness abhors the preference of one person over the other. When God made you, however, He likely made someone else more beautiful than you. This act of God is just and fair because God is the arbiter, or judge, of justice and fairness (Gen 18:25). We can never fully understand God's decisions (Isa 40:28). His plan is greater than we can comprehend (Isa 40:27–31). Genesis 29:17 compares the beauty of two sisters; the one is stunning and the other is homely. The Christian must accept this evaluation.

A Hebrew word (*yafeh*) almost always refers to physical beauty. The Bible uses this word to describe several women as beautiful: Abigail (1 Sam 25:3), Tamar (2 Sam 13:1), and Abishag (1 Kgs 1:3–4). It uses *yafeh* to describe men as well: Joseph (Gen 39:6), David (1 Sam 16:12; 17:42), and Absalom (2 Sam 14:25). Genesis 41:4 and 18 even describe healthy cows as beautiful. Some men, women, and cows are beautiful, but others are not. In fact, that few people are described as beautiful implies that most people are just average looking.

DIGGING DEEPER

Critics argue that beauty is subjective because different times and cultures have defined beauty differently. Within cultural differences, however, we see universal patterns. Roger Scruton writes, "Cultural variation does not imply the absence of cross-cultural universals. . . . Symmetry and order; proportion; closure; convention; harmony, and also novelty and excitement: all these seem to have a permanent hold on the human psyche," Roger Scruton, *Beauty: A Very Short Introduction* (New York: Oxford University Press, 2011), 119. Scruton's list of "universals" typifies definitions of beauty which appeal to general revelation. The Bible does not present a list of "universals," but assumes an objective definition of beauty from which a person can only *begin* to define beauty.

Blemishes

We can begin defining beauty by looking at the biblical descriptions of beautiful people. For example, Absalom is described as beautiful, and then the narrator states, "From the sole of his foot to the crown of his head there was no blemish [*mus*] in him" (2 Sam 14:25). The groom describes his bride in Song 4:7, "You are all beautiful [*yafeh*], my love, and there is no blemish [*mus*] in you." God required the priests who would draw near to Him to not have any major blemishes (Lev 21:16–21).

Also, the animal that has a blemish was not supposed to be sacrificed to the Lord (Lev 22). Blemishes are an effect of the Fall (of mankind) and are not beautiful.

Deformities, scars, imperfections, or abnormalities in the skin are not physically beautiful, but neither do they define a person. A believer's identity is in Christ, and this is our identity regardless of any physical deformities plaguing the body. If, however, you tell someone that his/her imperfection is beautiful, that is a lie. Blemishes are not beautiful; they are an effect of the Fall. And something about us humans knows this to be true. I (Tim) remember as a teenager an individual with a birthmark that covered half of the person's face. This person, however, had an engaging personality and was rarely alone. Some would say that this person was beautiful. What they meant, of course, was that the person was metaphorically beautiful, or had correctly ordered affections. The person with the birthmark had a servant's heart, loved the Lord, and loved others. The person was still beautiful, but his/her outward beauty was marred. That is ok! In fact, I could see how God was glorified through that person's imperfection (John 9:2–3).

Don't believe the lies of our culture and define yourself according to your physical appearance. We have five children, all of whom came into this world by way of a doctor's knife (cesarean section). Are the scars on Angela's body beautiful? No! They may represent something beautiful, but they are not beautiful. She was more beautiful on our wedding day because she possessed fewer flaws. I was more beautiful on that day as well! Most people possess some sort of marks, scars, or blemishes. Those blemishes are not beautiful. Most people do not have a flawless body, and the ones who do won't have it for long!

Youthfulness

Beauty is not only unblemished; it is young. Proverbs 31:30 reads, "Charm is deceitful, and beauty is passing; but a woman who fears the Lord, she will be praised." The original word *passing* is literally a *breath*. How is beauty a breath? It is a breath in that it does not last long. We don't like to hear it, but deep down, we all know it is true. People's beauty passes away as they age. They realize this truth, which is why the U.S. beauty industry makes billions selling anti-aging products. Recognizing the value of beauty and not wanting to lose it, people readily spend money to retain their youthful beauty.

What makes youth beautiful? Lack of blemishes? Soft skin? Firm body? The text does not say. This chapter, however, focuses on a biblical definition of beauty, and, biblically, all that can be said is that beauty is young. Are you young? If so, you are in the prime of your beauty. Enjoy these days, but remember your Creator as you take delight in them (Eccl 11:7—12:7). Is your beauty diminishing? Use your beauty for God's glory and not self-interest or vainglory.

Symmetry and Cleanness

In Song 4:1, 7 the man describes the woman as beautiful. Then in verses 2–6 he describes all the ways she is beautiful. One characteristic of her beauty is her teeth: "Your teeth are like a flock of shorn sheep which have come up from the washing; every one of them bears twins and there is not one missing." The first description of her teeth is that they are clean. The sheep (teeth) are shorn (not fuzzy) and washed. Her example sounds like good advice! It sounds pretty objective too—how many people and cultures like dirt and dirtiness? Even God's common grace exalts cleanliness. If you live in or are aware of a culture that does not exalt cleanliness, that culture is broken. God loves cleanliness (Lev 11—15), and as children of God, we should like cleanliness. It is beautiful.

The second characteristic of her teeth is that they are symmetrical. All her teeth have twins, meaning they are in order, and not one of them is missing. They all are beautiful. Many people have crooked or missing teeth. Many lack symmetry in the face; they have an ear or an eye that is a little higher than the other. Most people do not have a symmetrical body either; for example, one foot is bigger.

All kinds of minor deformities plague our bodies, marring beauty. When I (Tim) smile, one of my eyes scrunches up tightly, but the other opens wider. My eyes are asymmetrical. This irregularity is an imperfection. I have tried to open that eye more, but the muscles or something else is messed up, and I can't do it. I am guessing it is the result of getting hit by a hockey puck in my younger years. Should I be ashamed of this imperfection? Refuse to smile so people don't see it? Absolutely not! Rather, I smile, enjoy life as a gift from God, and enjoy the goodness of God (Eccl 2:24–25).

Healthfulness

Beauty is healthy. Western culture, however, has defined beauty as gaunt, though this ideal may be changing. The faces of models are often sunken, revealing that they are malnourished. The second half of Song 7:2 describes the Song of Songs woman: "Your belly is a heap of wheat." This woman is not a size 0. Her belly is a *heap* of wheat. In other words, she is healthy. Many young men today would call her overweight. Now if you are thinking she is a couch potato, you have the wrong idea in mind. She is active. In fact the husband describes her dancing in Song 7:1–6. She is healthy looking; she is beautiful.

We are highlighting this characteristic of beauty because we believe that Western culture has marred God's design of beauty by projecting an intentionally waifish woman as the ideal beauty. This view of beauty has had adverse effects on young women, some of whom have damaged their bodies because of malnourishment. Some young men have come to assume that gaunt is more beautiful and that if a young lady has a little meat on her bones, she is a lazy glutton. False! I remind you, Rachel was curvaceous.

Most people in the biblical world were thin because they did not have an abundance of food. Denying oneself necessary sustenance made a notable contribution to a person's family or community. Ruth was given food by a generous man. She ate only some of that food and then saved the rest for her starving mother-in-law (Ruth 2:18). In their culture, a curvaceous woman was beautiful. A woman typically acquires more curves by eating, but Ruth was not concerned with her appearance. She was thin when thin wasn't in.

God may have made you thin. That is ok! The point here is not skinny vs. not skinny. The point is healthy. And if you are healthy and thin, great! If you are healthy and not as thin, great! Ruth sacrificed her own beauty to love and serve others. At least for the time being, God has blessed Western culture with an abundance of food. Eat with moderation and a grateful heart, and be healthy.

Colorfulness

While it is not as clearly stated in Scripture, a case could be made that beauty is colorful. This characteristic would also be a sign of good health. The two times that David is described as beautiful, he is also described as "ruddy" (1 Sam 16:12; 17:42). Similarly, Song 4:3 describes the woman's lips as being "like a strand of *scarlet*." And Song 5:10

describes the man as ruddy. All these records connected to beauty describe something red. Having some color in your face is also a sign of being young and healthy. Aren't you glad God didn't create the world in only black and white?

Conclusion

This definition of beauty is incomplete because we limited our study to the biblical evidence. We hope, however, this definition of beauty gives you an idea of what beauty is and what beauty is not.

BEAUTY AND BLEMISHES

Everyone has beauty and blemishes. If you are flawless, give it time. There is a little shape shifting in all of us. Gravity and time will make your shape shift. To the woman in Song 1:5–6, her skin color was a blemish. She says, "I am black and lovely, daughters of Jerusalem; like the tents of Kedar, like the curtains of Solomon. Do not look on me because I am black, because the sun gazed upon me. The brothers of my mother were angry with me. They made me keeper of the vineyards; my vineyard which is mine I have not kept." First, her "blackness" is *not* a statement about her ethnicity but about her socioeconomic status and required activities in the home (1:6). In other words, she had to work outside and had a farmer's tan. In her culture, the "beautiful" maidens were fair-skinned. Their fathers were rich and hired others to work outside. The "fair" maidens stayed out of the sun and were the envy of young men. Over the last century, Western culture has glorified the tanned body, but agrarian cultures today still consider the untanned body more beautiful.

Conscious of her skin, the woman commands her husband to not look at her because the sun has gazed at her (Song 1:6). The reader can feel the woman's dissatisfaction through her use of hyperbole, or exaggeration. The sun does not make someone black; it makes someone dark. The woman, however, magnifies this perceived blemish through hyperbole. To her, this blemish is no small thing; it is everything. She isn't dark; she is black.

Women today continue to struggle with blemishes (perceived or genuine) in their appearance. Just like the woman in the Song, women today exaggerate their "flaws." Some perceived flaws are not even flaws. God made you with that pasty complexion, big nose, ethnic distinctive, or whatever it is you don't like about your physical appearance. These things are not even flaws; they are simply the way God made you uniquely you. The Song continues to teach women today how to handle imperfections (perceived or genuine) in their bodies. The Song of Songs wife also refers to herself as lovely. Every woman has beauty and blemishes. Whatever blemish you may have, acknowledge it, but also acknowledge your beauty.

Blemishes

The woman in the Song was forced to keep a physical vineyard, which resulted in her metaphorical vineyard (her body) being unkept (Song 1:6). Beauty takes time, money, and the right circumstances, and she didn't have those things.

As in ancient days, young women born into a high socioeconomic situation possess greater potential to enhance their beauty than those born into a lower socioeconomic situation. In Song 1:7, the woman is no longer a vineyard keeper but a shepherdess. She playfully banters with her husband and asks where he grazes and rests at noon. His response in verses 8–9 are the first words that he speaks in the Song of Songs: "If you do not know, O most beautiful among women, follow the tracks of the flock, and feed your little lambs by the tents of the shepherds. I have likened you, my sweetheart, to my mare among the chariots of Pharaoh." Modern readers may find this final compliment insulting, but the husband actually flatters his wife and teaches us some lessons about beauty. Remember that this woman is a shepherdess—this would be the least desirable occupation. Shepherds were outside all the time with their bodies exposed and marred by the elements. But look at how he describes her: "O most beautiful among women"! How could a shepherdess girl who cannot devote resources to beautify her body be beautiful? I remind you again: everyone has beauty and blemishes. This guy knew how to enjoy his wife's beauty by looking past the flaws and finding her beauty. This guy saw the whole picture and loved what he saw.

This husband was not only content with his wife's beauty, but he also admired it and was excited by it. In Song 1:9, he compares her to a mare among Pharaoh's chariots. He is flirting with her and creating a comparison to illustrate how her beauty has affected him. Pharaoh's chariot would be pulled by the biggest and strongest horses—stallions. Here he likens his wife to a mare/filly, or female horse. A little knowledge of hippology (the study of horses) can go a long way here. When a female horse comes near stallions, those stallions become excited. In this text, the wife's beauty has excited her husband in the same way. Her beauty—regardless of her blemishes—excites him.

Five Beauty Lessons

The Bible teaches five lessons concerning beauty from Song 1:5–11.

First, enjoy your wife's beauty. Does she have flaws? Certainly, and so do you! And as the two of you grow older together, you will both get more flaws. I encourage every married man to look at his wife—to really look at her and find the beauty. As I have said repeatedly, everyone has beauty. If there's a problem, it is not that a man's wife lacks beauty; it is that he is blind to it. The Song of Songs husband genuinely admires his wife's beauty and communicates that adoration to her. Obviously, this application directly appeals to married men.

Concerning single men, we are going to talk about flirting in a couple of chapters. In the meantime, do you—like Caleb in the introduction—find a young woman's appearance unappealing? Why? Is it because she is not the knockout that our culture has conditioned you to expect and look for? Could you learn to be physically attracted to a godly young woman?

Second, some flaws can be fixed. Christians may struggle with the ethics of beautifying what, presumably, God has given. In Song 1:11, however, the couple enhances the wife's beauty, showing that beauty can be adorned (more on this later). Flaws that are the effect of the Fall (such as warts, scars, moles, birth defects, crooked teeth, and lazy eye) may be fixed using modern medical intervention. "Flaws" that are *not* the effect of the Fall (such as the shape of your nose, your cheekbones, and your hip size) should *not* be fixed using modern medical intervention. Whenever you turn to modern medical intervention, analyze your heart. An engaged woman had a flaw on her face. Before she got married, the flaw "disappeared." She had enhanced her beauty using modern medical intervention as an act of love for her soon-to-be husband. Evaluating our motivation in these situations can be difficult. So lean on the wisdom of your parents and spiritual mentors. The next three lessons will help you grow in wisdom and help you make these decisions as well.

Third, beauty is not that important. Solomon surrounded himself with beauty. His vineyard cost one thousand silver coins for a reason!

> Whenever you turn to modern medical
> intervention, analyze your heart.

None of his women would have been a shepherdess/vineyard-keeper kind of girl with blemishes. Solomon learned over time that intimacy according to the order of creation is less related to beauty and more related to character. The Bible discusses another godly woman who worked in a vineyard (Prov 31:16–17). She is known as the excellent woman. The strong woman of Proverbs 31, the woman whom every man should want to marry, works with her hands (Prov 31:10–17). And when the Proverbs 31 woman worked with her hands, she sweat, stunk, and got dirty. She labored and probably developed some callouses. As she toiled through the day, the softness of her skin tightened, and the wrinkles in her eyes narrowed. But this woman, this blemished woman, this woman who works with her hands, this strong woman—she is the kind of woman a biblical man wants to find. Young man, you want to marry this woman: "Who can find an excellent woman? For her worth is far above rubies. . . . She considers a field and buys it; from her profits she plants a vineyard" (Prov 31:10, 16).

Young lady, God designed you to work. If you don't want to work because it may mess up your nails/hair/etc., you have more in common with Dame Folly (a foolish woman; we will talk about her more later) than with the excellent woman; you are not thinking biblically. And young man, if you aren't interested in a girl because her beauty is flawed, you are just a pathetic Solomon. You are valuing what Dame Folly has to offer and will never marry the Song of Songs woman—the excellent wife.

Remember Caleb? When he realized that Jill was a Proverbs 31 woman, he had a great awakening. He realized that he had been deceived by the world's definition of beauty and love. He learned to see the beauty that was always there in Jill. The problem was never Jill; it was him. This realization gave him confidence that she was definitely the woman he wanted to marry—she would be his excellent wife! She had become highly attractive to him. After this revelation, there was no way he was going to let her go.

> If you don't want to work because it may mess up your nails/hair/etc., you have more in common with Dame Folly than with the excellent woman.

Fourth, anyone, regardless of economic status, can enjoy beauty (Song 1:5–11). In Song 1:10–11, the scene completely changes. The lovers are no longer shepherd and shepherdess but king and queen. This literary device is called a merism. Solomon has presented the poorest people in the land (shepherds) and the richest people in the land (royalty). Who can enjoy beauty? Anybody. Whether a person is rich or poor, intimacy and beauty are gifts from God for all to enjoy.

Fifth, beauty is important and can be adorned. In Song 1:10–11, the lovers create ornaments, necklaces, and earrings to adorn the wife and provide greater enjoyment for the couple. These expensive adornments enhance the wife's beauty. The couple in the Song enhance the woman's beauty together because the husband likes to look at his beautiful wife, and she enjoys being looked at by him. A couple can use the financial blessings God has given them to enhance and enjoy beauty.

For singles, however, this point of application requires significant discernment. You are unmarried, so what is the purpose of adorning yourself? Our culture's system of dating rages against wisdom, promoting a beautification of women for their own exaltation and sexualization. Certainly, our culture has erred, but should the pendulum be swung in the opposite direction, and should Christian singles adopt an external form of piety that intentionally refrains from adorning their beauty?

PURSUING BEAUTY

It feels great to be wanted, to catch a second glance, or to be the center of attention. But why does it feel so good? Do these desires arise from the indwelling Holy Spirit or the flesh? Dame Folly uses her beauty to exalt herself and/or get what she desires. She uses her beauty as an instrument of war to conquer and subdue men. We will develop this Dame Folly character more in chapter seven. Essentially, she is the bad girl and represents the *disorder* of creation.

I was sitting at a basketball game and noticed an attractive young lady snapping selfie after selfie. Why? This woman does not fear the Lord like the Proverbs 31 kind of woman does; instead, she desires human praise. She was an attractive woman; I am sure she received that praise. Her behavior, however, is not how God ordered creation.

Some women have responded to the vanity of Dame Folly and have altogether cast beauty aside, saying it is neither relevant nor needed. The destitute but excellent woman Ruth worked hard in the fields (Ruth 2), but when she went to meet Boaz, she beautified herself (Ruth 3:3–5). Naomi, the elder mother-in-law, instructed Ruth to put herself together in the best way possible (which wasn't much because she was an impoverished widow) and to propose to the man who was required according to Deuteronomic law to marry her. There is a time to sweat and stink, and there is a time to adorn beauty. The excellent woman possesses the discernment to distinguish between these times.

The discerning single preserves beauty for the glory of God and future pleasure of his/her spouse. Preserve your beauty according to wisdom and prudence within your budget with the financial blessing God entrusted to you. Perhaps God has sovereignly ordained that you work on a farm. You may regularly have to work with your hands, under the sun, or in various beauty-damaging environments. Work just like the Proverbs 31 woman, but do what you can to preserve your beauty for your future husband.

As we have seen, the primary time for beautifying comes after marriage, rather than before marriage. Too often Christian women have this flipped around. Why do some married women adorn themselves only when they go out in public? The appropriate time for beautifying comes back to the purpose of beauty and connects to the power of beauty, which is the sixth beauty lesson from the Song.

Beauty is a powerful force in marriage. The woman's banter excites and arouses the Song of Songs man. And her beauty awakens sexual desire in him. In Song 4:9, the man states, "You have captivated my heart, my sister, my spouse, you have captivated my heart with one of your eyes, with one link of your necklace." The word *captivated* here means "to heart." It says literally, "You have hearted my heart." What caused the husband's heart to be "hearted"? His wife probably winked at him with "one of [her] eyes." So she winks at him, and what do you think happens to his heart? Probably something similar to Pharaoh's stallions when that mare came along (Song 1:9).

As we live in a fallen world and recognize the power of beauty, wisdom would say that at times a young woman should not beautify herself or maybe should even refrain from enhancing beauty. If you are one of the few young ladies who regularly have the guys fawning over you, think about why this happens. Beauty is a powerful force, and wisdom may be saying that you shouldn't beautify yourself. We are not saying you should go out in public looking and smelling like a junior camper who has no concept of personal hygiene. But the opposite is not necessarily appropriate. A young woman can adorn herself in such a way that makes heads turn. If you're that woman, what is motivating you? Be clean, but don't put on the tour de force either. Save that display for your husband. The looks you are getting from men are not the kind of looks you want to get. Be wise.

What about Jenny? Jenny learned through the wisdom of godly counsel how she can adorn the beauty God gave her. She recognized that the guys who can't see her beauty are not the selfless, sacrificial men who characterize the Song of Songs man and are not worth her time. She was liberated, freed from this world's enslaving standard— freed to rest in God's sovereign plan for her life and confident in the God who made her.

CONCLUSION

God made beauty and He delights in beauty. When Jesus returns to establish His kingdom here on earth, it will be a beautiful kingdom (Isa 60). The God of beauty wants us to enjoy beauty as He does, and to beautify the portion of this world over which we have authority. This involves beautifying yourself, your bedroom, house, office, etc. Consider the six lessons concerning beauty from the Song and be wise. Different people and situations demand different responses concerning when and how to beautify or not beautify. Beauty is important, but it also is not important. Be wise. Listen to your parents and/or spiritual mentors. Lean on their wisdom and trust them to guide you into making wise beauty decisions.

| DISCUSSION QUESTIONS:

1. Discuss the difference between external beauty and internal beauty.

2. What is subjective beauty?

3. What is objective beauty?

4. What is the emphasis of the popular maxim "Beauty is in the eye of the beholder"?

5. Is it fair of God to create a few people more beautiful than others?

6. How is beauty like a breath?

7. Discuss some aspects of physical beauty.

8. Is the woman of the Song satisfied with her appearance? Explain why or why not.

9. If you could change something about your appearance, what would it be?

10. How does the husband's description of his wife differ from her own description of herself?

11. What are the six lessons on beauty from the Song?

12. Who is another well-known woman of the Bible who worked in a vineyard?

13. How does Dame Folly use her beauty?

14. Is it ok to adorn your God-given beauty? If so, how should you go about doing that?

CH. 4

DO NOT DISTURB
(2:7; 3:5; 8:4)

Carrie was the girl Josh wanted to marry. He loved hanging out with her: working on their homework together, shooting hoops, and going on dates. But there was a problem; Carrie wasn't as excited about Josh as he was about her. She enjoyed hanging out with Josh and appreciated his company, but dating? When Josh asked Carrie if she would be his girlfriend, she politely declined. Josh was crushed! He asked why, sought counselors' wisdom, was completely confused, and asked, "Where did I go wrong?" It couldn't be their physical relationship; they didn't have one.

Stories like Josh's abound. Why are breakups so difficult, and what can be done to minimize the pain? Or is pain just part of the process? The Song of Songs teaches singles about the danger of awakening love too soon.

Jack and Amanda were struggling. Time after time, they progressed beyond the physical boundaries that their godly parents/mentors had encouraged and that they'd established for themselves. Now they were ashamed and embarrassed. They really liked each other but needed to get their physical relationship under control. How did things even get to this point?

> Many good Christian singles want to honor the Lord in their relationships but underestimate the pull of lust, which is disguised as love.

Jack and Amanda's struggle is similarly all too common. Many good Christian singles want to honor the Lord in their relationships but underestimate the pull of lust, which is disguised as love.

The Song provides answers to both of these situations and points Christian singles toward the path of purity. Love is a powerful force that no one should trifle with. The Song guides singles on how they can love according to the order of creation, avoid the guilt and shame of lust, and evade the pain of breaking up.

SETTING OF THE SONG OF SONGS

In the days of the Bible, most marriages were arranged by parents. Western singles cringe at the thought of their parents asserting so much authority in the selection of their spouse. But the biblical model of courtship and marriage, with rare exception, included the children's input. For example, Samson, while not a model to follow, told his parents whom he wanted to marry and asked them to take steps to secure the union (Judg 14:2). Notice that Samson had a choice, but his parents had to secure the union. What would have happened if they had refused? Deuteronomy 7:3 commands Israel, "Do not make marriages with [the Canaanites; foreigners]. You will not give your daughter to their son, nor will you take their daughter for your son." The primary characteristic of foreigners in that culture was that they did not believe in the God of Israel (Deut 7:3–4). The Israelite parents possessed veto authority in the selection of a spouse, so Samson's parents could have exercised that authority, since the Philistine young woman did not serve Israel's God. To avoid such choices, Proverbs 31 provides instructions from a mother to a *son* concerning what to look for in a wife.

Even with this overarching parental involvement in the selection of a spouse, singles fell in love in days gone past, as they fall in love today.

And God did not leave the unmarried without counsel concerning how to handle these desires. The clearest biblical exhortation concerning these desires comes from the Song of Songs.

THE ADJURATION REFRAIN

Song of Songs 2:7 and 3:5 read exactly the same: "I put you under oath, O daughters of Jerusalem; by the gazelles or by the does of the field; do not stir up, do not even awaken love, until it pleases." When a phrase is repeated in a small book like Song of Songs, that means it is an important phrase. It is called a refrain, kind of like a chorus in a song. Just like the chorus is repeated for emphasis, so also is this refrain. In fact, it is repeated a third time in a modified form in Song 8:4: "I put you under oath, O daughters of Jerusalem! Why would you stir it up? Why would you awaken love until it pleases?" Three times the woman directly pleads with the single ladies not to awaken love until the appropriate time. While this refrain is primarily directed toward the single ladies, the single men are not excluded. When the woman says, "I plead with *you*," the pronoun *you* is masculine. So, this refrain is directed to all, but the specific audience is young ladies.

Making an Oath

The first word of the refrain literally means "I make you swear an oath." The Song of Songs woman uses the word *oath* to emphasize the importance and commitment necessary to fulfill the plea. To bind an oath means to "put under an obligation" or "to constrain with legal authority." Notice the ones who bind the oath: "the gazelles and the does of the field." Now you may be thinking, "These are odd things to bind an oath. I mean, if you want to break the oath, couldn't you just go shoot Bambi, then be free of your oath?" Yes, these animals are odd things to swear by, but it isn't that simple. Normally, when someone swore an oath, that person would be bound to the oath by someone or something higher than himself/herself, such as a deity. For example, we would expect the refrain to read, "I plead with you, O daughters of Jerusalem, by the Lord of Armies and God Almighty." But that's not what it says. The woman created a pun here. In Hebrew, the word for *gazelles* is exactly the same as the word for *armies*. The Old Testament regularly identifies God as the "Lord of Armies." The original readers would have understood that *gazelles* stood for the Lord of Armies. Similarly, the phrase "does of the field" sounds almost exactly like "God Almighty" in Hebrew (El Shaddai). The woman is not asking the daughters of Jerusalem to swear by some animals but to make a solemn oath before the Lord of Armies, God Almighty!

This pun is important because God's name is excluded from the Song of Songs. The pagan religions of Solomon's day incorporated sexuality into their religions. It seems that Solomon intentionally omitted God's name from the Song so people would not associate sexuality with religion. It is a spiritual thing for a husband/wife to serve his/her spouse sexually, but it is not a sacramental or religious act. Intimacy is *not* a way that a person connects to God. The marriage bed should be undefiled (Heb 13:4), but being undefiled does not make it a place for people to draw near to God, who does, by the way, delight when He sees a couple drawing near to one another in the marriage bed and enjoying something He created for their pleasure (Song 5:1).

Awakening Love

Next the woman adjures the young ladies to not awaken love. This metaphor should make a reader pause and think. What does she mean by *awakening love*? Many well-intentioned Christians encourage purity through a virginity pledge, but these Christians have misunderstood this oath. This woman is pleading for way more than just remaining a virgin. She is encouraging the reader to not even *awaken* love. Understanding what it means to "awaken love" becomes of paramount concern to the unmarried Christian.

> Do not awaken love until you can go
> all the way.

Until It Pleases

The Christian should let love sleep until the appropriate time. The time, however, is not explicitly stated in the refrain. After all, when does love "please"? The Hebrew word for *please* has the idea of something a person delights in or takes pleasure in. One difficulty, or a peril, of love is that if you awaken it too early, it can create problems. You do not want to awaken love until you can take pleasure in it—until you can delight in it. The message of the adjuration refrain is clear—do not awaken love until you can go all the way.

DEFINING LOVE

So what is love, and how does a person not awaken it? When you think about love, consider what awakens it. Christian singles who care about their purity often want to know how far is too far. "How far can I go?" But singles should, rather, ask themselves, "Does this action awaken love? Does holding hands awaken love? Do hugs? Kisses? Dances? Intimate embraces?" We will answer some of these questions, but first, consider what love is.

Distinguishing Loves

Let's clarify for a moment what kind of love we are talking about. You should love everyone with a brotherly/sisterly kind of love. You should "love your neighbor as yourself" (Mark 12:31). That love for your neighbor (and whomever else the Lord has placed in your life) should be patient, kind, selfless, and all the other characteristics of a 1 Corinthians 13 kind of love. Every Christian should have this kind of a selfless, sacrificial love for all of those around him/her. Every Christian should regularly stir up and awaken this love for the Lord and for his/her neighbor. The Song of Songs, however, clearly speaks concerning a different kind of love.

The love of which the ideal woman speaks in Song 2:7, 3:5, and 8:4 is a permanent, exclusive, jealous, unquenchable kind of love. It is a love that is like death, as there isn't any going back. This kind of love is permanent. The love in the Song is also a jealous kind of love. It's a "He's/she's mine; back off" kind of love. This Song of Songs love is an exclusive love for another person. Maybe another way to think of it is like an unquenchable fire. This exclusive, permanent kind of love for another is like a fire that is never supposed to go out. When this fiery kind of love is awakened, it isn't meant to be put out. It rages within you and is designed to continue until one of you physically dies. We will talk about this love more throughout the book. Playing with this kind of love is like playing with fire. And it is quite likely that you and others will get burned. Consider Song 8:6–7, think about these metaphors, and note this kind of love that needs to sleep until it pleases.

SONG
8

> [6]Set me as a seal upon your heart, as a seal upon your arm;
>   because love is as strong as death;
>   jealousy is hard like the grave;
>   its flames are flames of fire, the flame of the Lord.
> [7]Many waters are not able to extinguish love;
>   and rivers cannot flood over it.
> If a man would give all the wealth of his house for love,
>   they would despise him for it.

> Love is something a person can create and cultivate. We can choose to stir it up and awaken it or *choose not to*.

Loving God: Thinking about Love

Let's think about love a little more. Consider Deuteronomy 6:5, "And you will love the Lord your God with all of your heart, and with all of your soul, and with all of your strength." In this passage, God commands Israel to love Him. Does that seem odd? Love is presumably a feeling, so how can it be commanded? Lovers often talk about "falling in love." This idea, falling in love, sounds accidental, a chemical or divinely ordained action, something that just passively happens to you. But in Deuteronomy 6:5, *love* has imperatival force. It is something that a person is required to do. Love is something a person can create and cultivate. It is almost as if we have control over love—we can choose to stir it up and awaken it or *choose not to*. Love isn't something that happens passively to us; it is an action we choose. Deuteronomy 6:5 teaches that you can and should create a love for God. So if you do not love God, you should do things to stir up a love for God.

Love for God entails obeying His commands. First John 5:3 states, "For this is the love of God, that we keep His commandments." Obeying God's commands is evidence that someone loves Him. While love for God includes obedience, it is not limited to obedience. Love for God actually empowers obedience. Psalm 42:1 reads, "As a deer longs for the streams of water, so does my soul long for you, O God!" The thirsty animal's *desire* urges it toward the waters; similarly, the believer's *desire* for God urges him/her toward God.

So, we continue to ask, "What is love?" Love for God is first intellectual. It involves something you know. From Deuteronomy 6, you have to *know* the law of the Lord. From Psalm 42, the one who desires God remembers things about God. And as one thinks about God, remembers who He is, and meditates upon His Word (Ps 1), that person cultivates affections (love) for God—affections that are both not fleeting, like a feeling, and deeper than mere knowledge. This affection for God propels a person to the ends of the earth—it leads a person to do the illogical. It leads a person into prison, banishment, or fire because this love transcends all loves. This is biblical love.

This love for God is the kind of love that a man should have for his wife. This is the kind of love a wife should have for her husband. This is the kind of love with which a woman desires to be loved. This is also the kind of love with which a man desires to be loved. It is an earnest, fervent, burning love, a love that transcends all other loves but one—love for God. It is a love that denies self and serves another, a jealous love that forsakes all others and seizes the one.

Just as this love can be fostered, created, and awakened in obedience to God's Law (Deut 6:5), so also can this love be intentionally denied and left to slumber, according to Song 2:7, 3:5, and 8:4. Don't even start love until "it pleases." If the ideal woman spoke today, how would she word it? What would she say? "Don't fall in love"? According to Song 2:7, 3:5, 8:4, a single should not love until it pleases. Do you want to remain a virgin until marriage? If you don't love, you probably won't make love! The Song encourages singles to make a conscious, intentional decision to let love sleep.

Western culture has, unfortunately, adopted a model for finding a spouse that is prone to awakening love. The relationships singles have with one another should be non-awakening relationships. They should be familial—loving a brother or sister in the Lord as a brother or sister in the Lord, with all purity (1 Tim 5:2). We encourage you to refrain from telling a significant other that you love him/her for a *very* long time. You think you love that person, but as we will discover in the Song, your love has not been genuinely tested. In fact, your love can't be tested until you have covenanted with that person to serve him/her sacrificially, selflessly, and jealously.

Josh realized that while he had never had a physical relationship with Carrie, he had let his thoughts wander and had cultivated an affection for Carrie that was not based on reality. He awakened a love for her through his own unchecked thoughts and desires. When Carrie did not reciprocate his affection, he was left to extinguish a fire that was never designed to be extinguished. We know that this is not an unusual situation. Working at a Christian college, we counsel young men and women like Josh and Carrie all the time.

Defining Physical Love

If you understand what we were just talking about, then defining the physical boundaries in a relationship should be a no-brainer. Nevertheless, many young singles would benefit from a more specific explanation of what awakening love physically looks like. While you work through this section, remember that Song 2:7, 3:5, and 8:4 are talking about more than just physical boundaries. Not awakening love involves a completely different approach to a relationship. And it applies to speech and thoughts because certain words awaken love and certain thoughts can awaken love as well. God's plan for purity includes words and thoughts. In fact, we will talk about the words in the next chapter.

For now, let's consider the question, "How far is too far?" Most singles ask this question because they desire a physical relationship. Ask yourself if the desire for a physical relationship comes from the Spirit of

God or from your sinful flesh. This question usually comes from a fleshly, worldly heart that desires affection before the appropriate time. If you desire physical affection, consider the source of that desire and an appropriate response to it (Col 3:5–6; James 4:1–10). How far is too far? We have decided to answer this question, praying that some of these specifics can help guide you onto the correct path. And to do that, we are going to ask and answer specific questions. As you think through them, keep in mind the biblical question, Does this awaken love? In fact, always keep that question in mind when you plan your time with your significant other. Do *not* wait until you are in the moment. You must have a plan. Sit down and talk with your parents, pastor, pastor's wife, and/or godly mentors whom the Lord has brought into your life; then set up those boundaries. Also get accountability in place to make sure you stick to those boundaries.

Can We Kiss?

The prince awakens the damsel with a kiss. A couple kisses passionately on a park bench. A young man gives his girlfriend a goodnight kiss. A father kisses his daughter goodnight. A kiss can mean different things in different situations. In Bible times, a kiss could be a sign of submission (Ps 2:12), or a kind of greeting, "Greet each other with a holy kiss" (Rom 16:16; 1 Cor 16:20; 2 Cor 13:12; 1 Thess 5:26). After a lovely date, is a holy kiss the kind of kiss a young person is bending in for? By the way, most of the kissing recorded in the Bible takes place between family members (for example, Gen 27:26; 31:28; 2 Sam 14:33). In Bible times, kissing was a cultural greeting. But the ancients were not naïve; they knew of a different kind of kiss. That kind of kiss is the subject of this section.

We can kiss one way in public, and nobody thinks anything about it. We could kiss a different way, and people might shout, "Get a room!"

Proverbs 7:13 describes this other, get-a-room kind of kiss. In Proverbs 7, a seductress seizes a naïve young man and kisses him. She is not his sister saying hello! She is seducing him to rob him of his money, maybe even his life. The kiss is the beginning then her words appeal to the fleshly desires of his heart. Her kiss awakens him.

Defining physical boundaries can reveal the deceitfulness of our hearts. Scripture never says, "Thou shalt not kiss"! So, is kissing ok? Even without a chapter and verse, singles should be able to discern the awakening effect of kissing.

The Song of Songs establishes this point. In Song 1:2, the wife propositions the husband: "Let him kiss me with the kisses of his mouth—for your caresses are better than wine." She wants his kisses because she enjoys his intimate caresses. She wants to have sex with him, so she says, "Let him kiss me!" And they progress to the chamber (1:4). This kind of kissing awakens love, and only married couples should enjoy this kind of kissing.

In Song 8:1, the wife again expresses desire for her husband's kisses: "If only you were like a brother to me, one who sucked upon the breasts of my mother; I would find you outside; I would kiss you! They would not despise me." This verse seems odd to the modern reader, but it is an excellent illustration of the different kinds of kisses. In their culture, the public did not despise the brother-sister kiss, but they did despise the public romantic kiss. The wife here desires to kiss her husband, not her brother. She wants to kiss him passionately wherever they are, which she cannot do in public without being despised. Clearly, she is referring to passionate kisses because in Song 8:2 she brings her husband to their house, where she offers him intimacy. Romantic kissing is again connected to sexual intimacy.

Romantic kissing is connected to sexual intimacy.

Romantic kissing is described two additional times in the Song of Songs, where it is again connected to sexual intimacy. In Song 5:16, the wife says, "His mouth is sweet." The Hebrew word for *mouth* refers to the palate, the inside of his mouth, which she considers "sweet." The word *sweet* is a metaphor for something sugary—something desirable. (It sounds as though he knew how to freshen his mouth!) In Song 7:9, the husband similarly says, "Your mouth is like the best wine." This time *wine* is a metaphor for intoxication. Tasting the inside of the other person's mouth is intoxicating—it causes a loss of control. So a couple proceeds down the path of "love" by participating in intoxicating (losing-control) activities. What is popularly considered "making out" is clearly connected to sexual intimacy in the Song of Songs.

Romantic kissing and making out awaken love. But it is not just the kissing that awakens love; it is the desire for the kissing. If you want to kiss, you need to identify this desire as fleshly, kill it, and cultivate biblical affections (Col 3:5–15). Talk to a pastor, parent, or mentor on how to have victory over these desires because the desire for romantic kissing is clearly included in the appeal to the daughters of Jerusalem to not awaken love (Song 2:7; 3:5; 8:4).

If you feel yourself rebelling against what you just read, God's Word should convince you that Angela and I are biblical here. If, however, you are still not persuaded, consider the words of Lauren Winner:

> I realize some readers will think that kissing ought to be off limits until you've said I do. If you're in the no-kissing camp, don't worry, I won't try to talk you out of it. I know people who've held to the no-kissing-before-marriage rule, and through knowing them I've moved from thinking they're nuts to having the utmost respect for them. But I never joined their cause. What's compelling about the no-kissing rule is its clarity. It is very, very clear. It admits no gray area. If you're not even smooching, you're unlikely to find yourself sliding down a slippery slope to sex itself.

> There is something decidedly un-natural about sparking desire and then arresting it, night after night. To refrain from kissing is to avoid not only temptation, but also the odd shocks, fits, and starts of interrupted desire.[1]

Winner's perspective is common among Christian dating books. The authors recognize the danger of kissing but fail to draw a clear line. Winner seems completely oblivious to the adjuration refrain in the Song of Songs, but she perfectly illustrates from her personal experience the danger of kissing: "To refrain from kissing is to avoid not only temptation, but also the odd shocks, fits, and starts of interrupted desire." Kissing awakens love. If you kiss, you have to do something completely *unnatural*—shut down the desire to go further. Romantic kissing leads to sex. This is the order of creation.

Have you ever wondered why a minister at a wedding says, "You may kiss the bride"? The kiss is a publicly appropriate symbol of the mysterious "two have become one" union of a husband and wife. A new family has been created. If you have already kissed, stop and wait to kiss again on your wedding. If you haven't, don't awaken love in this way. Save your first kiss for your wedding day.

Can We Dance?

Dancing, like kissing, needs to be defined before we address it. Dancing was a regular activity in the ancient world. Exodus 15 describes Miriam and the Israelite women dancing in celebration of the Lord's victory over the Egyptian army. In Song 7:1–9, the wife dances a dance very different from the one Miriam and the Israelite women danced. As we learn from Song 7, the wife dances before her husband, and she clearly has little or, more likely, no clothes on—except sandals (7:1). To simply pronounce

---

1   Lauren F. Winner, *Real Sex: The Naked Truth about Chastity* (Grand Rapids: Brazos Press, 2006), 107.

that dancing is right or wrong is naïve. We need to ask, "Will this activity awaken love?"

The dancing recorded in the Bible can be categorized primarily under two headings: celebratory and religious. Some of the dancing recorded in the Bible is carnal (e.g., the Israelites around the golden calf in Exod 32; Salome before Herod in Matt 14:6; Mark 6:22), but that is not the kind of dancing Angela and I want you to consider here.

In Exodus 15, Miriam and the Israelite women danced in celebration. Notice that only the women danced; this was not a coed dance. When David danced, he performed a religious solo dance before the Lord (2 Sam 6:14–26). Nowhere does Scripture present coed dancing as holy except between husband and wife in the Song of Songs. Jeremiah 31:13 even supports the separation of the sexes: "Then the young women will rejoice in dance; the young men and the old men together." The young men and old men dancing together implies that the sexes were separated during the celebratory dancing recorded in the Bible. Dancing is a very physical activity; so it would be wise not to dance with someone of the opposite sex. Proponents of dancing create a false analogy when they claim that coed dancing is ok because David danced before the Lord. David's dance was very different than a couple's romantic dance.

Dancing with one's own spouse is a different matter. We believe it should be encouraged. For one thing, it has a unifying effect. Dancing requires a couple to work together for mutual enjoyment. It literally is two people becoming one on the dance floor. We were once asked if we dance. Well, we try to dance; we aren't very good. We were asked if we tangoed. We're not that athletic. But we like to slow dance. I would never let my wife dance with another man. I assure you; dancing awakens love.

And what about Jack and Amanda? While they believed that anything beyond kissing was "too far," they realized that their regular kissing provided opportunities to make small, seemingly insignificant compromises that ended up taking them, well, "too far." They realized that their physical relationship wasn't based on love but lust. Scenarios like Jack and Amanda's are very complicated to resolve. The grace of God, however, is greater than any sin, and nothing is beyond the capacity of God to redeem. If you are in a situation like theirs, you can do two things that Jack and Amanda did: they repented of their sin and obeyed biblical counsel concerning the next step forward.

CONCLUSION

Perhaps you desire to participate in a form of physical affection with your boyfriend/girlfriend that we did not mention. We cannot discuss every form of physical affection, much less prove it by Scripture. So we encourage you to ask yourself regularly, "Does this word/thought/action awaken love?" The advice in this chapter should give you sufficient guidance to recognize awakening behavior and guide you in the path of life.

If you think, however, that everything is ok in your relationship because you aren't having sex, you are mistaken. Ezekiel has been called the porno-prophet because of the extreme sexual language he used. Modern culture has defined "virgin" too specifically. Ezekiel 23:2–3 reads, "Son of man, there were two women, the daughters of one mother. And they engaged in prostitution in Egypt; when they were young they prostituted themselves. There, their breasts were pressed; and there, their virgin nipples were fondled." Virginity applies to more than sexual intercourse. You shouldn't need us (or the Bible) to tell you that. If you need a verse like Ezekiel 23:3 to help you define a "line," you are blind in your sin and you need to repent. You need to separate from your boyfriend/girlfriend, involve your Christian community, seek repentance, slay the flesh, and begin walking in the Spirit. God created a beautiful place where this happens—the church. Get plugged in.

DISCUSSION QUESTIONS:

1. In Bible times, how were marriages secured and established?

2. What important phrase/refrain is repeated three times in the Song?

3. What does "by the gazelles and does of the field" mean?

4. What does it mean to "awaken love"?

5. When is the appropriate time to awaken love?

6. What type of love does the Song speak about?

7. How does the command to love God in Deuteronomy 6:5 help us understand the choice to love or not to love?

8. How should singles love the person of the opposite gender?

9. Discuss the danger of kissing and awakening love prematurely.

10. What are the different kinds of dancing mentioned in the Bible?

CH. 5 | AWAKENING THE SENSES
(1:12—2:7)

Art, poetry, and music appeal to the senses. Look around you. What colors do you see? Have you considered why God made grass green? Why such a variety of birds? Take a deep breath. What do you smell? Gently brush your hand across your arm and think about what you are feeling. Take a moment; what can you hear right now? Both Angela and I had piano lessons when we were children. Our parents sought to instill in us a love for music. I, however, despised aesthetics (beauty, the arts) and rebelled against this guidance. After three years, my parents gave up. It was not until I studied the Song of Songs that I recognized this defect in my character. The biblical worldview values aesthetics because God values aesthetics and designed humans to enjoy the senses.

> ## God designed intimacy as a sensuous experience.

Song 1:5—2:7 teaches the reader that God designed intimacy as a sensuous experience. Our evolutionary world, pornographic culture, and "man is a machine" anthropology indirectly, if not directly, teach that sex is simply a biological experience. Yes, biology is involved, but the Song teaches that God designed intimacy as a sensuous experience in which two people become one in more than just a biological way. God wants men to be strong and tough yet soft and gentle. King David not only fought Israel's enemies but also wrote many of the psalms. Biblical masculinity fights for what is right, but it also remembers what the man is fighting for—the beauty that God created. Singles, particularly single men, should cultivate their aesthetic tastes.

A SENSE FILLED EXPERIENCE

Song 1:12—2:6 invokes all five senses: touch, taste, smell, hearing, and sight. The sense of taste is found in Song 2:3–5, and the sense of touch in Song 2:6. We will examine the senses of smell, sight, and hearing more closely from Song 1:12–17.

Smell and Hearing (Song 1:12–14)

SONG
1

> *12While the king was around his table,*
> *my spikenard gave off its scent.*
> *13A sachet of myrrh is my lover to me,*
> *he spends the night between my breasts.*
> *14A cluster of henna blossoms is my lover to me,*
> *in the vineyards of En Gedi.*

In Song 1:12–14, the wife speaks of "the king" at his table. Her scent draws her husband to herself—"my spikenard gave off its scent." In the very next verse, however, the husband is a scent ("A sachet of myrrh is my lover to me"), and he is found intimately connected to her ("he spends the night between my breasts"). Notice that the two smells are combined, her spikenard with the bundle of myrrh, which represents the male lover. Through the sense of smell, the couple unites.

The imagery in this section also illustrates the power of words. But first a word of warning: young man, as you read what the Song of Songs woman says, take every thought captive to the obedience of Jesus the Messiah.

A woman in ancient days would place valuables or a fragrance in a sachet, which would then hang between her breasts. The Song of Songs wife likens her husband to the bundle of myrrh that rests in this intimate location. And she describes her good-smelling husband in v. 14:

"A cluster of henna blossoms is my lover to me, in the vineyards of En Gedi." The description seems rather innocuous, but it is actually quite erotic. We already talked about the meaning of the vineyards in chapter one. Remember how "sachet of myrrh" in verse 13 and "cluster of henna blossoms" in verse 14 correspond, while "between my breasts" in verse 13 corresponds to the "vineyards of En Gedi" in verse 14? This parallelism helps a reader understand and interpret the text. The "vineyards of En Gedi" are parallel with the wife's breasts, representing all of the sexual delights she offers her husband.. The literal En Gedi is an oasis of pristine natural beauty in southern Israel; it is surrounded by an excessively dry desert. The Song of Songs wife offers herself to her husband as a refreshing oasis (En Gedi) away from the trials and travails of life (arid desert). Her sexual delights provide refreshment to the man like water provides refreshment to an individual crossing a desert. The reader should easily understand how speech like this would be awakening for a man and perhaps be equivalent to a modern proposition, or invitation to have sex. Words are powerful.

We contend that hearing is the most powerfully arousing sense for both sexes. The sense of sight may capture a young man's attention, but the woman's playful proposition pulls him in. While men may seem most interested in sight, what they really desire is to be desired. The adulterous woman of Proverbs 7 knew this and used words to express her desire for the naïve youth (Prov 7:13, 21). The wife of the Song also uses words to awaken desire, her husband's desire. We will consider the implications for singles in a moment, but for now, let's see how the husband replies.

Hearing and Sight (Song 1:15)

SONG
1

>[15]*Look at you! Beautiful, my sweetheart;*
>   *Look at you! Beautiful, your eyes are doves.*

The man hears his wife's proposition and responds in Song 1:15 with a corresponding compliment of her appearance. Two times he repeats, "Look at you! Beautiful," which emphasizes the sense of sight. Then, somewhat oddly, he compliments only her eyes. Why her eyes? He is using a play on words, words that she has already used (Song 1:14). He was *listening* to her. She referred to herself as En Gedi. In Hebrew, the place En Gedi (*ayn gedi*) sounds like the word *eye* (*ayn*). This banter between them demonstrates that intimacy is more than biology. It involves all the senses—particularly the sense of hearing, through flirtatious banter.

BECOMING ONE (SONG 1:16–17)

SONG
1

>[16]*Look at you! Handsome! Surely, pleasant.*
>   *Surely, our couch is green.*
>[17]*The beams of our houses are cedar; our rafter is firs.*

After the husband compliments his wife's beauty, she responds by telling him he is "beautiful." Today the woman might have said handsome, but that's not the point. She has also been listening, and now she responds to his words in kind, calling him beautiful. She also describes their couch as "green," which seems rather odd to us. This is another wordplay. Her husband had called her "my sweetheart" (1:15); now she uses a word, *green*, which in Hebrew sounds similar to "my sweetheart." What would you call this dialogue between husband and wife; this complimenting of one another? Their dialogue doesn't end here, so through this section, you should be considering the power of words.

Then the woman begins talking about their house (1:17). The scene she paints is one of the Garden of Eden. The Song of Songs paints two pictures of love: ideal love and real love. This section describes ideal love—the way love is supposed to be. The En Gedi / Garden of Eden oasis setting thus creates a perfect environment for love the way God designed it. This setting recalls the instruction from Genesis 2:24: "Therefore a man will leave his father and mother and cling to his wife, and they shall become one flesh." Throughout this section, the two become one. They become one in smell in verses 12–14; then, by using the same word to describe each other's appearance, they become one in sight in verses 15–16; they also become one in speech by using wordplay and playfully bantering back and forth. Finally, they recreate the Garden of Eden and create an Edenic house—a place of bliss, felicity, and delight—where they can unite.

Song 1:17 reads awkwardly in the Hebrew because of the two-becoming-one wordplay. Song 1:17 literally reads, "The beams of our houses are cedars, our rafter is firs." Notice the *our* pronouns. It isn't "his" or "hers"; it is "our houses" and "our firs." Did you notice that *houses* is plural, but *rafter* is singular? You probably would expect a husband and wife to have a singular house with a plurality of rafters! This wording is awkward because the verse is moving from their closeness to their union. And one more point: Hebrew nouns have gender, and the genders are combined in the last word, *firs*. Song 1:17 reads, "The beams [fem.] of *our* houses are cedars [masc.], *our* rafter is firs [feminine/masculine]." This final word, *firs,* is used only here in the Hebrew Bible. Solomon created a wordplay to illustrate the two becoming one even through the construction of their Edenic house.

Consider how these words would make a young man feel. Also, consider their goal, particularly the goal in the Song. Why is the woman talking in this way? The answer may be obvious, but what implications might this way of talking have for singles, particularly in regard to the adjuration to "not awaken love."

This teaching of the Song concerning sexuality and intimacy has another application for singles today, and it flies in the face of the world's teaching on sexuality. You are not an animal that can go around having sex with anyone and everyone. God designed sex to work a certain way, and this (as described in the Song) is it! Becoming one involves more than biology; it involves the wrapping together of two souls who experience all of the senses together. This is ideal love. This is the way God designed intimacy. This is the order of creation.

> Becoming one involves more than biology.

POWERFUL WORDS (SONG 2:1-6)

SONG
2

> [1]I am a meadow flower of Sharon, a lily of the valleys.
> [2]Like a lily among the thorns,
>   so is my sweetheart among the daughters.
> [3]Like an apple tree among the trees of the forest,
>   so is my lover among the sons;
>   in his shade I desired passionately,
>   and his fruit is sweet to my palate.
> [4]He brought me to the house of wine,
>   and his banner over me is love.
> [5]Sustain me with raisin cakes;
>   refresh me with apples, because I am lovesick.
> [6]His left arm is under my head, and his right arm embraces me.

I remember my dad telling me, "Sticks and stones may break my bones, but words will never hurt me." This modern proverb intends to strengthen children's resilience so they are less affected by name-calling and verbal bullying. Modern critics have noted that the proverb teaches a falsehood, because words are powerful, and they do hurt. The unknown original author of the proverb likely knew quite well that words hurt and sought to strengthen children's resolve against powerful words. Yes, words are powerful, and Song 1:5—2:7 teaches the reader the power of words.

The division between chapters one and two in the Song is an unfortunate division. There is a transition between 1:17 and 2:1, but the transition is slight. The couple continues talking, teaching their readers about the power of words—the sense of hearing.

In Song 2:1, the woman states, "I am a meadow flower of Sharon, a lily of the valleys." Now that may seem like a compliment to us, but the man corrects her in the next verse: "Like a lily among the thorns, so is my sweetheart among the daughters." Did you see what he just did there? She is saying, "I am just another girl [lily], just like all the girls in the world [valley]." Then he comes in and says, "You are my girl, and all those other girls are thorns [and you don't touch thorns]." What would be the English word to describe this verbal wordplay? Consider how these words would make a young woman feel. Also, consider their goal, particularly the goal in the Song.

In Song 2:3, the woman responds to the man's compliment by complimenting his "shade" and "fruit": "Like an apple tree among the trees of the forest, so is my lover among the sons; in his shade I desired passionately; and his fruit is sweet to my palate." The other young men are trees in the forest; but only her husband is the apple tree, and she desires to sit in its shade. In the Old Testament, shade is a common metaphor for protection. The men of an ancient community would provide a measure of protection (shade) for the women of the community, but this woman greatly desires her husband's protection. And not only does he protect her, but he also provides for her as well (cf. Ruth 2—3 and Boaz's provision for and protection of Ruth). This special tree produces fruit—sweet fruit.

The woman expounds on this idea of provision and protection in Song 2:4–5. In verse 4, she says her husband takes her to the "house of wine." Wine is intoxicating, and she is intoxicated with his love. Consider what has been going on since Song 1:5. This husband and wife have been flirting back and forth. Through this dialogue, the wife's love is awakened; she is now intoxicated by her husband's love. She then states: "His banner over me is love." The banner would be similar to a modern flag (cf. Num 2:10, 17, 25). When an army conquers a city or territory, it raises the flag (banner) over the conquered territory. So the wife is saying, "You have conquered me!" In this way, the Song metaphorizes the sexual act, likening it to an army (the husband) conquering a city (his wife). This metaphor reappears in the Song (6:4–10; 8:10) and teaches several truths concerning biblical sexuality. The husband does not conquer through coercion, manipulation, lies, or force, but through *love*: "His banner over me is *love*." He does not say, "I have placed my banner"; rather, the wife declares, "his banner over me is love." Biblical sexuality includes a willing and submissive wife who desires her husband's *loving* and *peaceful* conquest. We will develop this thought further in our discussion of Song 6 and 8.

> The husband does not "conquer" through coercion, manipulation, lies, or force, but through *love*.

Talking, Flirting, and Sweet Nothings

Song 1:5—2:6 teaches singles about the power of love. It is a powerful force that, according to Song 2:7, singles should not awaken until the appropriate time. The chief sense that awakens love in this section of the Song is the sense of hearing. Through flirting, poetry, and wordplay, the couple grow in their affection for one another to the point that they are no longer two, but one. Their speech has an intoxicating effect, making them drunk with love.

In sum, the Song teaches Christian singles to be careful with their words. Unfortunately, this message has been lost in the Christian church. Phylicia Masonheimer writes,

> Then there is *flirtation*. In my conservative teen years, this was a cardinal sin. Girls wondered whether flirtation was okay, what it looked like, and whether or not their friends' actions toward boys qualified as flirting or just friendliness. Flirtation—I was taught—is inherently deceitful and insincere. But is that true?
> Once I started dating, these regulations on flirtation became a heavy burden to bear. I debated whether I could show interest, and if so, how much? Where was the line for a godly woman who just plain *liked* a guy? As I dug deeper into the Word, I couldn't find a solid case against flirtation when it was expressed to a person you genuinely wanted to date. There was nothing dishonest or unladylike about expressing interest in a man. And as I raked through history on relationships and dating, I discovered that a woman's initiation was more accepted and normal than courtship culture would have me believe.[1]

Masonheimer correctly encourages Christian wives to flirt with their husbands. The Song supports this message; in fact, in Song 1:7, it is the wife who begins the flirting! In Song 8:5, it is the wife who awakens her husband's affection! Repeatedly the Song encourages Christian wives to be the initiator. Masonheimer errs, however, by failing to apply the adjuration refrain ("do not awaken love") to flirting. Christian singles should ask themselves, "Does this speech awaken love?" Masonheimer's quote is helpful, however, because it illustrates the difficulty of determining whether speech is awakening or not.

A couple's speech should correspond to the level of commitment in their relationship. The wife in the Song propositions her husband. Playful banter of a sexual nature clearly awakens love and, therefore, should be reserved for married couples. The flirtation in Song 2:1–2 is of an exclusive nature: "Like a lily among the thorns, so is my sweetheart among the daughters." The man essentially says, "You are my beauty,

---

1   Lisa Jacobson and Phylicia Masonheimer, *The Flirtation Experiment: Putting Magic, Mystery, and Spark into Your Everyday Marriage* (Nashville: Thomas Nelson, 2021), xiv–xv.

and all those other girls are untouchable." Young lady, if a guy told you that, how would you feel? Would it awaken something inside you, particularly if it came from a guy you liked? At what point should a couple begin speaking about an exclusive relationship like the one the Song of Songs husband is describing?

Here is an example. In high school, the girls just plain liked Spencer. He was gregarious and genuine, and he played the guitar—there is just something about a guy and a guitar. He also had a reputation for hurting girls. Spencer knew he wasn't ready for a serious relationship, but he wanted to be ready when the time came. When Spencer was eighteen, he liked a young lady in his youth group and could see himself married to her in five-plus years. Through a text, Spencer asked her theoretically if she were to marry a guy like him, what would she be looking for? Then he shared this seemingly innocuous conversation with his mentor, which precipitated a conversation about how words awaken love. He never intended to hurt girls, but he hurt them nonetheless. Spencer needed an older man, not a teenage girl in youth group, to mentor him.

Think about how your words may affect the person with whom you are speaking. Also, if that person likes you, you should be even more careful. Awakening love concerns not just yourself but also the person you are speaking to.

We are not saying you should not talk or joke around with your friends. Enjoy the days of your youth! These are good years of your life (Eccl 11:9–10), but remember your Creator, who will "judge your motives and actions" (11:9 NET). Let wisdom guide your speech. What you should or should not say needs to be governed by the fear of the Lord (12:13).

And that guideline includes the three special words *I love you.* We all want to love and be loved by someone. When another person reciprocates our love, the world is a better place. But what is love? And do you really love that person? While some individuals may say, "I love you," simply to manipulate the other person, most couples believe they genuinely love one another. Again, what is love? And do you really love that person?

The Song of Songs defines love using provocative metaphors concerning the nature of love: "Love is as strong as death, jealousy is hard like the grave, its flames are flames of fire, the flame of the Lord. Many waters are not able to extinguish love; and rivers cannot flood over it" (Song 8:6–7). God designed romantic love to be a permanent, fierce, inextinguishably fiery affection. Do you really love that person? When would it be appropriate to say, "I love [have a permanent, fierce, inextinguishably fiery affection for] you"? Playing with love is like playing with fire.

CONCLUSION

Song 1:5–2:7 teaches that intimacy invokes all the senses. Develop your aesthetic tastes while you are single. Consider learning to play a musical instrument. Write a poem. Compose a song. Take writing/ music/speech/ classes. This understanding of Christian aesthetics transformed our ministry. We encourage the young men and women whom the Lord has entrusted to us to love art, music, and beauty. God desires for His creatures to enjoy His creation and then to worship Him as the Creator.

Finally, consider the power of words to awaken love, and be careful with your speech. We all want to be loved, but be mindful of how your words could affect another person. Speak to your parents, pastors, and godly mentors, and trust them to guide you with your speech. Then have fun and enjoy the days of your youth.

DISCUSSION QUESTIONS:

1. How does the Song highlight the sense of hearing?

2. In what ways are words powerful?

3. What are the husband and wife doing with their words in Song 2:1–3?

4. What do the metaphors shade and fruit mean in Song 2:3?

5. How is speech a powerful force in a guy-girl relationship?

6. When should flirtatious speech and actions be employed?

7. What should our speech be governed by?

8. What can you do to develop your aesthetic taste?

CH. 6 | FINDING YOUR HAPPILY EVER AFTER
(2:8–17)

Some well-meaning Christians promote the idea that singles only need to wait until they are married, then everything will be great! They claim that if you have sex before marriage, you will mess up the intimacy within marriage. This is only half true. Premarital sex only compounds a couple's existing problems. Even if the two let love sleep until the appropriate time, they will still have to work through issues in their relationship. Song 2:8–17 addresses this truth.

After the adjuration refrain in Song 2:7 ("Do not awaken love *until* it pleases"), the Song discusses a *time* to awaken love through metaphor—spring. Spring has sprung, and spring is the time for love (Song 2:10–13). Solomon uses grape blossoms (or "tender grapes," NKJV), which represent the beautiful intimate experience that God designed (Song 2:13). But in Song 2:15, jackals, little jackals, damage the blossoms. The jackals (sometimes translated *foxes*) represent not just the big things, but even the little issues that destroy intimacy. Blossoms are beautiful and fragrant but delicate and easily destroyed. The world feeds singles this idea that intimacy is easy and instinctual. A couple presumably becomes enraptured with love for each other, and sex seems instinctual, easy, and problem free. But because people are complex, they can quickly create problems that destroy intimacy. You are a sinner, and your future spouse is likewise a sinner. When sinners are put together, they get jackals, which destroy blossoms. While you shouldn't awaken love, you also need to learn how to deal with sin so you know how to catch the "jackals" that destroy "blossoms." Song 2:8—3:4 discusses some of these problems and teaches the real meaning of love.

In the meantime, let's address another false narrative, that is, that after you get married, you can enjoy intimacy whenever you want. While you *and your spouse* can enjoy intimacy whenever *you both want*, if either one of you does not want to be intimate or cannot be intimate, then the other one must respect that spouse's wishes and restrain the desire for intimacy. Sexual freedom is not unrestrained desire. Realistically, after you get married, you will not enjoy intimacy whenever *you* want.

> ## Sexual freedom is not unrestrained desire.

A person can prepare *for* marriage by learning to restrain sexual desire *before* marriage. Many singles, particularly young men but increasingly young women too, struggle with self-pleasure and sexual restraint. They falsely believe that after they get married, this struggle will go away. The Song teaches that different issues will impede intimacy and that every couple will have to work through those issues. In Song 2:8–17, the couple start out separate from one another, but they work their way through three impediments to intimacy.

SPATIAL SEPARATION

SONG 2

> *8The voice of my lover. Look! He comes!*
> *Leaping upon the mountains; skipping upon the hills.*
> *9aMy lover is like a gazelle or a young stag.*

Married couples do not spend all their time together. Couples go through seasons of life when they will be physically separated. A military or work assignment may require a husband and wife to be separated for months, even years. Love might demand one spouse leave and care for a sick friend or family member. Sexually, what should a couple do during these times? Resort to the self-pleasuring habits that defeated them during their unmarried years? What is right? Song 2:8—3:5 instructs readers concerning the *time* for sexual pleasure and the way to resolve issues in a relationship.

In Song 2:8, the husband and wife are separated physically, but the Song moves them from separation to union. The wife describes her lover's desire for intimacy using a gazelle (think *deer*) as a metaphor (Song 2:8–13). In Song 2:8, he is a gazelle—or to humanize it, a superman—jumping from mountain to mountain to get to her. Gazelles mate only at certain times of the year. However, when that time of the year comes, male gazelles go great distances to find their way to female gazelles. Living in rural New York and Iowa, Angela and I are very familiar with "the rut." Most of the time, a white-tailed deer has the sense to watch out for a vehicle. But during "the rut," those crazy deer have something else on their minds and pose a greater risk to commuters. The Song of Songs wife describes her husband's desire as being like that of a gazelle, and he seems willing and able to cross mountains to be with her.

THE TIME

SONG
2

9bBehold, he is standing behind our wall,
    looking from the window; gazing through the lattice.
10My lover answered and said to me,
    "Raise yourself, my sweetheart, my beautiful, and take yourself.
11Indeed, look! The winter has passed;
    the rain has passed, and it is gone.
12The blossoms have appeared in the land;
    the time of singing has come,
    and the sound of the turtledove is heard in our land.
13The fig tree has ripened its figs,
    and the vines have blossomed; they give a scent.
Raise yourself, my sweetheart, my beautiful, and take yourself!"
14My dove in the clefts of the rock, in the secret place of the cliff;
    show me your face; let me hear your voice;
    for your voice is pleasant, and your appearance is lovely.

Sometimes distance separates lovers; but sometimes the *time* simply is not right for intimacy. In Song 2:10–13, the wife tells us her husband's proposition. He entreats her, "Raise yourself" (Song 2:10, 13) because now is the right time. The husband implores his wife to come away *because* it is spring—the *time* of love. A wall, however, separates the couple from one another. At times, even in marriage, the time may not be right for sex. Perhaps one spouse is ill, the wife has had a child, a child is sick, or some other reason makes it the wrong time. Myriads of reasons exist why couples exercise sexual restraint even in marriage.

> At times, even in marriage, the time may not be right for sex.

To repeat myself (and biblical teaching), the only God-honoring sexual expression is the sexual expression between spouses, and sexual desire drives a couple together (Song 2:8–13). However, when a couple cannot experience intimacy because of time or distance, sexual temptations multiply and become more alluring. So a married person must always remember that intimacy outside of God's prescribed boundaries is a sin against God and against his/her spouse. Learning self-restraint while you are single will help prepare you to deny yourself when you are married and to better love your future spouse.

We do not intend to downplay the intensity of sexual desire, particularly the sexual desire of singles. In this Song of Songs passage, the husband possesses an intense desire. He is like a deer during the rut. In Song 2:14, he speaks for himself and reveals his desire to see her face and hear her voice, even explaining why he desires her presence. She, however, does not respond in kind. Another problem separates them, and they must catch it before they can enjoy intimacy according to the order of creation (the way God intended it; the wise way).

LITTLE JACKALS

| *¹⁵Catch us the jackals, the little jackals that ruin vineyards, for our vineyard is in bloom.*

Eventually, mountains have been crossed and the time is right; then the biggest problem presents itself—jackals. Jackals destroy living places then dwell in destroyed places. Lamentations 5:18 reads, "Concerning Mount Zion, which is desolate; jackals walk about on it." Throughout Scripture, foxes, which are often jackals, either ruin things or live in ruins (Judg 15:4; Ezek 13:4; Ps 63:10; Lam 5:18; Neh 4:3).

The garden and vineyard are metaphors for the woman and intimacy. The metaphorical "Garden of Eden" vineyard should be a place of life, aroma, fruitfulness, and beauty. But jackals—the things in life that destroy intimacy (usually sinful acts)—can enter the garden and transform the Garden of Eden vineyard into a desolate wasteland.

Depending where you live, you may be unfamiliar with jackals. They are small omnivorous carnivores of Africa and Asia that are larger than foxes. Jackals are not pets; they are wild and vicious. They are a fitting metaphor for the things in life that destroy intimacy. Pornography, premarital intimacy, affairs, addictions, and the like, are definitely jackals that make intimacy a barren wasteland. These issues represent large jackals. Certainly, these jackals need to be caught! But big jackals start out as little jackals.

> The real intimacy killers are the little things.

Notice in Song 2:15, the Song of Songs wife says it is the *little* jackals that ruin vineyards. The real intimacy killers are the little things. Little jackals embody sarcastic remarks, manipulation, negotiable requests that are really demands, and small acts of selfishness. The little jackals are extremely sneaky. They may be how a spouse smashes the toothpaste, puts the toilet paper on the toilet paper holder, or forgets to refill the toilet paper holder! You may be thinking, "Those things won't bother me!" What about when it happens again and again and again? What about when he fails to take care of his dirty clothes or clean his dishes, or he tracks mud into the house? The real intimacy killers are the *little* jackals. Even a desire for one's own dining or entertainment preferences can be a little jackal. And the list could go on and on. Usually, a wife feels as though she is being taken advantage of and used instead of being loved; and sometimes those feelings are legitimate. Jackals transform the verdant garden of intimacy into an unfruitful wasteland.

The essence of love is selflessness. Jesus explained that the greatest commandment is to "love the Lord your God," and the second is like it: "Love your neighbor as *yourself*" (Matt 22:37–38). Before the 1800s, the exhortation "Love your neighbor" synonymously meant "Be selfless." Nineteenth-century people defined love as selflessness. Today, when one spouse commits small acts of selfishness, he/she is essentially saying, "I love me; I don't love you." Genuine love is selfless. A believer should demonstrate this selfless love to everyone, most importantly to the person he/she has covenanted to live with for the rest of his/her life. A spouse may say, "I love you," but when that spouse's actions communicate "I love me," little jackals destroy the delicate blossoms of intimacy.

Up to this point, we have basically defined the jackals as issues that either a husband or a wife may create. Song 2:15, however, is primarily directed toward husbands (not exclusively though; the imperative is a plural—*y'all*). In Song 2:8–14, he wants to have sex, and in Song 2:15, she points out that they have problems. Men tend to be more oblivious to problems in a relationship. This is a generalization, of course, because sometimes the woman is oblivious. But generally, the guy is oblivious; furthermore, it is often the guy who has been selfish, ruling selfishly over his wife and taking advantage of her selfless love.

The jackal of sin and selfishness is decidedly subtle. For example, when a wife talks to her husband, he should be *listening*. Her trials at work, day with the children, or time running errands may be completely irrelevant to him. He may not be able to help her, assist her, or be of any service. He may have "bigger" issues in his life that draw his attention away from the conversation. He may even want to get to a game or some other amusement, and his wife is keeping him from something he desires more than he should. Failure to listen to his wife is a sin of selfishness. He places his desires and interests above his wife's. He is not loving her; he is being selfish. Failure to deny oneself an amusement or pleasure is selfish. Here is a generalization, not a promise: by selflessly and sacrificially loving his wife, the Song of Songs husband cultivates his wife and her vineyard blossoms.

Young man, while the best way to maintain the vineyard is to not create any little jackals, unfortunately, you are a sinner and will sin against your wife. What do you do when that happens? You do something that guys tend to really struggle doing—you confess your sin and ask her to forgive you. Then, young lady, if you're the wife, you need to forgive your husband. Confession and forgiveness are the essence of the gospel and illustrate the way jackals are caught.

The Gospel

The gospel is the good news that Jesus died on the cross for your sins so you can be reconciled and have peace with God (Rom 5:1). Because of your sin, you rightly deserve the wrath of God. If you confess your sin to God, ask Him to forgive you, and believe in His plan of reconciliation,

God will forgive your sin (John 3:36). This gospel is the way for you to be at peace with God, and it provides a pattern for how you can have peace with your future spouse. In Matthew 18:21–35, Jesus draws a direct correspondence between being forgiven by God and forgiving others who sin against you. Because God has forgiven you, you have an obligation to forgive your spouse. The unforgiving Christian is an oxymoron. Genuine Christianity requires genuine forgiveness. When you sin against your spouse, you need to confess that sin to God and your spouse. God will forgive you; and, hopefully, your spouse will as well. The vineyard-destroying "jackal" is then seized, the husband and wife are at peace, and they recreate the Edenic garden of love. Living the gospel corresponds to seizing jackals.

> Because God has forgiven you, you have an obligation to forgive your spouse.

Many times, however, we pursue a different path to reconciliation. By nature, a person is proud and does not want to admit that he/she is wrong. Instead, a husband may go to the flower shop and order the "I'm in the doghouse" bouquet or do some act of kindness to "make things right." The husband who does this is a gospel denier. He tries to tip the scales of "good works" to outweigh the "bad works."

To use the vineyard analogy, he is planting more vines but letting the jackal continue to run free in the vineyard. This approach fails because it does not address the sin that was committed. It does not seize the jackal. While the husband may think that the "good deed" outweighs the "bad deed," his wife may think it isn't enough. He needs to do more "good things" to fix the problem. And when you have two sinners piling good deeds and bad deeds on two sides of a subjective scale, what do you get? Fights. Peace fades away. Jackals multiply. The vineyard becomes a desolate wasteland—a habitation of jackals.

Belief in the gospel provides the foundation for seizing jackals. The person who refuses to believe in the gospel—God's plan of reconciliation—is not equipped to deal with either sin or forgiveness. Think about it. If one spouse refuses to admit that he/she has sinned, then that jackal will continually be spoiling the vineyard. Similarly, if one spouse refuses to forgive the other, there will never be peace between the couple. The gospel is the foundation for seizing jackals and enjoying intimacy the way God designed it.

Because the gospel is the foundation for seizing jackals and living according to the order of creation, you and any potential romantic interest of yours must be believers in the gospel. If you have never believed in God's plan of reconciliation, do so today. Talk to your pastor or Christian mentor and trust God's plan for peace today. Furthermore, purpose to never marry, date, or even cultivate interest in a person who does not believe the gospel. If you ever considered dating or marrying somebody who does *not* believe the gospel, recognize the absurdity of this sinful union (2 Cor 6:14), and never consider it again. Additionally, live the gospel today. Whom have you sinned against? Acknowledge your sin, confess it, ask that person to forgive you, and be reconciled. Your future relationship with your spouse depends on it. If you cannot humble yourself and ask for forgiveness today, then you will not be equipped to capture jackals in marriage. Further, if someone has sinned against you, forgive that person! Forgiving someone can be more difficult than asking for another's forgiveness. C.S. Lewis said, "Everyone thinks forgiveness is a lovely idea until he has something to forgive."[1]

---

1   C. S. Lewis, *Mere Christianity* (San Francisco: HarperOne, 2001), 115.

Denying forgiveness reflects a proud heart that says, "What you did to me is worse than what I have done to God." God forgave you your sin; the least you can do is forgive those who have sinned against you (Matt 18:21–35).

> Denying forgiveness reflects a proud heart.

Defining the Vineyard

Song 2:15 teaches the reader that the "vineyard" concerns more than a woman's physical body; it includes all of her—body, soul, and spirit. We have already noted that the vineyard represents the sexual pleasure that a wife offers to her husband. We saw in Song 1:5–6 that the Song of Songs woman guards literal vineyards, resulting in her body (her metaphoric vineyard) being physically damaged by the sun. So, the vineyard in Song 1:5–6 focuses on the woman's physical body. Similarly, the "vineyards of En Gedi" (1:12–14) represent the physical, sexual pleasure she offers to her husband.

In Song 2:15, however, the foxes or jackals do damage, not to the woman's physical body, but to the lovers' intimacy. This intimacy includes their emotional and spiritual union. So, the vineyard metaphorically represents the sexual pleasure that the wife offers the husband, not only in body but also in mind and soul. The husband greatly wants to have sex (2:8–14), but a jackal has come between him and his wife. Realistically, the husband could enjoy the physical union with his soft, supple, fragrant wife, but the "jackal" prohibits him from enjoying the soul-related intimacy with her because she doesn't really desire intimacy *with him*. The jackal prohibits her from desiring him.

Once again, jackals destroy the intimacy that God designed. But after the couple seizes a jackal, the ensuing bond of peace they create generates a union that transcends the physical senses. This union, or bond, manifests itself most profoundly after a couple seizes the jackal of sin. Then the wife offers not merely her physical body to her husband but all of herself to him—desiring him as he desires her. The gospel act of admitting sin, confessing it, and being forgiven creates the *shalom*—peace—which is the foundation of real love—real intimacy. Genuine confession requires humility and selflessness; it is a loving act. Similarly, genuine forgiveness requires humility and selflessness—love. This demonstration of genuine love binds the couple together. Unifying *shalom* transcends and enhances the biological experience of sex. Sex becomes not only a physical connection, but the natural conclusion to an intimate experience. The lovers connect intimately because they both want to. The biological union is not only the union of two bodies but also the knitting together of two souls. Each spouse loves not only sexually, but through the gospel act of confession and forgiveness, together they love each other selflessly. This is genuine love. When a couple loves each other in this way, the vineyard blossoms, desire increases and deepens, and the couple experiences sexual pleasure the way God designed.

This definition of sexual pleasure was what Solomon never experienced. Solomon did not personally take care of his "vineyard" (Song 8:11–12). He paid others to take care of the vineyard, which deprived him of the sexual union God designed. Solomon experienced sex at a sensory level. His wives and concubines were, no doubt, beautiful, fragrant, supple women who wanted to have sex with him. But the vineyard they offered was solely at a sensory level. These women did not love Solomon selflessly and sacrificially. Solomon planted a sensuous vineyard and harvested exactly what he planted, a sensuous vineyard (compare Prov 1:31; Gal 6:7). He had a vineyard of trophy wives.

Having learned his lesson too late, Solomon encourages each husband to not only cultivate the physical vineyard of his wife's body but also to irrigate the immaterial vineyard of his wife's soul. Husband, investing in your wife's body will yield a sensuous experience; investing in her soul yields an intimate experience.

The wife in the Song wants to have sex with her husband because she loves him. The harem girl wants to have sex with Solomon because of what she can receive from the relationship. Solomon harvested one thousand Dame Follies who "served" him sexually for a *reason*. And that *reason* was never genuine, selfless love. Solomon never experienced sexual pleasure the way God designed it because he failed to tend his own vineyard and personally seize the jackals.

UNION

SONG
2

> [16]My lover is mine, and I am his;
> the one who grazes among the lilies.
> [17]Until the day breathes its last and the shadows flee away;
> Turn! Liken yourself, my lover, to a gazelle or a young stag
> upon the divided mountains.

Song 2:16–17 describes the couple's resolution and union. Notice the two-becoming-one language: "My lover is mine, and I am his." He is hers and she is his. They literally possess one another. In Song 2:8, the wife described her husband metaphorically as a gazelle leaping on mountains. Now in Song 2:17, she invites her lover to be *like* a gazelle on the "divided mountains"—an intimate innuendo.

APPLICATION TO SINGLES

Singles are bombarded with messages of easy intimacy, but nothing could be further from the truth. Little jackals destroy vineyard blossoms. Blossoms are an appropriate, powerful metaphor for sexual intimacy because it is fragile, just like blossoms. A married couple could be on the path to intimacy, but one sarcastic remark, one selfish act, or one evil thought can ruin it. People joke about how little issues like toothpaste or toilet paper can generate great disagreements within a marriage. These little jackals grow up to become big jackals and destroy marriages. The problem, however, isn't toothpaste or toilet paper; it is selfish hearts. Selfishness manifests itself everywhere. Often couples go for marriage counseling because their intimacy has languished. But the lack of intimacy is only a symptom of a bigger issue—sin.

> The problem, however, isn't toothpaste or toilet paper; it is selfish hearts.

Sin makes people stupid and ruins sex. Learn to identify your sin, repent, and forgive today. When was the last time you confessed sin or asked someone to forgive you? When was the last time you repented of sin in prayer to God? You are an expert sinner; we guarantee it (Rom 3:23). We know you are an expert sinner because we are expert sinners. If you have not repented of sin recently, the reason isn't because you are a good person but because you lack spiritual discernment to recognize sin. Spend some time in prayer, ask the Lord to reveal the sinful desires in your heart, and then repent. Catching these little jackals does not begin when you get married; it doesn't even start today. Learning to catch jackals should have started when you were a child. You have been nurturing habits of selfishness since you were an infant. Prepare to enjoy Edenic intimacy with your future spouse by cultivating the process of slaying your flesh and living a life wholly devoted to the Lord—a life of selflessness.

Learn to live a life of selflessness *today*. Order your world. Clean, organize, and beautify the area of your world that the Lord has entrusted to you. When you marry, your spouse will be close to you. Prepare to serve your spouse by serving the ones closest to you right now. Serve those whom the Lord has placed in your life—your parents, siblings, or roommates. Look for opportunities of service to those who are closest to you (neighbors, classmates, friends, employers, coworkers). Serve in your local church. Be known as a person who loves and serves others.

Finally, learn to control sexual desire. Young men and women falsely believe that after marriage they will no longer struggle with self-pleasure. Song of Songs teaches that there will be seasons when a couple will not be intimate. The temptation to resort to self-pleasure will be strong. A friend polled the married men (young and old) at his Bible study and was shocked to learn that over 70% still struggled with masturbation. A struggle with masturbation will not go away after a person is married. Self-pleasure is selfish and sinful. God's design for intimacy concerns another person—your future spouse. God desires for you to live selflessly, which includes refusing to masturbate. Every married couple experiences times when they cannot enjoy intimacy because they are physically separate from one another, the time is wrong, or because jackals exist in the relationship. The worldly, selfish individual escapes to masturbation instead of resolving the issues in his/her marriage relationship. Learn to control your desires now so that when you marry and the time for intimacy is not present, you live in holiness before your spouse and your God. Pursue freedom from sexual sin today.

DISCUSSION QUESTIONS:

1. What are some false narratives about intimacy in marriage?

2. What are the three impediments to marital intimacy?

3. What do jackals represent?

4. Study and discuss the nature and destruction of jackals (Judg 15:4; Ezek 13:4; Ps 63:10; Lam 5:18; Neh 4:3).

5. Discuss what little jackals might look like in a marriage.

6. How should the gospel transform a marriage when it comes to forgiveness?

7. Why should a Christian marry a believer, not an unbeliever?

8. What is the foundation of real love?

9. Why did Solomon not experience sexual pleasure the way God intended it?

10. How can you learn to cultivate a life of selflessness?

11. Why is it important to learn sexual self-control before marriage?

CH. 7 | LOVE MADE ME DO IT (3:1–5)

Most couples marry each other because they are in love. But what is this thing that they call love? It is all a couple can do to keep their passions in check as they eagerly anticipate their wedding day. Some couples begin making small compromises. They rationalize, "We aren't having sex; besides, we are in love." What is this thing they call love? Other couples begin a sexual relationship and explain, "We are in love! We couldn't help ourselves." What is this thing they call love? Does love cause such actions? Then they marry, and their love begins to wane. They covenanted to love one another "in sickness and in health until death do us part," but the regular daily affairs of life expose a lack of love. This causes us to question whether the couple every really loved one another.

Song 2:8—3:5 teaches wisdom concerning the true definition of love. As we discussed in the last chapter, Song 2:8–17 teaches that love overcomes obstacles. The husband crosses mountains, entreats during the right time, and cultivates his wife's desire by seizing jackals. True love sacrifices and serves the spouse. The husband with biblical masculinity does not seize his wife and compel her to have sex with him because he "has a right" to her body. With biblical masculinity, a man denies himself and seizes jackals, thus cultivating his wife's desire for him. The pagan man, however, crushes his wife's sexual desire by compelling, manipulating, or coercing her to have sex with him. But the virtuous man cultivates his wife's sexual desire by exercising sexual self-control, seizing jackals, and sacrificially protecting/providing for her. Love makes him do it.

True love is deliberate and intentional. It chooses a difficult path when an easier way is available. True love obeys the Lord's commands not only when it is easy and convenient but also when it is difficult and presumably foolish. When everybody else says, "This is the right way!" true love looks to the Lord, who says, "Reject them! Trust me. Take the step of faith. I will help you" (for example, Isa 50:4–11).

While Song 2:8–17 primarily exhorts the husband to love his wife selflessly and sacrificially by cultivating the vineyard and seizing the jackals, Song 3:1–4 primarily exhorts the wife to love her husband even when he is unlovable. True love loves not only when loving is easy but also when it is hard. Love makes you do it.

> True love loves not only when loving is easy but also when it is hard.

SEXUALLY ASSERTIVE WOMEN

Today there is a Christian subculture that unintentionally depicts a wife as sexually passive but regularly available to serve her husband. Presumably, the "normal" sexual relationship includes an assertive, initiating, desiring husband, who regularly propositions his available and willing wife. This unbiblical sexual ethic stems from failing to preach the whole counsel of God (e.g., the Song of Songs).

Wholesome preaching against immorality from passages like Proverbs 5–7 correctly shapes the affections of a young man to forsake an immoral woman and pursue intimacy with his wife or, if he does not have one, to pursue a wife. Unfortunately, Christian young women have heard these messages as well and have been either directly or indirectly taught, "Don't be like this girl." Certainly! Good Christian young women should not imitate the behavior of the immoral woman, the Dame Folly we have been referring to.

But here's the thing. The sin of Dame Folly doesn't lie in her being sexually interested and assertive. It lies in her motivation and object of desire. The excellent wife in Proverbs 31 and Song of Songs reveals a similar interest, but in her husband only. The Song actually teaches that a wife should be assertive, initiating, and desiring, and should regularly proposition not only her available and willing husband but also her struggling, misguided, and lost husband. Love makes her do it.

SONG
3

¹*Upon my bed in the night,*
I sought the one whom my soul loves;
I sought him, but I did not find him.
²*I will rise now, and I will go about the city,*
in the streets and in the open squares.
I sought the one whom my soul loves;
I sought him, but I did not find him.
³*The watchmen found me, the ones who go around the city.*
"Have you seen the one whom my soul loves?"
⁴*Shortly after I passed by them,*
then I found the one whom my soul loves;
I seized him, and I would not release him
until I brought him to the house of my mother,
to the bedroom of the one who conceived me.

The father in Proverbs 5–7 instructs his son to be satisfied with his wife's breasts (Prov 5:19) and to avoid the seductress (Prov 5:20). Sounds like a great sermon that still needs to be preached today! In fact, young man, we encourage you to avoid the immoral woman. She doesn't really care about you; she just wants everything you have. You are simply another client ("a piece of bread," Prov 6:26).

> Proverbs 7 reveals what a young man should hate and avoid at all costs: the immoral woman.

Proverbs 7 explains that the immoral woman dresses like a harlot (7:10); has a crafty heart (7:10); is loud (7:11), stubborn (7:11), and does not stay home (7:11). She is in the streets (7:8) and open squares (7:12) at night (7:9) and seems to have her own "corner" (7:8, 12). She *seeks out* the young man and *finds* him (7:15). When she finds him, she seizes him, kisses him (7:13), and takes him back to the house of the grave and the bedroom of death (7:17, 22–23). This woman is sexually aggressive. She wants to have sex with the young man because she covets his wealth and will take everything she can from him, even his life. Proverbs 7 may have been written with Samson in mind. He was a mighty man (7:26) conquered by a dame folly. Proverbs 7 reveals what a young man should hate and avoid at all costs: the immoral woman.

The Song of Songs wife (Lady Wisdom) is sexually assertive just like Dame Folly. In Song 3:1–4, the Song of Songs wife *seeks* her husband but cannot *find* him (3:1–3). As a result, she does not stay home (3:2) but goes about the streets and open squares (3:2) at night (3:1). She seeks him out and finds him (3:4). When she finds him, she seizes him (3:4) and brings him back to the bedroom of life (3:4). This female lover sexually exemplifies the excellent wife who fears the Lord (Prov 31). She wants to sleep with her husband because she loves him. Though uninvited, she seizes him and drags him home. Song 3:1–4 teaches that a Christian woman not only *can* be sexually assertive but also she *should* be sexually assertive.

The similarities between Dame Folly and Lady Wisdom (the excellent, Song of Songs wife) are surprising. Neither stays at home but seeks a man in the streets and open squares at night. In the ancient world, streets and squares at night were not places of safety (e.g., Judg 19). But the excellent wife takes risks to be with the one her "soul loves."

Just like Dame Folly does with the foolish young man, the excellent wife seizes her husband and takes him to a place reserved for intimacy—the bedroom of life (conception).

SIMILARITIES BETWEEN PROVERBS 7 AND SONG OF SONGS 3:1–5		
	PROVERBS 7	**SONG OF SONGS 3:1–5**
Setting	⁹In the dark of *night*	¹Upon my bed in the *night*
Seeking and Finding	¹⁵I came out to *seek* your face, and I have *found* you	²I *sought* him, but I did not find him . . . ⁴I *found* the one whom my soul loves
Location	⁸passing by the *street* . . . ¹²at times in the *open squares*	²in the *streets* and in the *open squares*
Seizing	¹³She *seized* (*ahaz*) him and kissed him	⁴I *seized* (*ahaz*) him, and I would not release him
House	²⁷The way to the grave is her *house* . . . to the *bedroom* of death	⁴I brought him to the *house* of my mother, to the *bedroom* of the one who conceived me

Today our sexualized culture celebrates Dame Folly's sexual aggression. The Christian response has been "Don't be like this girl." Lady Wisdom, however, is sexually aggressive just like Dame Folly. In the privacy of the bedroom, she may even don the "attire of a harlot" (Song 4:1–7; 7:1–6). The Song of Songs wife speaks seductively (Song 8:14), dances suggestively (7:1–6), and rendezvous intimately (7:11–13). Potiphar's wife's appeal in Genesis 39:7, "Lie with me!" was a perversion of God's good design. Just as Potiphar's wife caught Joseph by the coat and propositioned him, so also does the Song of Songs wife proposition her husband and drag him to the bedroom (Song 3:1–4). The excellent wife is not sexually passive but sexually assertive. The world, the flesh, and the devil have twisted and perverted God's good creation—a sexually assertive wife.

> The excellent wife is not sexually
> passive but sexually assertive.

BIBLICAL LOVE

The Song of Songs wife frequently calls her husband "my lover" (Song 1:13–14, 16; 2:3, 8, 9, 10, 17), but she doesn't call him that in Song 3:1. The NET Bible mistranslates this verse: "All night long on my bed I longed for *my lover.*" The name *lover* is an intimate word that has sexual connotations. For example, in Song 1:2 the wife states, "Let him kiss me with the kisses of his mouth, because your *loves* [that is, caresses] are better than wine." The word *loves* in Song 1:2 is similar to the name "my lover." Both words are pronounced *dōd.* So, when the wife calls her husband "my lover," she is essentially saying "the one with whom I enjoy sex."

But the term she uses in Song 3:1–4 is not my lover (*dōd*). Instead, she creates a relative clause to describe her relationship to him: he is "the one whom my *soul* loves." She uses that wording four times in Song 3:1–4. The translation "the one whom my soul loves" may be wordy, but it is necessary, since it conveys a very different idea from "my lover." Song 3:1–4 is describing a soulish love, not necessarily an erotic love.

Song 3:1–4 may be one of the most difficult sections of the Song of Songs, particularly for young ladies. I (Angela) have taught this section in the past and have heard young women respond something along the lines of "I don't want to get married." But sex is a beautiful thing that God made (Song 1:5—2:7). He ordained sex within the covenant of marriage to be enjoyed and celebrated (Song 3:6—5:1)! Unfortunately, sin has made a mess of everything, including sex. And the Song doesn't talk just about the ideal; it also talks about the real. Within the real world, where dame follies abound, the Song instructs young women how to be a lady wisdom and create ideal love in a real world. All you really need is love! A real love. A deep-seated, servant-hearted, self-sacrificing, "take up your cross and follow me" kind of love for the one whom your soul loves.

♥ DIGGING DEEPER

Proverbs presents two women: Dame Folly and Lady Wisdom. Lady Wisdom is a composite character representing the way God made the world (wisdom), the excellent woman (Prov 31), and the ideal wife in the Song of Songs. Lady Wisdom functions as a synecdoche (a part for the whole) for the most important and most difficult part of living according to the way God made the world—an excellent wife. The wife who models the excellent wife is her husband's Lady Wisdom. For more information on the intertextual resonance between these women, see Timothy Little, "Finding Lady Wisdom: The Excellent Woman (אשת חיל) as a Synecdoche for the Order of Creation and Interpreting Ecclesiastes 7:28" *JETS* 66, no. 1 (March 2023): 53–71. The illustration below displays the correspondences between these women.

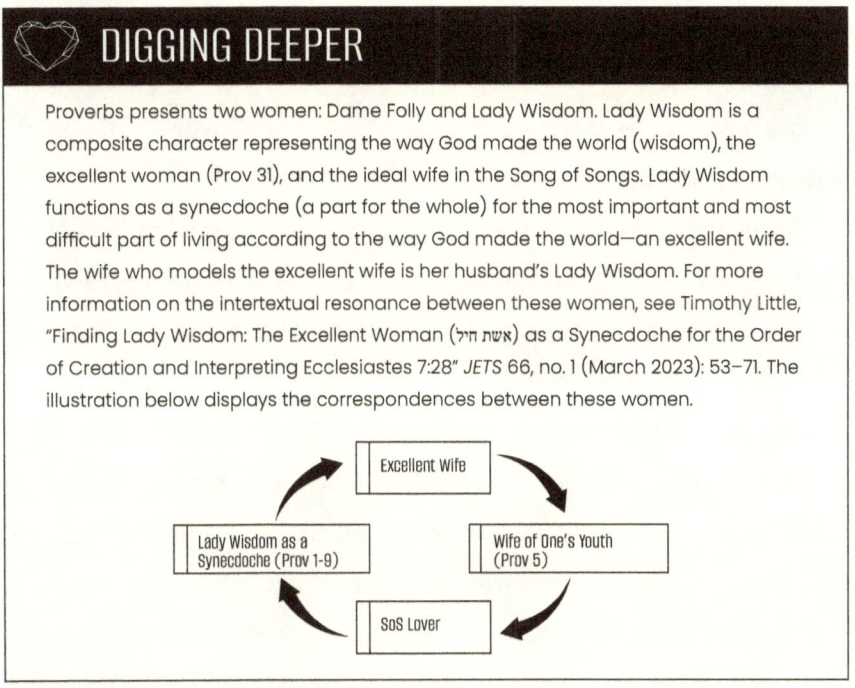

Soulish Love

Yes, the Song of Songs wife loves her husband. But even deeper, her *soul* loves him. Can you feel the depth of that phrase? He is not her "lover" here; he is the one her very *life* is connected to. The excellent wife's life is woven by covenant with his life. They are one. And the knowledge of that covenant, combined with a faith in the God of Israel, drives this woman to do the illogical. It drives her to do what this world simply calls foolish. This woman is the Proverbs 31 wife who fears the Lord and rejects the world's wisdom. Love makes her do it.

While the dame follies of the world want to take a man's "life," or soul (it is the same Hebrew word), the excellent wife is not like that. In Song 3:4, the wife drags her lover "to the house of my mother, to the bedroom of the one who conceived me." This terminology seems out of place and strange to us, but the woman is highlighting the *life-/soul-creating* potential of their relationship. Dame Folly destroys life. But when the covenanted couple weave their *lives* together, they may literally create a *life*. The Song contrasts the life-destroyer (Dame Folly) with the life-sustainer/creator (Lady Wisdom).

Dame Folly and Lady Wisdom (the excellent wife) are not the only ones out on the street (Song 3:3). The Song of Songs woman says, "The watchmen found me." These guards are kind of like modern police. They walk about the city and make sure everything is ok. Because they are walking around the city, they may have seen her husband. So she asks them, "Have you seen the one whom my soul loves?" The watchmen are flat characters, meaning they represent only one character trait, righteousness. The watchmen enforce justice and righteousness in the streets. She entreats them concerning the location of "the one whom my soul loves," then they disappear. The watchmen are arbiters of righteousness in the city; they have the power to decide a dispute about what is right. In Song 3:3, the woman has done nothing wrong, so they pass her by. She then immediately finds her lover (3:4). We will talk about these watchmen more when they reappear in Song 5, but here they reinforce that the woman is not doing anything wrong; rather, her search for her husband is right (just, righteous).

Finally, the woman finds and *seizes* "the one whom my soul loves" (Song 3:4). Just as Dame Folly seized the young man (Prov 7:13), here the excellent wife *seizes* her husband. Her earnestness and jealousy (He is mine!) is on display as she then states, "I would not let him go." She is not giving him an option in this situation. Imagine her clinging so tightly to him that if he wanted to be loosed from her grasp, he would literally have to peel her off. The excellent wife does not take *no* for an answer here. She insists and then hauls him off to the "bedroom of conception."

Unconditional Love

The excellent wife, the woman who fears the Lord, builds up her house. So why isn't her husband at home? Why is she finding him in the streets and open squares? What is he doing there? The text does not say why he is there. It only states his location. The Song lets the reader deduce that the husband is in a dangerous situation. The woman, being an excellent wife, doesn't let her husband wander around where that other woman is hunting for him. Rather, she gets out of bed, placing herself in an uncomfortable and dangerous situation (on the city streets). She searches earnestly for her husband. She doesn't just walk around the block and then go back to bed. Four times she says, "I sought him." She doesn't stop searching for him. When she finds him, she seizes him and doesn't take *no* for an answer. She takes him back to the bedroom of

> Young wife, sometimes your knight in shining armor needs some help getting back up on his horse.

conception. Young wife, sometimes your knight in shining armor needs some help getting back up on his horse. The foolish wife leaves; the "spiritual" wife says a prayer; but the excellent wife prays and does something about it. She gives him a boost back up on his horse. Love makes her do it.

The father in Proverbs 5:19–20 exhorts his son to be satisfied sexually with his own wife and to not be enraptured with the immoral woman.

Young lady, you will not only be your husband's source of sexual satisfaction, but you may also be his last line of defense. A husband walking around the street at night is in a dangerous situation, and he needs you. This husband may have ignored the advice of the father in Prov 5 and is dangerously walking about near Dame Folly's corner. Lady Wisdom, the excellent wife who fears the Lord, loves her husband not only when he desires her but also when he desires something he should not. She goes out into the street at night and seizes him. She does not let him go. She brings him back to the bed chamber of conception, the bedroom of life. She sexually serves him even when he doesn't deserve her love. This is soulish love for "the one whom my soul loves." The excellent wife builds up her house and intervenes when her husband is in danger of tearing *their* house down. Love makes her do it.

How does a "soul" love? Song of Songs 3:1–4 teaches the reader the meaning of true, servant-hearted, self-sacrificing, "take up your cross and follow me," soulish kind of love. It connects with the modern reader in very difficult situations. Modern technology creates regular access to a multitude of dame follies. Much has been written on pornography, but few authors acknowledge the power of a wife to either help her husband reject Dame Folly's proposition or naïvely ally with Dame Folly and destroy her husband. Certainly, the Christian wife should pray for her husband and encourage him spiritually, but when Dame Folly is pulling on his heart, he doesn't need his wife to mention another jackal that needs seized; he simply needs his wife to seize him. Song 3:1–4 gives a wife practical insight concerning how she can help her husband who struggles with Dame Folly's allure. She has sex with her husband. She sacrificially loves him and drags him off to the bedroom. Wife, put yourself in her shoes: You wake at night. He isn't there. What do you do? Say a prayer and hope for the best? Or get up (Song 3:1), find him (3:1–4), remind him of your unconditional love ("the one whom my soul loves"), and selflessly have sex with him (3:4). You are not *the* solution to his problem, but your selfless, sacrificial love could be part of what God uses to deliver him from Dame Folly's grasp.

Who can find an excellent wife? The excellent wife pleases first and foremost the God who sent His Son to die for her. As Jesus died and rose from the dead, she also dies to self and rises in service to others. The gospel motivates the excellent wife. She fears the Lord and trusts Him to help her through this trial. The Lord empowers her to love the unloving. So, young woman, when "friends" seek to ease you from the trial that a sovereign God has ordained you to walk (Isa 50:4–11), bring them to Song 3. May your illogical, foolish love for the one whom your soul loves be a testimony to the gospel of Jesus the Messiah (1 Pet 3:15). Believe the gospel; live the gospel. Love makes you do it.

BECOMING WISE TOGETHER

We saw that Song 2:8–17 explains that a couple needs to seize the jackals in order to enjoy intimacy the way God designed it. But if the husband is wandering around Dame Folly's street corner, that is a big jackal! It is rather hard to want him to be a "gazelle on the mountains" (Song 2:17) when he is wanting to pounce around on someone else's mountains! The Song anticipates this tension and combines Song 2:8—3:5 to teach couples how to grow in wisdom together. The verb in Song 2:15, "*Seize* the jackals," is the same verb in Song 3:4, "I *seized* him." Wife, when your husband refuses to seize the jackals (problems), you seize him anyway.

Similarly, husband, you are accountable before God for your actions regardless of your wife's actions. Even if your wife regularly refuses your advances, you do not have an excuse to flee into the arms of Dame Folly. You can never rationalize porn, masturbation, or any type of abusive behavior. You do not manipulate, threaten, coerce, or punish your wife in any way because she isn't giving you want you want (e.g., sex). Do you really love her? Do you have a deep-seated, servant-hearted, self-sacrificing, "take up your cross and follow me" kind of love for the one whom your soul loves? Deny yourself and follow Jesus' example.

> Even if your wife regularly refuses your advances, you do not have an excuse to flee into the arms of Dame Folly.

You may be like that gazelle, the time is right, you are taking care of jackals, but your wife always finds/creates more jackals. The vineyard is constantly in a state of disarray! What do you do? You fear the Lord and trust Him. Lead your wife to help you seize the jackals. Do not consider the world's counsel. Reject the unbiblical counsel of friends. Fear the Lord; do not fear your wife. You are accountable before God and God alone; love God first and trust Him to work in your wife's heart.

When a husband unconditionally loves his wife, willingly surrendering any "right" that he possesses, and when a wife unconditionally loves her husband, willingly surrendering any "right" that she possesses, the couple has found the way of wisdom—the way of peace. Neither spouse fights to get what he/she wants from the relationship; instead, both of them fight over who will serve the other. The couple recreates Eden. Peace reigns. Their trials strengthen and deepen their love for one another. They no longer trust one another in word only, but in deed, which enriches their sexual relationship. They are no longer two bodies; they are two souls uniting in a mutually enjoyable sexual experience. Many married couples testify that their sexual relationship enhances after 10–15 years of marriage. The shared trials the couple has had to endure deepen their love for one another and enrich their sexual experience. This is how a husband becomes a wise man. This is how a wife becomes the excellent wife.

> The shared trials the couple has had to endure deepens their love for one another and enriches their sexual experience.

When jackals appear in a relationship, greet them, not as enemies, but as opportunities to grow in love for God and one another. Don't fight your spouse to get what *you* want; instead, fight your spouse to serve him/her. A person becomes wise through the unconditional, selfless, sacrificial love for his/her spouse. When a husband and wife love each other selflessly and sacrificially in a covenanted, exclusive, heterosexual, monogamous relationship, then they live at peace (*shalom*) according to the order of creation—the way of wisdom.

CONCLUSION

The last verse of Song 2:8—3:5 contains the adjuration refrain in which the woman adjures (earnestly advises) readers to not stir up or awaken love until it pleases. This section defines love in a very different way than Song 1:5—2:7 does. In that passage, the couple are flirting with one another in a "Garden of Eden" kind of setting. Everything is the way it should be, and the power of love is communicated to the reader. With this power in mind, the woman instructs readers to not awaken love until "it pleases."

Song 2:8—3:5, however, discusses love realistically. Here, love is a deep-seated, servant-hearted, self-sacrificing, "take up your cross and follow me" kind of love for "the one whom [your] soul loves." Dating couples do not love each other this way. They can't. Engaged couples? Do you love your fiancé? Not in this way. You can't love him/her in this way yet. Furthermore, think about the feeling of love that you experience when your significant other does something affectionate. What is that feeling? Is that love? Biblical love is choosing to shut down that feeling because of jackals in the vineyard (Song 2:15). And the opposite is true. Biblical love is choosing to awaken that feeling when every part of your being doesn't want to. Love is a choice, and after you marry, you will have to choose to love your spouse even when he/she is unlovable. And the best training to prepare you to shut down that feeling or learn to awaken it at the right time comes during your single years. Love, as a choice, can remain asleep until the appropriate time. With this self-sacrificing, intentional, servant-hearted love in mind, the Song of Songs woman instructs readers to not awaken love until "it pleases."

DISCUSSION QUESTIONS:

1. Study Song 3:1–4 and note any repeated words or phrases.

2. Read Proverbs 7:6–27 and compare it to Song 3:1–4.

3. How is Dame Folly like the Song of Songs wife, and how is she different?

4. What is the difference between the names "my lover" and the name "the one whom my soul loves"?

5. How does a soul love?

6. What do the flat (uncomplicated, nonchanging/undeveloped) characters, the watchmen, represent?

7. What is the difference between the world's definition of love and the Song's definition of love?

8. What drives the excellent wife to go after her husband when he is struggling or in danger?

9. How does a couple become wise together?

CH. 8 | I NOW PRONOUNCE YOU HUSBAND AND WIFE! (NOW WHAT?)
(3:6—5:1)

After those last two chapters, you may be thinking, "I don't know if I can do that! I don't know if I want to get married." You are not alone. When Jesus taught the Pharisees concerning marriage and divorce, His disciples responded in Matthew 19:10, "If this is the way of the man with his wife, it is better not to marry!" God, however, created man and said, "It is not good for man to be alone" (Gen 2:18). God's order in creation involved a man and a woman covenantally bound together as one flesh (2:24). This is God's design, and it is a good design. Marriage should be a joy and delight, and God gave you the Bible to help you make it a joy and delight. If you submit to His will and follow His way, you have a high probability of experiencing a marriage that is both a joy and a delight. But you are guaranteed nothing. After all, you will marry another person to whom God gave a will, or choice, to do whatever he/she wishes. But if you do what God says, the risk of marrying a rebel (or being one!) is lower.

In Song 3:6—5:1 Solomon presents an ideal wedding, including an ideal bride in an ideal union. This illustration won't describe your wedding, or your groom, or your bride; and it likely will not describe your union! It does, however, celebrate the goodness and beauty of marriage and sex the way God designed them, while it teaches principles to newlyweds concerning beginning married life together. It also dispels some of the expectations and mutes some of the fears. Through this imaginary day and night, the Song teaches the reader about the desires and expectations of the wedding (night). The Song also teaches that if you emulate the lovers, you can enjoy being a selfless, sacrificial lover from the very beginning.

Premarital counseling typically includes a concluding lesson where the older man (typically a pastor in the church) talks to the young man and an older woman talks to the young woman about sex. These conversations help the couple begin a sexual relationship well. Often, the couple is given a book that they take on their honeymoon, which they should read out loud together and discuss openly as they learn various aspects of each other's bodies. This book would be essentially a sex manual. The book explains how to have sex and provides tips concerning common newlywed struggles. After the couple returns from the honeymoon, the older man may reconnect with the new husband to answer any of his questions, and, similarly, the older woman may reconnect with the new wife. The two couples may reconnect throughout a six-month and/or have a one-year "checkup" just to give the newlyweds an opportunity to talk with someone who is experienced and more knowledgeable. This pattern is effective and is one that we recommend.

The Song of Songs, however, is not a sex manual. The Song cultivates desire for God's sexual design instead of explaining, "This is how to have sex." God's design for sex concerns way more than just mechanics. The single Christian must *believe* that God's design is good

> The single Christian must *believe* that God's design is good and is the best design.

and is the best design. After a couple marry, a plethora of spiritual and/or physical issues can either crush a person's desire for sex or lead the couple away from God's design for sex. The newly married Christian must remember that God's design for sex is good and is the best design regardless of the difficulties he/she encounters or the feelings he/she possesses.

Even while single, some Christians possess strong *feelings* for a sexual design that is contrary to God's design. While a person's *feelings* may be *real*, those feelings may *not* be true. The Christian *believes* the truth even when his/her *feelings* communicate a different truth. It all comes down to *belief*. Whether married or single, the Christian must *believe* that God's design is the best, and a Christian may have to earnestly pursue it. Maturing Christians "understand the fear of the Lord and find the knowledge of God" (Prov 2:5). They reject the world's knowledge concerning love, marriage, and intimacy and enjoy the peace and serenity that come with the fear of the Lord and God's knowledge concerning sexuality. Through metaphor, Song 3:6—5:1 teaches God's design for sexuality and cultivates the single's affections for intimacy according to God's design.

Song 3:6—5:1 is one of the most erotic sections of the Song of Songs. As we work through this section, remember to take every thought captive to the obedience of Jesus the Messiah. This section of the Song has important lessons for singles to learn. Come to the text with a humble heart, desiring and willing to learn, and remember to be thinking purely and biblically.

GOING TO THE CHAPEL!

SONG
3

⁶Who is this coming up from the wilderness?
Like pillars of smoke, a fragrant cloud of myrrh and frankincense
*   with all the merchant's fragrant powders.*
⁷Look! It is Solomon's couch!
*   Sixty valiant men surround it, from the warriors of Israel.*
⁸All of them hold swords, being well-trained in war;
*   each man has his sword on his thigh,*
*   because of terror in the night.*
⁹King Solomon made for himself a palanquin
*   from the wood of Lebanon.*
¹⁰Its pillars were made of silver, its back of gold,
*   its seat of purple, its interior is inlaid with love*
*   by the daughters of Jerusalem.*
¹¹Go out, daughters of Zion, and see King Solomon
*   with the crown which his mother crowned him*
*   on the day of his wedding*
*   and on the day of the gladness of his heart*

Marriage has fallen upon rough times in Western culture. Fewer and fewer people marry. Those who do marry are waiting until they are older, educated, and/or established. The ones who do marry divorce. With all this bad news, is getting married worth it? The biblical answer is yes. Marry a godly person and enjoy an intimate relationship with your spouse. Marriage has its challenges, but it is a good thing. We encourage you to follow God's plan for marriage and intimacy going forward.

Young man, I want to talk to you for just a moment. Too many young men are following the spirit of the age and not marrying. Should a man be unmarried at 22, 25, 30? Maybe you are working ninety hours a week on an advanced degree, and you plan to marry in a few years. That may be fine, but what I see is a lot of men working regular jobs and going nowhere fast. Maybe you've tried and been rejected. Talk to your pastor and/or mentor. You may need to address sin in your life or reevaluate what you are looking for in a wife. The Jewish rabbis said that the unmarried twenty-year-old man was living in sin and/or cursed! Granted, that is a bit of an overstatement. But that sentiment reflects God's design for man. It is not good for man to be alone (Gen 2:18; Prov 18:22). God's plan is for most men to marry and for each one to serve his wife, children, and church. Too many men think they have the "gift of singleness," which is really their license to live a selfish life. We will discuss the gift of singleness more in chapter fourteen. Many young women want to marry, but guys don't pursue them, leaving them frustrated and listening to the ticking of their biological clocks. What are you waiting for? Submit to the clear teaching of God's Word, marry a God-fearing woman, selflessly and sacrificially enjoy sex with her, have children, serve in your church, and glorify God through it all. This plan is God's design for most men; submit to it and pursue it. It is a good life.

Ok, let's talk about weddings. Big wedding? Small wedding? Can we just elope? Marital union is a big deal, and you should treat it as a big deal. Certainly, some exceptional circumstances may require a couple to elope, but this kind of union should be the exception, not the rule. When a man leaves his father and mother and is joined to his wife, the couple is creating a new family unit, and this event should be celebrated.

The ancient wedding was very different from weddings today. The groom would go to the bride's house, where there would be a celebration. A wedding chamber would be set up where the couple would consummate the marriage. The family would celebrate for a specified time. We read about this celebration in Jesus' parable of the ten virgins in Matthew 25:1–13. (You can read more about weddings in the apocryphal book of Tobith.) After the celebration, the groom would take the bride back to his house. A snippet of this process is probably found in Song 8:5. Song of Songs 3:6–11 may be a royal variation of this wedding procedure. Solomon is the king, and it appears his bride is being brought to him. We will discuss these two weddings more in chapter twelve.

The wedding in Song 3:6–11 is the wedding par excellence. The approaching bridal caravan is burning so much incense that the air around the travelers looks like smoke. People can smell them coming. The beautiful smells accentuate the importance of both the group and the event. Furthermore, the armed guard enlisted to protect the bride highlights the important cargo. And, finally, as the retinue draws nearer, onlookers observe that the transport is Solomon's own palanquin. (A palanquin transported VIPs and usually consisted of an enclosed litter borne on men's shoulders by means of poles.) The description of this luxurious bridal transport reflects the preeminent nature of this wedding (Song 3:10).

Weddings are an important part in the sexual union of a husband and wife, so it is not surprising that the Song of Songs includes a magnificent wedding. This wedding is the one of young women's dreams. The bride marries the king with pomp and circumstance. Family members (mother) are present and approve the union. A side lesson here is that because marriage is important, it is fitting for families to celebrate the event in *proportion* to how God has blessed them financially.

The wedding described here may be *Solomon's* wedding, but it is *not* the wedding of the female lover in the Song of Songs. In Song 3:11, the woman states, "Go out, daughters of Zion, and see King Solomon with the crown with which his mother crowned him." The female lover commands (permits) the daughters of Zion to go and watch the beautiful wedding. She, however, seems quite distant from the event and is not the bride in the palanquin. Poetically, Solomon's wedding serves as a type of the richest, most extravagant wedding. Solomon gets *a* girl, but he doesn't get *the* girl. Furthermore, young lady, you may have dreamed of a wedding like this your entire life. Something inside every young lady may yearn to marry Prince Charming in pomp and circumstance, just like this woman is doing. But the Song teaches that you do *not* want to marry a Solomon. (This thought will be developed later.)

O, HAPPY DAY!

Weddings are happy days! Celebrate! Have fun! Enjoy your wedding! The Song celebrates the joy of the wedding. The very last line of Song 3:11 reads, "On the day of [Solomon's] wedding, on the day of the gladness of his heart!" What, however, made Solomon so happy? Remember, the Song of Songs was primarily written to virgin women to teach them matters concerning love and sex. The Song continues to teach us lessons today.

People enjoy weddings for different reasons. Grooms are usually happy for one reason. Put simply, sex makes a guy happy. Solomon is happy because he knows what he will be experiencing in a little while. Brides, on the other hand, look forward primarily to the wedding day, the day a bride may have dreamed about since she was a little girl. The groom, however, looks forward to the wedding night, the time when his dreams (he hopes) come true. A pastor told me he would ask couples during premarital counseling how important sex was to them. On a scale of 1 to 10, the young woman would say it was around a 4 and the guy would say probably a 7. We both just laughed! Bride-to-be, it isn't a 7 to your groom. It is a 10. Or maybe a 20. And it is likely higher than a 4 for you as well. A young man knows it sounds shallow to say he is marrying you because he wants to have sex with you. And I am sure he is marrying you for more reasons than sex (or at least he should be). But on the wedding day, something he has been anticipating for a while is right around the corner. Sex is a big reason he is marrying you, and that reason isn't weird or perverted. Read the Song. His desire for sex is not creepy or depraved. While a mature man knows that sex is not the sum total of a marriage, sex still makes a guy happy. God made it that way.

We went to a wedding where a groom showed great affection for his bride. His fawning all over her got her a little perturbed with him! We laughed together on the drive home: it was Song 3:6—5:1 being lived out before our eyes! Here was this beautiful bride, adorned to the hilt, a princess on her day, and the groom's eyes were all over her. He did restrain himself, but we guests knew what was going on in his head. Though both a bride and her groom look forward to the whole wedding day, typically the bride's attention concerns the wedding, while the groom focuses on the wedding night.

Young lady, the wedding is your day to shine! Have fun! Adorn yourself. Be beautiful! And that evening, be a veritable garden for your groom. This is the order of creation.

HERE COMES THE BRIDE

SONG
4

[1]*Look at you, beautiful! My sweetheart!*
Look at you, beautiful! Your eyes are doves.
[2]*Your teeth are like a flock of shorn sheep,*
which have come up from the washing;
every one of them bears twins,
and there is not one missing.
[3]*Like a strand of scarlet are your lips,*
and your mouth is lovely;
like a slice of a pomegranate
is your open mouth behind your veil.
[4]*Your neck is like a tower of David, built for an armory;*
on which hang a thousand shields,
all of the shields of mighty men.

SONG
4

> ⁵*Your two breasts are like two fawns;*
>   *twins of a gazelle,*
>   *who graze among the lilies.*
> ⁶*Until the day breathes, and the shadows flee away,*
>   *I will go, myself,*
>   *to the mountain of myrrh and to the hill of frankincense.*
> ⁷*All of you is beautiful, my sweetheart;*
>   *and there is no blemish in you.*

In Song 4:1–7, the groom extolls the beauty of his bride. He begins by talking about her eyes, hair, teeth, lips, and mouth. He focuses on her face—the most distinct anatomical part of her body. Then he proceeds down her body and comments on her neck, which is bedecked in jewels, and ends with her breasts. He stops saying "you" and "your" at this point and begins saying "I will," revealing his intention to go further: "I will go, myself, to the mountain of myrrh and to the hill of frankincense." The couple is alone in the wedding chamber; she is absolutely beautiful (4:7), and he extolls her beauty. This is a good thing.

Modern brides often spend weeks and months beautifying themselves in preparation for their wedding day. This beautification can be extravagant, elaborate, and rather wasteful! But the Song of Songs recommends this extravagance and presumed waste—not for the ceremonial gathering of witnesses but for her husband's enjoyment. She is her new husband's joy and delight. It is appropriate, then, for the new bride to go through a process of beautification and adornment in celebration of this moment but in proportion to God's financial blessing. In Song 4:1–7, the bride appears to be wearing some kind of jewelry around her neck. She is adorned to the hilt, a princess on this day. Visually, the bride arouses her husband sexually using her allure. But sometimes the bride is more hesitant. So the Song poetically describes the newlywed's first night and instructs future lovers.

ALLURE AND DESIRE

Often modern weddings are accompanied by a personal shower, where close friends shower the soon-to-be bride with articles of lingerie. This is appropriate. Notice in Song 4:1–7 that the bride's body is adorned with a sheer veil, but her husband can still see her eyes and mouth. Apparel that reveals but also conceals creates allure.

One honeymooning couple went to France and, to their horror, discovered that their hotel overlooked a nude beach. Partway through their honeymoon, the bride asked her groom about the temptation. To her surprise, he attested that there was very little temptation. Nudity exposes the entire body leaving nothing to the imagination. The artful concealing of the body creates more allure than brazen nudity because it creates interest.

Provocative apparel tantalizes the imagination, provoking the voyeur to look closer in hopes of seeing something more. Young man, when a woman dresses or acts provocatively, she is trying to manipulate you. By gazing upon her body, you become a naïve pawn in her hands; she exercises power over you. Your lust for her beauty can lead to your destruction (Prov 6:25). Rather, understand what this woman is doing and pity her. She does not realize that her evil will lead to her own destruction (Prov 5:6).

Young lady, your feminine appeal is powerful. Some women know that, but some don't. We are going to talk about this some more in chapter ten. Your sexuality empowers you. Be careful with it!

The wife in the Song of Songs intentionally tantalizes her husband. She doesn't do this to tease him and walk away, awakening a desire in him that she has no intention of fulfilling. Instead, she creates allure, awakens his desire, and then fulfills it. Some have begun to challenge the cliché, "Men are visually oriented." These writers and speakers are misguided. Men are more easily sexually awakened through sight than women, and the Song supports this view. By artfully revealing and concealing her body, the new bride awakens her husband.

As we look more closely at this passage, let's talk about the elephant in the room: a woman's breasts. Remember to take every thought captive to the obedience of Jesus the Messiah, particularly when we discuss more erotic sections of the Song. While talking about female body parts may be awkward, the Bible frequently refers to a woman's breasts. If you are wondering what is up with the *fawns* and the *lilies* in Song 4:5, well, scholars aren't sure either. So don't wonder about it. Discuss it with your spouse on your honeymoon. God gave women breasts. Their breasts perform a dual function in this world—a source of sexual pleasure for the couple and a source of physical nutrition for an infant. Through metaphor, Song 8:1–2 discusses both functions of the breasts. The Song regularly refers to the breasts as a source of sexual pleasure. As such, they represent the woman's whole sexuality, though they're only a part of it.

Naïvely, some within the world have sought to desexualize the female breast under the guise of feminine liberty and empowerment. The world contends that the sexualized breast is a socially constructed remnant of a once-powerful and coercive church. Folly! Nature itself mocks them. The truth is that breasts awaken desire. France has noted significant decreases in toplessness. Women have become weary of men leering at them. Cultures that have desexualized the female breast are broken cultures. These cultures have corrupted God's design of sexuality, usually by oppressively depriving women of the sexual pleasure which God ordained for them to enjoy. Yes, a woman's breasts do provide nutrition for children, but they also provide sexual pleasure for the couple. Do not be deceived the Bible supports this cross-cultural message.

THE DISTANT BRIDE

SONG
4

[8]Come with me from Lebanon, spouse, with me from Lebanon;
descend from the top of Amana,
from the top of Senir and Hermon,
from the lairs of the lions,
from the mountains of the leopards.
[9]You have captivated my heart, my sister, spouse,
you have captivated my heart with one of your eyes,
with one link of your necklace.
[10]How beautiful are your caresses, my sister, spouse;
how much better than wine are your caresses,
and the scent of your perfumes
are better than all spices.
[11]Your lips drip honeycomb, spouse;
honey and milk are under your tongue,
and the scent of your garments
are like the scent of frankincense.

Young man, here is something for you to consider on your wedding day. You may be super "happy" admiring your bride and anticipating that evening. She, however, will likely be more hesitant than you are. While your bride's focus may be on the big day and your focus on the big night, the time for selfless, sacrificial love for both of you begins immediately. In Song 4:8, the woman is both on the top of the mountains and in the lions' den. Lions and leopards are beautiful animals, but they're also dangerous! Song 4:8 is essentially saying that the bride is distant and dangerous. A foolish groom goes charging into the cave and enrages the lion! The wise groom, however, does not drag her off the mountain; rather, he gently coaxes her out of the cave.

A wise groom uses his mouth to capture his bride's affection through speech and kisses. In Song 4:9–11, the husband lavishes sincere praise upon his bride. He describes how he is completely smitten by her appearance (4:9), intoxicated by her smell (4:10), and desirous of her sweet mouth (4:11). Song 4:11 describes passionate kissing ("honey and milk are *under* your tongue"). This kind of kissing awakens love. The bride is not really distant and dangerous, but she may not be quite ready for what her husband is ready for either! The selfless and sacrificial groom woos his bride down from the mountain and out of the cave through his affectionate speech.

I COME TO THE GARDEN ALONE

SONG
4

> ¹²*A garden enclosed, my sister, spouse;*
>   *a spring bolted shut, a sealed fountain.*
> ¹³*Your plants are a garden of pomegranates*
>   *with pleasant fruits, henna with nard.*
> ¹⁴*Spikenard and saffron, calamus and cinnamon,*
>   *with all the trees of frankincense,*
>   *myrrh and aromatic aloes, with all the best spices.*
> ¹⁵*A fountain of gardens, a well of living waters,*
>   *and streams from Lebanon.*
> ¹⁶*Awake, north wind! And come, south wind!*
>   *Blow upon my garden; let its spices flow.*
>   *May my lover come into his garden,*
>   *and may he eat its pleasant fruits.*
> ⁵:¹*I have come into my garden, my sister, spouse;*
>   *I have gathered my myrrh with my spice;*
>   *I have eaten my honeycomb with my honey;*
>   *I have drunk my wine with my milk.*
> *Eat, friends; drink and be drunk, lovers!*

As we have seen time and time again, the Song of Songs communicates love through metaphor—both revealing and concealing. We already talked about the vineyard metaphor in Song 1 and 2. In Song 4:12—5:1, the bride is referred to as a garden. The groom describes her as a "garden, spring, and fountain" (4:12). These things are locked/enclosed, shut up, and sealed. These verbs communicate that this

> *Locked* means nobody is allowed into the garden!

woman is a virgin. *Locked* means nobody is allowed into the garden. This woman has sexually saved herself for marriage. Now that she is married, the garden unlocks for only one, her husband.

Notice that the husband doesn't break into the garden! Super important point here, young man. Even on that first night, with all of that desire for that beautiful princess, the groom does not break into the garden. He draws his bride down from the top of the mountains. He coaxes her out of the cave. His speech, kisses, and touches arouse her. Then, in verse 16, she invites him, "Blow upon *my* garden, that its spices may flow out. Let *my* lover come into *his* garden." Notice the change in the pronouns. The garden is *her* garden then it is *his* garden. Finally in Song 5:1, the groom says, "I have come into *my* garden." The text then talks about eating and drinking delicious things. By the way, if you are wondering about what the honey, milk, or plants refer to, thinking long and hard about them is something better reserved for your honeymoon. Many commentators believe they are only general metaphors for sexual pleasure. This veritable garden provides a fitting metaphor for sexual union. This garden is *her* garden, and he only enters the garden when she invites him into *their* garden.

ALL GLORY BE TO CHRIST

You may be thinking, "Whoa! This is a little much. I mean, is God ok with all of this?" Yes! God created sex; why would He have a problem with it? The end of Song 5:1 reads, "Eat, friends; drink and be drunk, lovers!" "Friends" refers to the couple. Who is speaking to them, calling them friends? Who in the world is watching them? God—the omnipotent, omniscient, and omnipresent God—sees the couple enjoy intimacy according to the order of creation. When you sin, God sees it. When you transgress God's sexual boundaries, He knows about it! And when you selflessly and sacrificially serve your spouse in the marriage bed, God sees that. God is God. He knows all and sees all. And when He sees a husband and wife "eating" and "drinking," enjoying sexual union according to the order of creation, He literally says, "Be drunk." God created sexual union to be an uninhibited experience. It is a time when a husband and wife find the act of intimacy intoxicating. When God sees a couple enjoying intimacy in this way, it gives Him great delight.

> When God sees a couple enjoying intimacy according to His design, it gives Him great delight.

Our worldly culture has propped up various perversions of sexuality. But God's design for intimacy is good. Simply submit to God's design for intimacy and trust Him to help you with any feelings that contradict His design. The intimate relationship in Song 3:6—5:1 involves a woman who possesses a garden and the man who enters the garden. You may possess real feelings that desire a different design. While your feelings may be real, if they contradict God's design, they are not true. Believe God's design for intimacy. When everyone tells you to believe yourself, to live according to your feelings, submit to God's design for intimacy. Trust Him because He knows what is best for you.

DISCUSSION QUESTIONS:

1. Why are fewer and fewer people in our modern culture getting married?

2. Why should most unmarried Christians seek to be married?

3. What must a Christian do when his/her feelings are real but contrary to God's design for sexuality?

4. Why are weddings important?

5. How is feminine appeal powerful?

6. What does it mean that "the garden is locked"?

7. What does God think of marital intimacy?

CH. 9 | FALLING OUT OF LOVE IS JUST ANOTHER EXCUSE
(5:2—6:3)

Sexual compatibility is a myth. Every marriage will experience times of sexual incompatibility. The husband may want intimacy, but the wife does not. Or the wife wants it, but the husband does not. The Song of Songs does not remain silent concerning this issue. Song 5:2—6:3 provides guidance, particularly to young women, concerning sexual incompatibility.

This may be a little shocking to you, but, generally, the husband wants sex more frequently than the wife does. It isn't always this way, but 95% of the time it is. We are not going to get into all the reasons for this. Some of the reasons are biological; others are practical and often spiritual. Young people marry with false expectations, which feed sexual incompatibility. The world's sexual message, a person's flesh, and premarital sexual desire contribute to these false expectations. God's sexual order of creation needs to be recovered, and Song 5:2—6:3 *begins* to teach couples how to recover God's lost design for intimacy.

Song 5:2—6:3 creates a scene where the couple has not been intimate for a while; the husband desires intimacy, but the wife does not. This scene reflects 95% of real-world marriages. One lesson from Song 5:2—6:3 is that a husband or wife should generally not deny the other spouse's sexual advances. This text/statement has been abused by male chauvinists, hated by feminists, and mocked by the world. The Song, being wisdom literature, communicates generalizations, so exceptions certainly exist. The Old Testament Law even stipulated certain times when a husband was *not allowed* to be intimate with his wife (e.g., Lev 15:19–24). A husband and wife, however, should be having regular sexual relations—a truth the New Testament affirms (1 Cor 7:2–5). Song 5:2–8 teaches that a wife sins against her husband when she rejects his proposition (5:3) after he has been outside for a long time (5:2).

SELFLESS LOVE

SONG
5

> ²*I was sleeping, but my heart stirred,*
> *the sound of my lover, knocking,*
> *"Open for me, my sister, my sweetheart,*
> *my dove, my perfect one;*
> *because my head is filled with dew,*
> *my locks with the droplets of the night.*
> ³*I have taken off my tunic; how can I put it on?*
> *I have washed my feet; how can I defile them?*
> ⁴*My lover sent his hand from the hole,*
> *and my feelings roared concerning him.*
> ⁵*I, myself, arose to open for my lover;*
> *my hands dripped myrrh, my fingers with myrrh passing over,*
> *on the handles of the lock.*
> ⁶*I myself opened for my lover,*
> *but my lover had gone and turned away;*
> *my soul despaired when he departed;*
> *I sought him, but I could not find him;*
> *I called for him, but he did not answer.*
> ⁷*The guards found me, the ones who go about in the city;*
> *they struck me; they bruised me;*
> *they took away my veil from upon me,*
> *the ones who guard the wall.*
> ⁸*I charge you, daughters of Jerusalem, if you find my lover;*
> *what should you tell him? I am sick with love.*

In Song 5:2, the woman speaks, saying, "I was sleeping, but my heart stirred." She might have been dreaming, or she could have been sleeping and her husband's knocking woke her. He asks her to "open." He desires intimacy with her and is poetically asking to have sex with her. He wants to have sex because "his head is filled with dew." In other

> ## Selfish love has consequences.

words, he has been outside the house for a long time—long enough for the dew to collect on his head. The two haven't been intimate for a while, and he is propositioning her.

The wife responds in verse 3 and gives two excuses for why she does not want to have sex. She states, "*I* have taken off *my* tunic; how can *I* put it on again? *I* have washed *my* feet; how can *I* defile them?" First, note in her reply that she says *I* and *my* six times. These pronouns reveal a selfish, unloving heart. Selfishness is the opposite of love. Second, look at her actual excuses. She first says, "I'm naked so I can't have sex with you." A propositioning husband might hear this excuse and be completely bewildered. How could this possibly be a problem? Then she says, "I've taken a shower so I can't have sex with you." While this excuse may be a little more understandable, from the propositioning husband's perspective, her reply, "I just showered" would awaken desire, not shut it down. These excuses are reasons to have sex rather than to not have sex.

So how do we know the wife is in the wrong? The meaning becomes really clear in verse 7, when the watchmen encounter her. Remember, the watchmen are flat characters who judicially enforce righteousness. That is all they do. They walk about the city, punishing the wicked, standing guard on the wall, and protecting the city from enemies who may do it harm. Previously, in Song 3:3, the guards found the wife on the city streets at night, but they simply passed her. She was not doing anything wrong in Song 3:3, so the guards simply came and left. In Song 5:7, however, the wife has been a selfish lover. In this text, the guards punish her. They poetically say, "What you did was wrong." Her punishment at the hands of the guards directly corresponds to her

selfish rebuff in Song 5:3. Mark McGinniss explains,

> [The watchmen] are the ones who discover the woman and they
> take seemingly violent action against her. But even in this, they are
> presumably acting in concert with their character. It would not be
> unusual for city watchmen to discover and mete out the proper
> discipline. Since the woman makes no complaint against their actions
> and there are no other comments by other characters or the narrator,
> the reader is left to assume that their actions are justified, albeit
> unsettling to modern sensibilities. In any case the guards act simply as
> guards. Their actions are usual and predictable for their function. They
> are one-dimensional or flat characters.[1]

The four first-person verbs in Song 5:3 (*have taken, can put, have*

washed, and *can defile*), which explain what the wife did, correspond

to the four direct objects (*me* 3 times and *my veil*) in Song 5:7, which

explain what happened to her (*found me, struck me, bruised me, took*

my veil). Because she acted selfishly (5:3), she was disciplined (5:7).

McGinniss explains that "[Solomon] might be making the case that

the discipline inflicted by the watchmen was in direct response to her

negative response to her lover."[2] McGinniss also states the conclusion:

"When a spouse fails to respond to the other unselfishly, the marriage

relationship suffers."[3]

CORRESPONDENCE BETWEEN SONG 5:3 AND 5:7	
SONG 5:3	SONG 5:7

I[1] have taken off my tunic;
    how can I[2] put it on?
I[3] have washed my feet;
    how can I[4] defile them?
	The guards found me,[1]
	    the ones who go about in the city;
	they struck me;[2] they bruised me;[3]
	    they took away my[4] veil from upon me,
	        the ones who guard the wall.

You might take great offense that the wife is chastised here.

Remember, she isn't really being struck. She may be dreaming, and

---

1   Mark McGinniss, *Contributions of Selected Rhetorical Devices to a Biblical Theology of
     the Song of Songs* (Eugene, OR: Wipf & Stock, 2011), 188.

2   Ibid., 73.

3   Ibid.

even if she isn't, she is a poetic character employed to teach the reader wisdom. Here *she* teaches the reader not to be a selfish lover, and the succeeding chapters of the Song teach additional wisdom lessons concerning selfishness. This passage is *not* promoting the beating of women. The guards, not the husband, chastise the wife. A husband should never administer corporal punishment to his wife. Ever. If a wife sins sexually against her husband, he needs to do exactly what the husband does in Song 5:6—walk away. The husband never barges into the house. Ever.

We recognize that you still may not like the instruction found in this section. But consider, when one spouse denies the sexual advance of the other because he/she doesn't "feel it" tonight, what is happening? We live in such a selfish, "My body, my choice" kind of world that we don't even stop to think that this scenario would be considered selfish. The wife puts her own feelings, desires, and affections above her husband's. True biblical love treats another person as oneself. The Song rebukes the wife for being selfish and not loving her husband.

Selfish love has consequences. One immediate consequence of the wife's selfishness is that she created an opportunity for Dame Folly to ambush her husband (Prov 7:5–27). The wife may not want to have sex with him, but Dame Folly does. Notice that the husband is now walking around the city streets at night alone (Song 5:4–6). Her rejection created a dangerous opportunity of temptation for him to fall into the arms of Dame Folly. Many "Christian" feminists absolutely abhor this teaching (that the selfish wife put her husband in a vulnerable position). They claim that if she doesn't feel it, then he simply has to deal with it. The wisdom instruction in Song 5:2–7, however, directly assaults their theology and condemns their practical instruction. Remember that in Song 3:1–4, the wife is sacrificially and selflessly out on the streets trying to find her husband to save him from Dame Folly's grasp. Here a similar setting is created. This time, however, the husband was trying to come home, but was denied by the very one who was supposed to help him stay away from Dame Folly. While a husband is *always* responsible for his own actions (Prov 5:18–23), Song 5:2–7 teaches that a wife's sexual rejection provokes an opportunity for her husband to become ensnared by Dame Folly.

Remember, Proverbs teaches young men that wisdom (the order of creation) will protect and guard them against immoral women. Proverbs 7:4 reads, "Say to wisdom, 'You are my sister!'" Putting together Proverbs 7:4 and Song 4, where *sister* is a term of endearment between lovers, we can conclude that personification of wisdom as a woman could also refer to the man's wife. Proverbs 7:5 goes on to say, "for the purpose of keeping you from the immoral woman." So, Wisdom as wife keeps the young man from the immoral woman. The same correlation is found in Proverbs 5:19: "A loving doe, a graceful female deer, may her breasts satisfy you *at all times*; with her love may you be enraptured *continually*." The young man's source of sexual pleasure is his wife. Her sexuality should satisfy him "at all times" and "continually." Yes, a young man needs to learn to be content with the sexual pleasures of his wife. But if a wife is not providing a husband *consistent* sexual pleasure, that wife induces an opportunity for Dame Folly to ensnare her husband (Song 5:2–7). Proverbs 5:20 continues, "But why should you be enraptured, my son, by an immoral woman?" The young man who is regularly enraptured with the affection of his wife is *less likely* to become enraptured by the immoral woman.

The New Testament and nature support this message. The Apostle Paul wrote, "Do not deprive one another, except with consent for a time, in order to devote yourselves to prayer. Then be together again so that Satan may not tempt you because of your lack of self-control" (1 Cor 7:5). Withholding intimacy should be consensually and temporally agreed upon. Even good men can struggle with purity because their wives deny their sexual advances. According to the message of Song 5 and 1 Cor 7, these women are sinning against their husbands.

> Even good men can struggle with purity
> because their wives deny their sexual advances.

JUST WALK AWAY

Let's notice the man's response in Song 5. Remember, the husband and the wife function as characters to teach the reader lessons. The husband in Song 5 provides an example of how to respond to sexual rejection. A strictly word-for-word translation of Song 5:4 would be, "My lover sent his hand away from the hole, and my inner parts roared for him." The hole would be either a keyhole or a peephole. The husband asks to enter and sticks his hand in the door; she denies him, so he walks away. Two lessons can be learned from this verse.

First, when one spouse is selfish and denies the sexual advances of the other, the other must respect that person's decision. The husband in Song 5:4 does not barge into the house! He walks away. We have said this before, but it bears repeating. If a wife denies her husband intimacy, the husband denies himself intimacy. He will not die if he doesn't have sex. This denial can be very difficult, particularly if it is an ongoing trial. A wife's sin does not give a husband permission to sin as well. Regardless of one spouse's sin, each person has a responsibility before God to love his/her spouse even when that spouse is unloving. We Christians can love the unloving because God first loved us (1 John 4:19). The gospel

 ## DIGGING DEEPER

Interpreters disagree concerning the husband's response in Song 5:4. The NET Bible translates, "My lover thrust his hand through the hole, and my feelings were stirred for him." This translation, however, is unlikely for two reasons. First, whatever he does in vs. 4 affects her (4b) so that she arises to open in a state of sexual readiness (5) but finds he departed (6). If he sticks his hand in, it doesn't make sense that he is gone in vs. 6. Second, the preposition (מן) denotes motion *away from* the hole, not *into* (ב) the hole. The NJPS translation reflects a movement away: "My beloved took his hand off the latch." Estes agrees, "Because his hand is being extended 'from' (*min*) the hole and not into the hole . . . it may better mean that he turns away from her after her words in v. 3," Daniel Estes, "The Song of Songs," in *Ecclesiastes & the Song of Songs*, AOTC 16 (Downers Grove, IL: InterVarsity, 2010), 397.

empowers a person to love as God loved. This principle is the essence of biblical Christianity.

So the husband simply walks away, but he does not walk into Dame Folly's house. Song 5 teaches that sexual denial provides only an *opportunity* for Dame Folly. Regardless of a wife's sin against her husband, he does not have permission to visit or look for Dame Folly. Proverbs 5:21 reads, "For the ways of a man are in front of the eyes of the Lord." God sees what is going on; and regardless of a wife's actions, the husband has a biblical responsibility to fulfill his marriage vows and remain wholly devoted to his wife. He may find himself in a sexless relationship. He still has a biblical responsibility to fulfill his marriage vows and remain wholly devoted to his wife. The Christian never has an excuse to sin.

> The Christian never has an excuse to sin. Honor God by loving your spouse *unconditionally.*

Second, the woman's response to her husband's selfless, sacrificial love illustrates how selfless, sacrificial love *normally* works. But it does not work this way all the time! The Song is wisdom literature; this principle is not a guarantee. A husband's genuine, selfless, sacrificial love *normally* endears his wife to him. But genuine, selfless, sacrificial love must be an expression of *unconditional* love for your spouse, not an act of manipulation. Honor God by loving your spouse *unconditionally*. Trust a sovereign God to change your spouse's heart. In Song 5:4, the husband's selfless, sacrificial love rekindled the wife's desire for him.

LEARNING TO LOVE; LEARNING TO DESIRE

Christian "sex" books talk a lot about sexual incompatibility and provide various ideas concerning how a couple can rekindle desire. These books have value for married couples. Rarely, however, does one of these books reference the Song of Songs. Song 5:8–16 provides guidance for a young woman on how to rekindle desire for her husband.

Desire awakens in men and women differently. The married wife awakens sexual desire in her mind. For this reason, many have claimed that the most important sexual organ for a woman is her brain. In Song 5:8, the wife suddenly summons the "daughters of Jerusalem" and uses them as literary characters to exult in her husband. By thinking affirmatively about her husband, remembering who he is, and speaking positively about him with the daughters of Jerusalem, the wife rekindles affection for him.

SONG
5

¹⁰My lover is dazzling and ruddy, standing out from a crowd.
¹¹His head is fine gold; his hair is curly, dark as a raven.
¹²His eyes are like doves by streams of water,
*   bathed with milk and fitly set.*
¹³His cheeks are like a garden bed of spices,
*   growing forth scents;*
*   his lips are lilies, dripping liquid myrrh.*
¹⁴His hands are rods of gold, fitly set with Tarshish stones;
*   his abdomen is carved ivory, inlaid with sapphires.*
¹⁵His legs are pillars of marble,
*   established on bases of fine gold.*
*   His appearance is like Lebanon, chosen like the cedars.*
¹⁶His palate is sweet, and all of him is desirable.
*   This is my lover, and this is my friend, daughters of Jerusalem.*

The wife describes her husband in an orderly way. She begins with a general description in verse 10 and then describes his body from his golden head to his golden feet (5:11–15). The meanings of some of these words are difficult to discover (for example, *dazzling* and *curly*). Some of the metaphors are puzzling too (e.g., abdomen with inlaid sapphires??). Other points, however, are clear, like the "raven" colored hair and the "carved ivory abdomen." This guy is chiseled! He is strong. His cheeks have been scented! Some young men need to take lessons here. If you have facial hair, keep it groomed and clean. Smell nice for your wife. Take a shower and put on a cologne she enjoys. Watch what you eat and go to the gym. Look good for your woman. The Song of Songs guy's physique makes it a lot easier for his wife to desire him. The biblical husband adorns the beauty God has given him in order to please his wife.

The wife ends in verse 16, describing her husband's mouth, which is actually the palate (inside) of the mouth, calling it sweet. The Song often refers to the oral parts of the body during sexual awakening. The inside of someone's mouth is not normally sweet, so her husband did something to make his mouth sweet to the taste.

She also describes him as "my" lover and "my" friend—pronouns that correspond to her excuses in verse 3. She is no longer jealous for her comforts, but is jealous for her husband.

> Nothing kills a wife's desire faster than remembering her husband's flaws.

Notice that the wife remembers and thinks about her husband's *positive* details. Nothing kills a wife's desire faster than remembering her husband's flaws. This woman *thinks about* her husband's positive features *with her brain,* which awakens desire in her. In this way she is teaching the female reader how to awaken desire when she has no desire.

This wife summons the daughters of Jerusalem, who prod her to reflect upon her husband. The wife remembers and ponders why she likes her husband, thus awakening desire for him. She praises him in front of her girlfriends rather than belittling him. It is difficult for a wife to complain and be ungrateful when she intentionally stops to consider the ways God has blessed her.

The daughters of Jerusalem reappear in Song 6:1, desiring to help the wife find her husband. The appearance of the daughters of Jerusalem here may communicate another way in which a wife can awaken or destroy affection for her husband. A wife who fellowships with women who constantly belittle and disparage their husbands will likely not desire her husband. Similarly, a wife who fellowships with women who praise their husbands will be more inclined to think highly of her own husband and thus awaken desire for him.

So, when a wife does not desire intimacy, the Song does not just say, "Awaken desire!" It gives advice on how to do it. Remember who your husband is, reflect upon the reasons you like him, and rouse (awaken, excite) desire for him.

The Song of Songs wife's description of her lover provides instruction also to young men. You could be a saintly person, but if you are unkempt, ungroomed, and unscented, well . . . intimacy is still something physical. The apostle Paul explained that bodily exercise profits little (1 Tim 4:8). Bodily exercise may not be as profitable as godliness, but it is still profitable. The Song of Songs husband possesses a good name, but he also takes care of his body. Young man, be fit spiritually *and* physically! In Song 1:3, the wife exults in the smell of her husband's *reputation,* but in Song 5:10–16, she exults in his *muscles, taste,* and *cologne.* Intimacy is a physical experience. The selfless, sacrificial husband—the *godly* husband—stewards his body to be a delight for his wife. In Song 5:16 the wife says her husband is altogether desirable. A bedraggled, stinky husband is not altogether desirable. Live according to the order of creation and take care of yourself for your wife's pleasure and the glory of God. Work with what God has given you and order your world!

CONCLUSION

As quickly as an issue arises between the Song of Songs husband and wife, so also is their issue resolved. After the woman exults in her husband and the daughters of Jerusalem are summoned again, they ask where her husband is (Song 6:1). The wife responds that her husband is now with her (Song 6:2–3). These abrupt transitions—guards, daughters of Jerusalem, husband—may argue that this is a dream. Regardless, this text teaches important theological lessons: Love serves, even when a person doesn't want to serve. And a woman can awaken desire even when there hasn't been any desire.

DISCUSSION QUESTIONS:

1. Why is sexual compatibility a myth?

2. When a wife selfishly dismisses her husband's advances, what does this communicate to her husband?

3. What are some consequences of selfishness when it comes to love?

4. How should a husband respond to his wife's sexual rejection?

5. How can a wife awaken desire for her husband?

6. How can a wife's friends influence her view of her husband?

7. Is it vain for a husband to make himself desirable for his wife? Why or why not?

CH. 10 | LOVE AND WAR: IT'S ALL FAIR, RIGHT?
(6:4—7:10)

Women possess a great power that they can use to either build up or destroy, and intimacy can be a woman's most powerful weapon. With sex, Delilah slew Samson, and with intimacy, Solomon's unbelieving wives led him away from the Lord. But the Song of Songs wife uses intimacy to build up her house and protect her husband (Song 3:1–4). Intimacy may not be a woman's *only* weapon, but it is her sharpest. This sword is forged from man's desire, so a husband's desire for his wife empowers her. She possesses something he wants—her affection and intimacy.

> Intimacy may not be a woman's *only* weapon, but it is her sharpest.

The intimate experience God designed before humanity sinned involved a submissive wife desiring her husband's *loving* and *peaceful* leadership. After mankind sinned, recreating God's original design became more challenging to practice. The Song picks up on this idea in a few places, one being Song 5:2, where the husband entreats his wife, "Open for me." This verb calls upon the submissive wife to open the door and *allow him in*. He does not barge into the house or break down the door. He waits for her to *let him in*. And Song 5:2—8:3 teaches that intimacy according to the order of creation requires a submissive wife to let her desirous husband inside the house.

A wife's desire to rule over her husband is one effect of sin. According to Genesis 3:16, a wife has a natural desire to assert authority over her husband. We will explain this more later. Because the act of intimacy requires a wife to allow her husband into the house, she will have a natural aversion to permitting him into the house. A wife who doesn't want intimacy just because "she doesn't feel it" is living in accordance with the Fall. She needs to learn to create the "feeling" (Song 5:9–16). This teaching may be contrary to her desires or nature, and it is definitely contrary to the message promoted by the world.

The husband whose wife refuses his advances may respond in a similar fleshly way by using his strength, manipulation, coercion, or threats to get what he desires. This husband is similarly living according to the effect of the Fall mentioned in Genesis 3:16; he is "ruling" over her in an unbiblical way.

♡ DIGGING DEEPER

The organization of Song of Songs is vigorously debated, particularly in this section of the Song. Many commentators believe Song 6:4 introduces a new section unrelated to Song 5:2–7. The wife's names, however, in Song 5:2; 6:4, 9 function as catchwords and communicate that Song 6:4—10 is related to what happened in Song 5:2–3. The name "sister" connects back to Song 5:1, "sweetheart" connects to the beginning of the next section (6:4), and "my dove, my perfect one" to the end of the next section (6:9–10). The chart below illustrates these catchwords.

CATCHWORDS BETWEEN SONG 5:1–6:10	
SONG 5:1	I have come into my garden, my sister,[1] spouse
SONG 5:2	Open for me, my sister,[1] my sweetheart,[2] my dove,[3] my perfect one;[4]
SONG 6:4	You are beautiful, my sweetheart,[2]
SONG 6:9	She is unique, my dove,[3] my perfect one;[4]

This couple is living out the broken relationship that is a consequence of the Fall. Both husband and wife are fighting against one another, seeking to get what each desires. The husband's greatest weapon is his God-given authority, but he is using it to serve himself, not his wife. The wife's greatest weapon is sex, but she is using it to serve herself, not her husband. Both feel justified in the wielding of their weapons of war. The battle of the sexes rages in most marriages in varying degrees of severity. Song 6:4—7:10 provides wisdom primarily to the wife concerning her power to create peace and to live at peace with her husband.

Remember, we already discussed that there are legitimate times and situations when a wife should deny her husband sex, but Song 5:2 is *not* one of those situations. Love according to the order of creation is an exclusive, desirous love. This kind of love is fragile and can be easily broken (Song 2:15). Song 5:2-7 describes a common way that love can be easily broken.

The wife's rejection disheartens the husband (Song 5:5-6; 6:5, 11-12) and threatens the exclusivity of their love (5:6; 6:8-10). The disheartened husband recounts his wife's beauty in Song 6:4-10 with descriptions reminiscent of his previous descriptions in Song 4:1-7, but he stops short! In Song 6:4-7, he only compliments her face, whereas in Song 4:1-7 he continued the description to her breasts—the representative of intimacy. Something seems wrong. In Song 4:9, the bride's eyes arouse the groom, and he declares his desire for her. In Song 6:5, however, her eyes affect him, but he commands her to not look at him. Why doesn't he want to look at her? Her rejection in Song 5:2 has created a problem. So now, in Song 6:4-10, Solomon teaches his readers about another aspect of the nature of love.

EFFECTS OF THE WOMAN'S EYES IN SONG 4:9 AND 6:5	
SONG 4:9	SONG 6:5
You have captivated my heart, my sister, spouse; You have captivated my heart with one of your eyes, with one link of your necklace.	Turn your eyes away from me, because they have made me defiant.

THE POWER OF LOVE

SONG
6

4You are beautiful, my sweetheart, like Tirzah;
lovely like Jerusalem, terrifying like banners.
5Turn your eyes away from me,
because they have made me defiant;
your hair is like a flock of goats, which move down Gilead.
6Your teeth are like a flock of ewe lambs,
which have come up from the washing;
all of them are bearing twins,
and there are none missing among them.
7Like a slice of a pomegranate is your open mouth
behind your veil.
8Sixty are they—queens, and eighty concubines,
and virgins—innumerable.
9She is unique—my dove, my perfect one;
she is unique to her mother,
she is the pure one to the one who bore her;
the daughters saw her and blessed her;
queens and concubines, and they praised her.
10Who is this? The one who looks down like the dawn,
beautiful like the moon, pure like the sun,
terrifying like banners.

Women possess a lot of power. More than you may realize. Because sexual desire is a very strong desire, you could use sex to get your husband to do things for you. The Song, however, teaches the young woman that she should not exert this power over her husband, because it is contrary to the order of creation and because it will damage her relationship with her husband. Furthermore, wisdom teaches that if a wife uses sex in this way, she could jeopardize her exclusive union with her husband (for example, in the Old Testament world, he might have married another woman). First Kings 11:3 reports that Solomon did

♡ DIGGING DEEPER

Several commentators do not believe Song 6:4 represents a hostile relationship. Exum, for example, correctly interprets the imagery: "Like KJV 'terrible as an army with banners,' it is a striking and memorable poetic image that calls up a picture of the two royal cities as strongholds, with troops streaming out of them—an image of power suggests the woman's 'conquering,'" J. Cheryl Exum, *Song of Songs*, OTL (Louisville: Westminster John Knox, 2005), 190. Nevertheless, she finds this interpretation "troublesome" and rejects it. Three textual observations, however, argue that the couple has a conflict. First, the word "terrifying," second, personified cities are women (cf. Isa 37:22; 47:1; 52:1), and third, "banner" represents a military unit (cf. Num 1:52; 2:2, 18, 25). Compare the city in Song 6:4 with the one in Song 8:10, where the wife is again a city, sexually at war with everyone *except* her husband: "I became in his eyes like one who finds peace." In Song 8:10, he looks at her and sees peace, but in Song 6:4, he looks at her and sees "terrifying like banners."

not have an exclusive love; neither did most of the prosperous men in the ancient world. For a woman in that world, the wife in the Song possessed a precious gift—an exclusive love with her husband.

But in Song 6 she does not appreciate this gift. In fact, she is at war. The Song even uses military imagery to describe her power. She is a fortified city at war with her husband. Song 6:4 and 10 contain the phrase "terrifying like banners." The phrase occurs at the beginning and end of this section, marking it off as a unit. The word *terrifying* is also found in Hab 1:7: "[The Babylonians] are terrifying and frightening." The word *terrifying* in this context refers to an invading army. The same idea is present in Song 6:4 and 10. The "banners" refer to an army's banners. In Song 6:4, the husband describes his wife as beautiful, lovely, and terrifying! This couple is metaphorically at war.

It has been said that one of the most fragile things in the world is a man's ego. A guy does not like to be rejected, and he certainly doesn't want to be considered a bad lover. When a wife rejects her husband, she could be saying, "I just don't want to have sex tonight." That may sound harmless, but to a guy it is essentially saying, "I don't like having sex with you." Other times, however, implicit in a rejection is the thought, "I have something you want, and I'm not going to give it to you." Neither of us have ever heard of a wife actually saying this, but think about what is happening. Does she have something he wants? Is she refusing to give it to him? Can or should any other person in the world give it to him? And how strong is his desire? Her rejection can dishearten her husband and negatively affect their relationship.

A rejection like the wife's rejection in Song 5:3 can create hostility in a relationship. Sometimes a wife may not even realize what she has done, but she has asserted power over her husband and damaged the desire he should have for her. The next time a husband desires his wife, if he desires her at all, he will likely be looking for nonverbal cues to determine if she is interested. And if she is on the top of the mountain or hanging out in the lion's den (Song 4:8) and doesn't seem to want to open the door (5:2–3), the husband may not make his desires known or may refuse to awaken desire (6:5). He is *afraid* of being rejected and hurt by her again. Fear has entered the relationship, where it should not exist. A cold war has been waged. Peace is gone. This marriage is now disordered.

A husband may respond to rejection by crushing his own sexual desire. When desire would otherwise be encouraged, he shuts it down. Remember back in Song 4:9, the wife looks at her husband, and her look lights the fires of desire! But in Song 6:5, he doesn't want her to look at him, because he knows what that look does to him. He doesn't want that desire. She is beautiful but also terrifying. If he doesn't awaken desire, then he doesn't have to shut it down. Many marriages become sexless, become nearly sexless, or end in divorce/affairs for this reason. I remember reading about a husband describing the trials of his early married life. He remarked how good all the single guys had it. He went to bed every night and slept next to his beautiful wife, but if he dared to touch her, she'd kill him! That couple had a lot of jackals to seize, but that relationship illustrates the connection between beauty, desire, power, and fear. He wanted his wife; he desired her, but he didn't want to desire her. Do you see how Song 6:5 was being fulfilled in their marriage? He didn't want to even sleep next to her. He thought the single guys had it better than he did because they didn't have to sleep next to this beautiful, terrifying army.

Even in a good marriage, rejection can crush desire. I was talking to a pastor about intimacy, and he mentioned how difficult it was for him to proposition or even talk to his wife about sex. He wanted her but would go night after night not telling her because he didn't want to be rejected. The last thing most guys want to talk to their wives about is sex. Fear paralyzes the sexual relationship ("terrifying like banners"). The pastor wasn't asking to do something weird in the marriage bed either; he just wanted to have sex with his wife. He was terrified to ask for fear of being rejected. He explained the struggle with temptation for pornography and masturbation during that season of their relationship as well (threats to their exclusive union, Song 6:8–10).

Now the Song does not encourage wives to lie. If a wife doesn't like something, she is sick, or she has some other legitimate reason, she needs to communicate with her husband. She should not live in fear that if she says no, she may destroy her marriage. Intimacy is learned. A couple will have to communicate and learn how to love together. They should speak *the truth* in love and not give up. Biblical intimacy is nothing like what the world portrays. The order of creation is that the two slowly, patiently, learn how to love one another. They should never lie! If the wife doesn't like something, she should say so. Intimacy gets better as the years progress. The trials, troubles, and travails could split the couple or, if they respond biblically, bind them closer together, driving their sexual relationship deeper. The couple possesses an intimate relationship, and the sexual aspect of the relationship represents only one aspect of their union. This deeper, closer intimacy cannot be experienced at the beginning of a marriage. So, when you are a wife and encounter problems, speak *the truth in love* and don't give up; your marriage will mature through the problem. And young men, when you are a husband and encounter problems, listen to your wife; don't shut her down or think it is "her problem."

One time I was talking to a husband whose marriage was struggling. He was being selfish and needed to address his personal sin. I inquired how he was doing with purity and intimacy with his wife. I wasn't really expecting a favorable response. He told me his wife was still affectionate toward him despite their marital challenges. I was shocked! Unaware of the instruction from Song 6:4–10, this wife had purposed that she would never use sex as a weapon in their marriage. She had realized the exclusive, powerful nature of love and had chosen to live in wisdom even through marital problems. As she made those problems known to her husband, he sought biblical counsel. Song 6:4–7:10 encourages a wife to follow a similar pattern.

EXCLUSIVE LOVE

As we've mentioned before, weaponizing sex can destroy the exclusive union that God planned for a husband and wife. The Garden of Eden included one man and one woman. God created the blueprint for love, marriage, and sex—one man and one woman for life. Jesus repeated the blueprint in Matthew 19:4–6. Regardless of either spouse's sin, this remains the pattern. This pattern for love, marriage, and sex is reflected in the Song of Songs.

Song 6:4–10 celebrates this exclusivity of marriage. And Song 6:8–10 specifically describes the wife's unique and special status: she is better than "sixty queens, eighty concubines, and numberless virgins." Two times the husband says she is "the only one." She is his exclusive one! Further, she is blessed and praised by other women. What she has (an exclusive marriage relationship) is what all those other women want. Each wants a man who will love *only* her. This is the order of creation.

Since using intimacy as a weapon could endanger this exclusive union, a wife has a decision to make. Song 6:10 sits at the crux between two options for a woman. She could choose to use her beauty to exercise authority over her husband like a harem girl would (3:6–11), or she could use it to recreate the Garden of Eden as the female lover in the Song of Songs (Song 7:11—8:5). The question "Who is this?" occurs three times in the Song (3:6; 6:10; 8:5) and presents the female reader with these two options.

Young woman, the Song intends to shape your affections so you desire the relationship of the Song of Songs lover and refuse the allurements of being like a harem girl. Who do you want to be? The text presents your options by describing two women coming up from the wilderness (Song 3:6, 8:5).

"WHO IS THIS?"		
SONG 3:6	SONG 6:10	SONG 8:5
Who is this coming up from the wilderness? Like pillars of smoke, a fragrant cloud of myrrh and frankincense.	*Who is this?* The one who looks down like the dawn,	*Who is this coming up from the wilderness,* leaning upon her lover? Under the apple tree I awakened you;

One woman comes with abundant smells, security (sixty armed men, 3:7–8), and a luxurious seat (3:9–10). She is the envy of the daughters of Zion (3:10). The other comes simply, leaning on her lover and awakening him under the apple tree (8:5). Song 6:8–9 teaches that while the daughters of Zion may envy the harem girl in Solomon's palanquin (3:11), the sixty queens, eighty concubines, and numberless virgins (6:8–9) envy the wife who has the exclusive love that the male lover of the Song has for his one and only wife.

Those women who marry the king envy the common wife who possesses an exclusive union with her lover. Young women often prefer the power and luxury that a Solomon could provide. The Song of Songs wife "looks down" upon the queens, concubines, and virgins like the rising sun looks down upon the land (Song 6:10). She outshines the night sky like the moon in its beauty (Song 6:10). The message from the Song is clear: do not use your beauty to terrify your husband. May your union be exclusive and fearless instead.

> The female lover of the Song is not a victim to her circumstances.

The female lover of the Song also teaches in Song 6:8–10 how a wife can cultivate love for her husband by thinking about their exclusive union. Just as we saw in Song 5:10–16, the Song doesn't just tell a wife, "You need to love him!" No! It instructs her how to cultivate *desire* for her husband. The female lover of the Song is not a victim to her circumstances. She is a strong woman who overcomes obstacles and conquers difficult situations. She is not powerless; she is powerful! She isn't some handmaid servant girl who labors around the house. She is *her husband's* unique *one*. She is his dawn who looks down upon all other women. She may clean the house and take care of the children, but those privileges and responsibilities are secondary to her status as her husband's lover. A husband could pay another person to clean the house, do the laundry, or even take care of the kids. The wife alone possesses this amazing thing that he desires—her affection. Even illicit sexual encounters cannot compare to the freely offered, desirous, and sacrificial love of the Song of Songs wife. Unlike the harem girl, she *desires* intimacy with her husband without obligation, compensation, or manipulation. She genuinely wants to experience an intimate encounter with him. She is his "only one"! Remembering her special and unique relationship to her husband cultivates desire for him.

Many wives have never been taught how to love their husbands in this way. The church taught them the duties of the Proverbs 31 and Titus 2 woman, and they falsely concluded that raising godly children, keeping a clean home, and managing household affairs were a wife's primary responsibilities. All these tasks are important, but a wife desiring a sexual relationship with her husband transcends them all.

On a blog post, an anonymous husband complained that his wife does a great job cleaning the house but never wants to have sex with him. Several other husbands noted similar sentiments. One husband countered, "Our sex is great, but I can't get her to clean the house." The other husbands retorted, "Shut up, and hire a maid!" This comical interaction illustrates how most wives mis-prioritize the intimate relationship with their husbands. Carolyn Mahaney testifies,

> Several years ago at a church leadership conference, I hosted a panel of pastors' wives at a women's session. We fielded questions on a wide variety of topics—from childrearing to counseling women in crisis situations.
> Then a woman from the audience posed the question: "What is one thing you have learned that encourages your husband the most?" As the other women on the panel answered, I pondered my response. *I know what C. J.'s answer would be, but dare I say that?* And then it

was my turn. "Make love to him," I blurted out. "That's what my husband would say if he were here!"

The room erupted into a wave of nervous, knowing laughter.

It's true! Engaging in this physical expression of marital intimacy and union is one of the most meaningful ways I can encourage my husband.[1]

Young lady, you will be your husband's "En Gedi," his oasis in a dry and barren desert (Song 1:14). What makes a wife uniquely *his* wife is her *power* to fulfill something that *only* she can fulfill—intimacy. *The* primary way that a wife *loves* her husband is by cultivating sexual desire for him.

> *The* primary way that a wife *loves* her husband is by cultivating sexual desire for him.

THE DESIRE FOR PEACE

SONG 6

[11]*To the garden of nuts I went down,*
to see the vegetation of the valley,
to see if the vines have sprouted,
if the pomegranates have bloomed.
[12]*I did not know what happened;*
my soul put me in the chariots of my noble people.
[13]*Return! Return! Shulamite!*
Return! Return! So that we may look at you.
What would you see in the Shulamite,
like the dance of the two camps?

Every marriage will have conflict. This conflict destroys the peace and intimacy that God would have a couple enjoy. Song 6:11 paints the picture of the "garden" being visited, but then suddenly someone is out of the garden and in a chariot (6:12). Even scholars are puzzled by exactly what is going on here. The garden is the place of intimacy (Song 4:12—5:1; 6:2), so leaving the garden represents lost intimacy. The chariot imagery could be something majestic, but it more likely represents terror. The chariot was an instrument of conflict, a vehicle of war. So this relationship has a problem; there is a conflict.

---

1   Carolyn Mahaney, *Feminine Appeal: Seven Virtues of a Godly Wife and Mother* (rev. ed; Wheaton, IL: Crossway, 2004), 82.

Several military metaphors appear in Song 6:4–13. First, the wife is a "terrifying army of banners" in verses 4 and 10. Then this chariot appears in verse 12. Finally, Shulamite dances the "two camps" dance in verse 13. The "camp" is usually associated with a military encampment. Scholars are at a loss to explain the "two camps" dance, but considering the couple's disputing in these verses, a reference to two war camps seems plausible. The couple have a dispute, like two camps at war, but what they want is peace.

MILITARY TERMINOLOGY IN THE SONG OF SONGS	
SONG 2:4	His banner over me is love
SONG 6:4, 10	Terrifying like banners
SONG 6:12	Chariots of my noble people
SONG 6:13	Dance of the two camps
SONG 8:10	I am a wall, and my breasts are like towers (wife as city metaphor)

In Song 6:13 (and only here) the wife is named Shulamite, a clear play on words with *Solomon*. Remember, Solomon's name means "peace." He is Mr. Peace (*Solomon*), and he is looking for Mrs. Peace (*Shulamite*). So also does every married couple, because they live in a perpetual "battle of the sexes" effect of the Fall (Gen 3:16), but what they really want is peace.

Instead of using her beauty and body to fight her husband, the Song of Songs wife exults in her husband's desire for her (Song 7:1–6). She does not desire to lead her husband (Gen 3:16), but lives so her husband desires to lead her (Song 7:10). The Song of Songs wife uses her sexual power to create peace with her husband.

The world celebrates female empowerment, but the Song exalts a different kind of female empowerment. Mrs. Peace sets down her sword and picks up her dancing shoes. The husband describes the beauty of her body, and his desire skyrockets (Song 7:1–6). He begins with her feet and ascends to her head. Finally, he exults in her breasts—again a representative of her sexuality, just like what we read in Song 4.

In Song 7:8, the husband no longer describes his wife's body but his intention and desire to partake of her body. In Song 7:10, the wife explains, "I am my lover's; and over me is his desire." The exclusive love exulted about in Song 6:8–10 is realized as the wife submits herself to her husband's desire over her (7:10). The world teaches a woman to use sex to love herself, but the Song teaches the wife to use sex to love her husband. The irony is that when she uses sex to love her husband, she *usually* discovers her husband genuinely loving her.

POWER, AUTHORITY, AND THE FALL OF MAN

Chapter five introduced the idea that the biblical husband sexually "conquers" his wife and that this "conquest" is not by force but by love (Song 2:4). The husband does not say, "I have conquered"; the wife says, "I have been conquered." This conquest is not violent but loving, for the wife says, "His banner over me *is love*." Song 2:4 teaches that a husband places a "banner" over his wife. She is his.

Song 8:10 uses similar terminology and explains the means of conquest. In the ancient world, a woman was a common metaphor for a city, and a "virgin" city was an unconquered city. For example, Isaiah 37:22 states, "She despises you, she ridicules you, the virgin daughter of Zion; she shakes her head behind your back, the daughter of Jerusalem." Jerusalem is personified as a virgin woman who mocks the invading Assyrian king (see also Isa 47:1; 52:1–2). Likewise, the wife is a fortified city. She says, "I am a wall, and my breasts are like towers, then I became in his eyes like one who finds peace" (Song 8:10). Her breasts are towers representing her sexual maturity and unconquerable defenses. She is fortified and defies anyone who tries to enter the city through force, flattery, coercion, or manipulation. She is unconquerable to all, except one. But the one who conquers does *not conquer by force* like an invading army but with a treaty (covenant) that creates peace: "I became in his eyes like one who finds *peace*" (8:10). The husband enters the city, not as a conqueror, but as a desired and invited leader. He raises his banner over the city and claims it as his own (Song 2:4).

These ideas of power, conquest, and authority are interwoven throughout Song 5:2—7:10 and resonate with the implications of the Fall in Genesis 3:16. The Lord explains that after the Fall, a wife will naturally be inclined to assert power over her husband: "And for your husband will be your *desire*, but he will rule over you" (Gen 3:16). This "desire" is connected to power, authority, and rule, which is why the next line states, "he will rule over you." Genesis 3:16 teaches that after the Fall, a woman would have a natural inclination to assert authority over her husband. Before the Fall, the husband (Adam) was the divinely appointed leader of his wife (Eve). Ever since the Fall, he continues in this role, but the wife possesses a desire to lead her husband. The easiest way for a woman to assert authority over her husband and lead him is through the marriage bed. The Song teaches the daughters of Jerusalem not to use intimacy to lead (rule over) their husbands. The wife who weaponizes intimacy lives out the Genesis 3:16 effect of the Fall. The wife who never "feels it" similarly lives out the Genesis 3:16 effect of the Fall.

> The easiest way for a woman to assert authority over her husband is in the marriage bed.

Connecting to the idea of authority and rule is the word translated *desire* in Song 7:10. In Genesis 3:16, the wife desires to rule over her husband: "And for your husband will be your *desire*, but he will rule over you." In Genesis 4:7, sin desires to rule over Cain: "Sin lurks, and toward you is *its desire*, but you should rule over it." And in Song 7, the wife rejoices in her husband's rekindled *desire* to lead her.

DESIRE IN THE BIBLE	
GENESIS 3:16	To the woman [the Lord] said, "I will greatly increase your hardship; in pain you will give birth to children; and toward your husband will be *your desire*, but he will rule over you."
GENESIS 4:7	If you [Cain] do well, will you not be accepted? But if you do not do well, at the door, sin lurks, and toward you is *its desire*, but you should rule over it.
SONG 7:10	I am my lover's; and over me is *his desire*.

In Song 5:3, the wife lives according to the effect of the Fall by refusing her husband intimacy. But in Song 7:10, she rejoices in her husband's leadership over her, and in Song 7:11—8:3 she uses her sexual power to recreate the Garden of Eden with him.

CONCLUSION

Our world promotes an idea of equality and fairness that contradicts the message of Song 5:2—8:3. The world claims that men and women are equal and that neither is the leader of the other. Within God's grand plan of redemption, men and women are equal before God (Gal 3:26–28), but during our lives on this earth, God has appointed specific roles to men and women. The theological word for this view is complementarianism (Eph 5:22–33). The world's idea of equality—egalitarianism—is false and fuels the battle of the sexes. God appointed the husband the head of the house.

In the Song, the wife is always the city; she is always the garden. These are gendered metaphors; they reflect gender differences and gender roles. The husband enters the city and consumes the garden. The city and garden become his. The Song teaches the husband to cultivate the garden (Song 2:15) and lovingly and peacefully enter the city (2:4; 8:10). The Song of Songs husband uses his divinely appointed authority to *serve* his wife, not selfishly serve himself. The wife *delights* to sit under the shade of his protection and to consume the fruit of his provision (2:3). The biblical man uses his divinely appointed authority to protect and provide for his wife. Similarly, the biblical wife desires her husband's leadership over her (7:10). Together the husband and wife recognize God's gendered design, submit to the order of creation, and love (serve) one another. This couple is not at war; rather, they have recreated the Garden of Eden—the place of peace.

DISCUSSION QUESTIONS:

1. Discuss how intimacy is a woman's most powerful weapon. How can she use it for good? For evil?

2. How and why is the wife in the Song terrifying to her husband (Song 6:4, 10)?

3. How is female power in the Song different from the female empowerment promoted by the world today?

4. What is the easiest way for a woman to assert authority over her husband?

5. How should a man use his divinely appointed authority over his wife?

6. Compare the three descriptions of the female lover (Song 4:1–7; 6:4–7; 7:1–7).

7. In Song 6:8–10, what does the appearance of 60 queens and 80 concubines teach the reader?

8. In Song 6:8–10, the husband describes his wife as his "only one" two times. What unique power does the wife possess that only she can fulfill in marriage, and what does this teach the reader about priorities in marriage?

9. What does the name Shulamite mean, and why does it appear in Song 6:13?

CH. 11 | YOU CAN RECREATE THE GARDEN OF EDEN
(7:11—8:4)

In the Garden of Eden, Adam and Eve lived in perfect harmony, peace, and security. Genesis 2:25 summarizes their experience this way: "The two of them were naked, the man and his wife, and they were not ashamed." But sin entered the world, and God expelled them from the Garden of Eden. The couple in Song 7:10, however, metaphorically reenter it. Song 7:11—8:3 describes Edenic intimacy and teaches the original design for intimacy.

THE EMPOWERED EDENIC WIFE

SONG
7

> ¹¹*Come, my lover, let us go out to the field;*
>   *let us spend the night in the villages!*
> ¹²*Let us rise early to the vineyards;*
>   *let us see if the vine has sprouted,*
>   *the buds of the vine have opened,*
>   *the pomegranates have bloomed;*
>   *then/there I will give you my love.*
> ¹³*The mandrakes give a scent,*
>   *and over our doors are all choice fruits.*
>   *New fruits! Also, old ones!*
>   *I have stored up for you, my lover.*

The Song of Songs female lover entreats her husband to an intimate encounter where she offers him a desirable and diverse intimate experience. She does not wait for her husband to proposition her but seizes control of the situation and offers him her "love." The word *love* in Song 7:12 is a plural in Hebrew (*loves*, cf. Song 1:2) and refers to sexual caresses. The empowered Edenic wife takes control of the sexual relationship with her husband, awakens his desire, and leads him to the apple tree (Song 8:5). This wife recognizes the power of sex and uses it to build up her house, not tear it down (Prov 14:1; cf. Song 5:2—8:3). The female lover of the Song desires intimacy with her husband and compels him to join her for a tryst.

For too long our Christian subculture has played into Dame Folly's tactics, teaching the lie that the husband, as the leader of the home, controls his wife, compelling her to submit to him by selflessly and sacrificially having sex with him whenever he desires. Baloney! While sometimes a wife may dutifully serve her husband, this is not the *normal* pattern. The wife is not a doormat, an object for her husband's sexual pleasure. The wife of the Song of Songs corresponds to the Proverbs 5:19 wife, whose husband is continually captivated by her, which protects him from Dame Folly (Prov 5:20). She is an active participant who not only says *yes* to her husband's proposition (Song 5:2–3) but also sexually *leads* her husband (8:2) and *awakens* his sexual desire (8:5). In the Garden of Eden, the husband was the head of the household, but the wife was the leader of the bedroom.

> The wife is not a doormat, an object for her husband's sexual pleasure.

This teaching has massive implications for the husband as well. In essence, husbands need to back off and let wives lead in the bedroom. And, single young man, when you pressure a girl to get physical, you are messing up God's entire design for intimacy. Pressuring her for physical affection *teaches* her a false sexual ethic that says, "The man is in charge of the physical relationship, and you need to do what I want when I want it." This sentiment crushes a wife's sexual desire, making sex dutiful instead of delightful. You are teaching her to want you because she *has to*, not because she *wants to*.

Meanwhile, like every other husband, you want not only sex but also for your wife to want you. By teaching a wife that she should simply be available to her husband's sexual whims, the church has unintentionally created an opportunity for Dame Folly to gain a voice in a husband's heart. The husband who *wants* his wife to *want* him is not perverted. His desire is normal. And if his wife doesn't *want* him, Dame Folly does. According to Proverbs 7:15, *he* is *the one* the woman is seeking. She doesn't want just anybody; she wants *him*. She *desires* him. Of course, she is lying, but it is a lie he wants to believe. And according to her, God has even "providentially" brought the two of them together! He is her soulmate, and now she has found him. She then entreats him, *"Come! Let us drink deeply with lovemaking until the morning; let us delight ourselves with love"* (7:18). And their rendezvous lasts until the *morning*.

Rather than encouraging wives to be the female lover of the Song of Songs and to desire their husbands, Christians have been influenced by asceticism, romanticism, and/or feminism. The ascetic wife tolerates intimacy only when absolutely necessary. The empowered, romantic feminist defines sex as a "feeling," and if she doesn't "feel it," then her husband is not getting it. She essentially uses intimacy for her own affection and/or personal gain. The female lover of the Song, however, cultivates sexual desire for her husband. She goes after him, initiates sex, sets up a rendezvous, and lures him away for a time of pure intimacy. The wife's proposition in Song 7:11–13 contains a striking correlation with Dame Folly's proposition in Proverbs 7. (See page 129 for a comparison between the Song of Songs woman and Dame Folly.)

EDENIC DIVERSITY

More than using some of the same words that Dame Folly used, the Song of Songs wife uses diversity to recreate the Garden of Eden. In Song 7:11–13, she presents different places, times, and fruits of pleasure. The Song of Songs wife entreats her husband to get out of town with her, suggesting, "let us spend the night in the villages." This wife is not a corpse, making herself available to her husband; rather, she desires him and entreats him to go off to another place for love. Not only does she want to "spend the *night* in the villages," but she also wants to "*rise early* to the vineyards." "Love" is something enjoyed not only at night but also in the morning. It is something done not only in the villages but also in the vineyards. Early in the morning the wife gives herself to her husband in the vineyards ("then/there I will give you my love"). Whether it is morning or evening, in the villages or in the countryside, the Song of Songs wife desires intimacy with her husband and appeals to him to join her in different places at different times.

The wife, however, does not limit the diversity to places and times. In Song 7:13 she tells him, "Over our doors are all choice fruits. New fruits! Also, old ones!" In the ancient world, fruits were stored above a door. The unique adjective here is *old*. Who likes old fruit? But in Song 7:13, the wife offers old fruit as something favorable that her husband would like. In our household, bananas are one of the most difficult fruits to keep on the shelves. Either the kids vanquish them, or suddenly nobody wants to eat them. The bananas get old then; they get older and older and older. Old bananas are undesirable. Likewise, old fruit is undesirable.

The fruit in Song 7:13, however, refers to erotic pleasures. And the *old fruit* refers to erotic pleasures the couple has enjoyed in the past. The wife has "stored up" these erotic pleasures and anticipates enjoying them with her husband again. Similarly, *new fruit* refers to erotic pleasures the couple has *not* enjoyed in the past. Hence, the adjective *new*. The Song of Songs wife's diversity extends beyond places and times, even to pleasures.

The marriage bed is a place of freedom. The couple is free to enjoy intimacy whenever and in whatever way they consensually desire. Intimacy should be a regular part of marriage, not an "every once in a while" kind of thing. During premarital counseling sessions, Angela and I recommend married couples should be intimate on average *at least* two times a week. Life gets busy, particularly with young children. Make intimacy a priority.

Couples need to prioritize not only intimacy but diversity as well. The marriage bed should be a place not only where old fruits are enjoyed but also where new fruits are tasted. Kiwis look disgusting, but they taste great! Some intimate fruits are that way. Something you didn't think you would ever like may become an old fruit that you enjoy for the rest of your lives. Other fruits are kind of like cranberries. They look so beautiful and tasty. But when you sink your teeth into those beautiful red fruits, you quickly learn how you were deceived! But you never know if you have a kiwi or a cranberry until you have tried it.

The proliferation of pornography has unfortunately polluted young minds. A caution is in order. Young man, cleanse your mind. Remember the other principles concerning intimacy in the Song. The "order" of intimacy in Song 4 is a relational, sensuous experience enjoyed by both individuals ("Eat, friends; drink and be drunk, lovers!" Song 5:1). Those pornographic images are dame follies. They are liars. If your spouse doesn't like a particular "fruit," believe your spouse. Don't be deceived by the pornographic actor. Cleanse your mind and enjoy intimacy according to the order of creation.

Real husbands and wives are different. One couple may like cranberries and not kiwis. Another couple may like kiwis and not cranberries. That is ok. Enjoy whatever fruit you enjoy. Don't compare! Be content and enjoy your fruit. God made people with different tastes, touches, and sizes. Marriage is a time for you to explore those senses. See what you enjoy together and enjoy the journey. Just make sure you are regularly eating some fruit. It's healthy for you!

Love is an act of service. The marriage bed is a place of peace. Whatever the couple decides, it is the couple that decides. Each of you has veto authority. If he likes only cranberries or she likes only kiwis, try an apple! Furthermore, if she likes kiwis, why can't you serve your wife sexually and give her kiwis? Each spouse should look at the diversity of the marriage bed as an act of service. The marriage bed is a place of variety and service.

Finally, you may have noticed that the wife recreates the Garden of Eden through diversity. Remember, the Song is wisdom literature. It isn't always this way, but usually husbands are more adventurous in the marriage bed than wives are. Husband, you have an entire lifetime to get to know this treasure that God has gifted to you. You will learn, and then she will change. You will learn again, and then she will change again. Female sexuality is way more complex than male sexuality. Furthermore, intimacy changes as you age. You may learn to like cranberries! You may get sick of kiwis. Be kind, loving, and gentle. Be kind, compassionate, and gentle. Be kind, patient, and gentle. Husband, if you want to try a new fruit, particularly at the beginning of your married life, tell your wife you would like to try a different fruit, but let her choose. Follow the pattern of the Song and let her take the *lead*.

Young man, one of the best ways you can love your future wife is to learn to control your sexual desire now. After you marry, let your wife awaken your sexual desire. If your sexual desire is always awakened, you are making it very difficult for her to love you according to wisdom. The wife in Song 8:5 awakens her husband's desire. In Song 7, she dances and awakens him, rejoicing in his desire for her. In Song 1:2, she entreats him to kiss her because she wants to make love with him. In Song 1:7, she propositions him for a midday tryst. In Song 8:1–2, she desires to kiss him openly and then states, "I would lead you; I would bring you to the house of my mother." Notice those verbs in Song 8:2— *lead* and *bring*. Have you ever considered that the pre-Fall, Garden of Eden, order of creation for sexual union was an awakening wife?

> Young man, one of the best ways you can love your future wife is to learn to control your sexual desire now.

In marriage, things tend to work better when the husband gives his wife the space and freedom to take the lead. Instead, young men think they constantly "need" or possess a "right" to have sex all the time. During his single years, he masturbates all the time. He thinks that a wife will solve this problem, so he looks for a wife, thinking they will have sex all the time. Problem solved! Then this guy marries some poor girl, and his insatiable appetite crushes her desire. His pornographic mind crushes her creativity and pushes her away. She begins to hate sex, and he naïvely wonders why. Young man, learn to control your sexual desire before marriage. Dethrone the god of sex. After you marry, let your wife awaken your desire. Focus on your mission, which should include work, church, family, and serving others (including your wife outside of the bedroom). Your focus on your mission gives your wife room to come along and say, "Come, my lover! Let's go!" Then she whisks you off to the Garden of Eden. This is the order of creation.

Young woman, after you marry, lead like the Song of Songs wife. This is the order of creation. Throughout the Song, when things are "right," the woman takes the lead. After marriage, particularly when children come along, you may have to be very intentional to do this. Don't leave your husband standing outside with dew on his head (Song 5:2). You may have to be very creative. Awakening your husband's sexual desire should be just as important to you as going to church. That means it is more important than everything else in your life (work, laundry, children, church ministry, etc.). You love God by loving your husband.

The most important way you can demonstrate love to your husband is by rejoicing in his affection for you. Yes, work hard, be the Proverbs 31 and Titus 2 woman; but the one thing that only you can fulfill is his desire for intimacy (Song 6:8–10). It will strengthen and enhance your marriage. Phylicia Masonheimer noticed her marriage growing cold and took *intentional* and *consistent* steps to flirt with her husband. She testified, "Day by day my marriage grew sweeter."[1] She took the lead in the bedroom, and her marriage blossomed into an Edenic garden. Young woman, you have a lot of power. Make intimacy a priority in your marriage.

Through all of this, you and your spouse will need to communicate. Tim and I are not saying a husband can never initiate an intimate encounter; in the Song, the man initiates three times (Song 2:8; 4:1; 5:2ff). At the beginning of your marriage, you are going to need to talk a lot. What the Song teaches and what we have experienced is that intimacy works better when the wife takes the lead. Husband, focus on your mission and entrust the bedroom to your wife; and wife, don't leave your husband standing outside covered in dew.

---

1   Lisa Jacobson and Phylicia Masonheimer, *The Flirtation Experiment: Putting Magic, Mystery, and Spark into Your Everyday Marriage* (Nashville: Thomas Nelson, 2021), xvii.

> Husband, focus on your mission and entrust the bedroom to your wife; and wife, don't leave your husband standing outside covered in dew.

EDENIC DESIRE

Edenic intimacy focuses on desire. A newly married groom is rightly excited for intimacy (Song 3:11). Every groom, however, quickly learns that intimacy is more than the physical act. Song 4 teaches that intimacy is a relational, sensuous experience enjoyed by both individuals. A husband does not just want satisfaction; he wants to be desired. This is the order of creation.

The Song presents desire in patterned ways. In Song 4:1-5 the husband describes his wife's beauty, but then in verse 6 he asserts what he will do: "I will go, myself, to the mountain of myrrh, and to the hill of frankincense." Similarly, in Song 7:1-7, the man again describes his wife's beauty and in verse 8 asserts his intention: "I said, 'I will climb the palm tree.'" Desire builds through the description of the wife's beauty until the husband can contain himself no longer; then he declares his intention to partake of her beauty. He desires her. But this sexual desire is not a one-way street. The wife, similarly, describes the place, time, and fruits of love in Song 7:11-13, but then in 8:1-2 she seemingly can contain herself no longer and declares her intention to make her husband consume her. This sexually assertive, excellent wife does not just make her body available to her husband; she compels him to consume her because she also desires him. This is the order of creation.

> ¹If only you were like a brother to me,
>   one who sucked upon the breasts of my mother;
> I would find you outside; I would kiss you!
>   They would not despise me.
> ²I would lead you; I would bring you,
>   to the house of my mother; she taught me.
> I would make you drink from the spiced wine;
>   from the sweet wine of my pomegranate.
> ³His left hand is under my head,
>   and his right hand embraces me.

SONG 8

Song 8:1 presents a small snapshot of ancient perceptions of public displays of affection. Family members could kiss, but public kissing between lovers was frowned upon. You may get a little grossed out by the *brother* and *mother* terminology. The wife does *not* want to kiss her brother! She wants to kiss her lover! Note that the figure of speech is a simile: "If only you were *like* a brother." She wants to kiss him. Note this is an expression of her physical affection. She desires him. This is the order of creation.

The reason she wants to kiss him is given in verse 2. She brings him to her mother's house, where she would make him drink her intoxicating beverages. As a mother's breasts provide physical nutrition to a child, the wife's pomegranate juice provides sexual intoxication to her husband. She awakens his desire and makes him intoxicated with her love. This is the order of creation.

As we said before, biblical sexuality is not a one-way street. Both lovers should enjoy intimacy. Just as the man describes love and then asserts his intention in Song 4 and 7, so also does the wife describe love and then assert her intention in Song 8. Most singles think they will love sex. They highly anticipate intimacy after marriage. Many, unfortunately, must work through physical or spiritual problems. We would encourage you to not give up. Serve your spouse. Desire your spouse. And we pray God allows you to enjoy intimacy according to the order of creation.

EDENIC EDUCATION

Almost on cue, the Song recognizes that intimacy is complex and that learning to love can sometimes be difficult. In Song 8:2, a Hebrew word sticks out. This word is translated "she taught me." This one word provides guidance, particularly to young ladies, on how to love even when there are problems. God's design is that mothers teach their daughters about marriage, love, and sex. Female sexuality is more complex than male sexuality. The divinely placed person to help a new bride with sex is her mother. This is the order of creation.

Interestingly, parents today often do not like talking to their children about sex. Typically, in our culture, whoever does the premarital counseling often includes a "sex talk" near the end of the counseling sessions. Then, when a problem arises, a pastor or his wife may get an urgent call on a couple's wedding night or a day later asking for advice. In the ancient world, the mother and daughter would live nearby, and the mother would be the source of sexual education for the new bride. Song 8:2 reinforces the idea that the primary teacher for a new bride should be her mother. In ancient times, love, marriage, and intimacy were much more of a family matter. The marriage was typically consummated at the bride's parents' house (read the Apocryphal story of Tobith). And the mother was readily available for continued education. While in many situations today, the mother may not be available or spiritually qualified to provide that instruction, the Bible guides young women on how to get advice on how to love their husbands: "The older women, likewise, should exhibit reverent behavior, not slanderers, nor given to much wine, but teachers of good things so that they might teach young women to love their husbands and children" (Titus 2:3–4). God has ordained the parents first, but the church second, to teach young people concerning matters of sexuality. When you have more questions, talk to your parents. If that is not an option, talk to a church leader of the same gender.

RESOLUTION AND CONCLUSION

The section that began in Song 5:2 concludes in Song 8:4 with the third and final adjuration refrain. This adjuration refrain, however, is a little different. This time the wife does not mention the "gazelles" or "does of the field" and changes the last line to a rhetorical question: "I put you under oath, O daughters of Jerusalem. Why would you stir up; why would you even awaken love, until it pleases?" By using the rhetorical question, the wife communicates the absurdity of awakening love prematurely.

We want to end this section with a caution concerning premarital affection. Engaging in premarital affection creates problems in marriage. That is why you have a rhetorical question in Song 8:4—"Why would you awaken love?" The woman of the Song asks the question to bring the reader into agreement with her. Young man, when you pressure a young lady for premarital physical affection, you are teaching her "the way intimacy works." Not only is your action contrary to God's Law, but it is also contrary to the way intimacy is supposed to work. The excellent wife is supposed to awaken you! By pressuring her, you are teaching her that you are in charge of the affectionate side of the relationship, and you'll decide when you'll be intimate or not. Then you marry. And you have created a mess that you are going to have to work through. Your wife will have to relearn what God's order of creation is supposed to be, and that is your fault.

> # Engaging in premarital affection creates problems in marriage.

Young lady, lust drives your desire for physical affection right now, but after marriage, that same sinful desire will drive you away from intimacy. Genesis 3:16 explains that the flesh will fight against you. After you marry, you will have to slay this same flesh. You will have to speak truth to yourself, employ some of the awakening practices of the Song of Songs lover, and learn to awaken your husband's love. The same flesh that drives you to be intimate right now will drive you to be lazy and indifferent after marriage. Heed the warning of the Song of Songs, and do not awaken love!

DISCUSSION QUESTIONS:

1. How has our Christian subculture been affected by the tactics of Dame Folly?

2. Discuss how the husband is the head of the household, but the wife should be the leader in the bedroom.

3. Compare Dame Folly's proposition in Proverbs 7 to Lady's Wisdom's proposition in Song 7.

4. Is it ok for the wife to be creative in her intimate encounters with her husband? Why or why not?

5. How has pornography affected young minds when it comes to "fruits"? (Be careful with this question.)

6. Why should a wife make intimacy a priority in marriage?

7. Who should be a young woman's primary teacher of intimacy?

8. Discuss why parents often abdicate their role when it comes to appropriately teaching their children about intimacy.

9. How does your flesh affect your intimate desires before marriage? After marriage?

CH. 12 | BEGINNING LOVE CORRECTLY, PART 1
(8:5–10)

God designed marriage into the order of creation. Singles regularly ask us what they should look for in a spouse. Song 8:5–14 corrects singles' thinking concerning what they should desire. Remember Song 1:3: "Oil poured forth is your name; therefore, the virgins love you." In sum, young woman, you want to marry the Song of Songs man. Young man, similarly, you want to marry the Song of Songs woman. Consider Song 8:13: "The one who dwells in the gardens, companions are listening for your voice. Let me hear it!" The "companions" are the other young men who are looking for the excellent wife; they want to find the Song of Songs female lover! The earnestness of the young man to find this woman is articulated in the last phrase, "Let me hear it!" The Song begins describing a husband that single virgins should want to marry and ends describing a wife that single men should want to marry.

> There is no mathematical marriage formula
> that guarantees you a problem-free marriage.

Remember, finding a spouse is a wisdom decision. There is no mathematical marriage formula that guarantees you a problem-free marriage. We have seen seemingly godly people marry and divorce. Similarly, we have raised our eyebrows when some couples marry, and then we have seen them mature and remain faithful to each other for as long as we have known them. More often than not, we witness couples who follow God's plan for love, marriage, and intimacy enjoy happy marriages. But we do see couples follow a worldly path and then struggle through difficult years in marriage or give up altogether. Only God knows hearts. Marriage is only the beginning, and the trials/difficulties of marriage reveal a person's true identity. Every marriage has problems. Ours has had problems. Yours will too. Many singles, however, naïvely walk into trouble. They sow seeds of sin during their unmarried years and collect crops of corruption during the early years of their marriage. Selecting a spouse is a wisdom decision, so if you listen to God's instruction concerning the selection of a spouse, you have a higher *probability* of enjoying a peaceful marriage.

GROWING IN WISDOM

Wisdom decisions are based upon risk assessment. Consider the wisdom in Ecclesiastes 10:8–10: "One who digs a pit may fall into it; one who breaks through a wall may be bitten by a snake; one who quarries stones may be hurt by them; one who splits wood may be endangered by it; if the ax is dull, and one does not sharpen it, then he will have to exert more strength, but wisdom brings success." Notice that Solomon does not say that a person should *not* split the wood! Instead, he says to use wisdom to be successful. Danger lurks in every aspect of life. If an employee walks to work, that person may have to cross a few streets to get to the job. Walking across streets can be risky. A driver may hit and kill that person! Maybe the employee should just stay home? Maybe that would be safer? Solomon teaches to cut down the tree, but to not be a fool! Sharpen the ax! So go to work, but follow the traffic signals. Use wisdom to decrease the risk.

Some professions are very risky. For example, a snake charmer could die if he/she fails to charm the snake: "The snake may bite if it is not charmed; then there is no advantage to the snake charmer" (Eccl 10:11).

Similarly, the electrician needs to make sure the power is off, or he/she might get zapped! Some jobs are more dangerous than others. People pay higher wages for dangerous services, and the individuals who work those professions must exercise greater wisdom to be successful. Their lives depend on it.

USING WISDOM TO FIND A SPOUSE

Many young singles do not know how to make decisions, much less wise decisions. Christians talk about the "gray areas" of life. Gray areas do not exist for God. The closer you draw near to Him, the smaller the so-called gray areas become. The mature Christian discerns right from wrong even when God does not give a specific command (Prov 2). Don't believe us? Study the fear of the Lord (Deut 5—6; Job 28; Prov 1—2; Isa 50:4–11)!

God does not tell you who you are supposed to marry; instead, He wants you to think, make a wise decision, then trust Him. Angela and I were just reading a book that talks about how God reveals to some people who they are supposed to marry. Wrong! If someone tells you that God divinely told that person that you are "the one," nicely tell your friend that he/she has been deceived and that God expects you to use wisdom to determine whether a person would make a good spouse. People who believe God "told them" whom to marry are high-risk marriage partners because they do not understand how God teaches wisdom to His children (Prov 1:20–33; 3:11–12; Jas 1:2–8).

So how can a person use wisdom to find a spouse? Let's use a young woman looking for a husband as an example. First, a man who regularly attends church, faithfully serves in his local church, and humbles himself before the teaching of God's Word would be a low-risk husband. He evidences submission to the teaching of God's

Word; so, when he sins, he knows to submit to God's Word and live in obedience to it. This man is a low-risk man and reflects several of the characteristics of the Song of Songs husband whom every virgin should seek to marry (Song 1:3).

Second, a man who sporadically attends church, claims that he is a Christian, but regularly imbibes the world system (games, sports, videos, etc.) would be a medium-risk husband. Marriage may make or break this guy. Young lady, you are the one to find out if he would truly submit to God's Word or not. After marriage, some of these worldly guys mature in their walk with the Lord. Some of them do not. Unfortunately, there are a lot of guys in this category.

Finally, the young man who never attends church and rejects God's way of salvation would be a high-risk husband. This man is a god to himself. Sometimes a guy like this does figure out that life will be better if he lives selflessly. Sometimes such a guy may act "good" because of God's common grace. But this man would serve his wife because he knows it will be better for *him* if he does. After all, "Happy wife = happy life." His love isn't biblical, unconditional love, and his headship isn't biblical male headship. This man's fleshly desires drive him, and his wife is just along for the ride. The biblical principle that a husband should love his wife as Jesus loved the church (Eph 5:25) would be irrelevant to this man because he does not believe in Jesus. Submitting to this man and regularly having sex with him will likely be extremely difficult. This man serves himself and usually demands that his wife serve him sexually.

These three categories of men are obviously painted in broad brushstrokes. People are not machines. They are not completely predictable. But each person submits to some kind of an authority, and if a man refuses to submit to God's teaching on marriage, then that man is an authority to himself. Who knows where that kind of marriage could go.

The believer who submits to the teaching of Scripture should love his wife selflessly and sacrificially. He should honor his marriage vows and support his wife regardless of the trials they may encounter. A wife would more easily be able to desire her husband because he loves her inside and outside of the bedroom. He leads her spiritually with the Word of God and by his example. A wife would have no guarantee, because men are not machines, but wisdom would consider the godly man a very low risk.

Well, that all sounds good, but it is more easily said than done. You may be wondering, "How do I go about finding that person?" Song 8:5–14 gives several practical tips to help singles find the Song of Songs lover.

AN EXCLUSIVE LOVE

SONG
8

> [5]Who is this coming up from the wilderness,
>   leaning upon her lover?
> Under the apple tree I awakened you;
>   there your mother conceived you;
>   there she conceived and gave birth to you.

Young woman, what are you looking for in a husband? A strong man? A rich man? The popular guy that all the girls like? Song 8:5–10 primarily speaks to young women. (Young man, we will get to you in the next chapter.) The question, "Who is this coming out of the wilderness" (8:5), also occurred in Song 3:6. A beautiful woman comes out of the wilderness accompanied by luxurious smells (3:6), surrounded by impressive security (3:7–8), and settled in a luxurious seat (3:9–10). Even in our democratic age, royal weddings receive massive attention. Why? Statistics regularly reveal that over 80% of romance novels are purchased by women. Why? I have worked in Christian retail for over fifteen years and can't remember a romance novel ever marketed to a man. Why? Something within most women wants a Song 3:6–11 relationship—marriage to the prince, billionaire, or hero. This woman's posh and prominence make her the envy of the other girls, the "daughters of Zion" (3:11).

Further, all the onlookers want to know who is coming out of the wilderness, so the Song of Songs wife tells the daughters of Zion to go and watch the wedding (described in Song 3:11). The daughters of Zion love the beauty, grandeur, and opulence of the event. Something in them desires it for themselves, and they vicariously enjoy the experience through that woman. (Romance novels function in a similar way.) Song 3:6–11 never identifies this woman who married King Solomon, because her identity doesn't matter. That woman represents every woman. She represents every virgin that wanted to be in that carriage and marry the king.

Let's jump ahead to Song 8:5. Who is coming out of the wilderness now? A woman. She is an ordinary, recently married girl who is returning with her lover and leaning on his arm. She is coming up as his exclusive wife, the one who awakens his love and raises an heir for him just as his mother has done. She does not live for the moment (the big wedding, the night with the king). Instead, she lives on through generations, just as his mother does. This woman coming out of the wilderness doesn't come in opulence and extravagance like the woman in Song 3:6–11. She doesn't come with a military escort on a bed of ease. No, she comes with something much better. She comes with the man who loves her exclusively. She comes with her ordinary, faithful, low-risk male lover from the Song of Songs.

The phrase "who is this" also occurs one other time, in Song 6:10. Chapter ten mentions it (p. 178–80). Song 6:8–10 distinguishes the female lover of the Song of Songs from other women. Verse 8 states, "Sixty are they, queens; and eighty concubines; and virgins innumerable." Look at these two women coming out of the wilderness! One is about to be a queen (Song 3:6–11)! The other has just married the man who will love her exclusively for his entire life (Song 8:5). The woman in Song 3:6–11 was just another woman who married Solomon— Mr. Peace. But the woman in Song 8 is an impenetrable fortress except to the one, the only one, in whose eyes she is the only Mrs. Peace. The Song asks you, young lady, "Which woman would you rather be?"

UNAWAKENED LOVE

SONG
8

> ⁶*Set me as a seal upon your heart, as a seal upon your arm;*
> *because love is as strong as death;*
> *jealousy is hard like the grave;*
> *its flames are flames of fire, the flame of the Lord.*
> ⁷*Many waters are not able to extinguish love,*
> *and rivers cannot flood over it.*
> *If a man would give all the wealth of his house for love,*
> *they would despise him for it.*

God wants what is best for you. He created sex and designed it to be enjoyed in marriage. The Song of Songs reflects this truth, particularly in 8:5–10. Remember the adjuration refrain in Song 8:4, "Why would you *stir* up, why would you even *awaken* love, until it pleases?" In the very next verse, the wife "awakens" the husband; she tells him, "Under the apple tree I *awakened* you." So Song 8:4 says not to awaken love "until it pleases," while Song 8:5 says the time to awaken love has come. Marriage is awakening time.

Notice the reference to the seal. The seal represents the marriage covenant and the confidence that helps a wife trust her husband and be the Song of Songs female lover. The seal "upon your heart" represents the internal love a husband should have for his wife. The seal "upon your arm" represents the physical manifestation of that internal love. A wife should know that her husband loves her by his *attitude* and *actions*.

> A wife should know that her husband loves her by his *attitude* and *actions*.

The three metaphors (death, grave, and fire) that follow descriptions of the seal convey the nature of love and teach readers two truths: how they should love in marriage and why it is foolish to awaken love before marriage.

First, you should not awaken love because love is like death. God designed love to be a permanent, lifelong bond—"strong as death." Death is permanent; love is supposed to be as well, with a person loving his/her spouse and never stopping. This is the order of creation. Falling in "love" with one person, then another, and another, is *not* the order of creation. God designed humans to love one person jealously until physical death separates them.

A second reason to wait to awaken love is that jealousy is cruel, like the grave. This permanent love is connected to jealousy because a "jealous for my lover" love is a biblical love. Scripture often condemns jealousy, but in two situations, it is a biblical character trait: the Lord is a jealous God (Ezek 8:3) and is jealous for the love and devotion of His chosen ones. In the same way, a spouse should be jealous for the love and devotion of his/her spouse (Num 5). The Old Testament word for jealousy contains the idea of a competitive, aggressive zeal. The Messiah has a jealous zeal for the Lord (Isa 42:13; 59:17). The believer should be completely devoted to the Lord and to the Lord alone (Deut 6:4; Zech 14:9; Jas 2:19).

Similar to God being jealous for those He loves, a spouse has a jealous zeal for his/her spouse. Believing spouses should be completely devoted to each other. For example, my wife is *my* wife, and if another man comes after her, my biblical love generates a jealous zeal that seeks to protect our union. The Christian subculture has lost this idea of a jealous zeal for one's spouse.

If a person awakens love before the seal/covenant/marriage, this jealous zeal has no basis. And if "the object of one's affections" refuses to reciprocate that jealous love, that jealous zeal becomes a cruel feeling, particularly when the awakened person sees the other person but cannot have him/her. It is kind of like a loved one who has died and is buried. You know where that person is physically located, but you cannot get or bring that person back no matter how much you want.

Third, you should wait to awaken love because love is a flame of fire. This is the order of creation. This is the way God designed love. Love is an inextinguishable fire! This metaphor builds on the previous two. Imagine a river, and in the middle of the river is a fire. When the water hits that fire, the fire is so strong that the water evaporates. The water cannot extinguish the fire. This is the picture of true biblical love from Song of Songs. It is an affection for the other person that endures any storm. An entire river cannot extinguish it. When you awaken this love, you awaken a fire that was never supposed to go out. This "permanent like death," jealous/zeal kind of love was designed to be an inextinguishable kind of love. Why would you awaken this love?

> When you awaken this love, you awaken a fire that was never supposed to go out.

When this permanent, jealous/zeal kind of love is awakened, the person who has it would do nearly anything to demonstrate his/her love for the other person. The most tangible means to demonstrate such love is through showering gifts on that person. But love can't be bought! The end of Song 8:7 reads, "If a man would give all the wealth of his house for love, they would despise him for it."

The attempt to buy love has led to a multitude of sins. Paying for a meal or a sentimental trinket is not "buying" love, but trying to manipulate someone into loving you is. The Song teaches that you cannot manipulate someone into loving you. Giving money, gifts, etc. is the most logical manner of proving your love to someone. But if someone "loves you" because you are constantly showering gifts on that person, he/she doesn't really love you. True, biblical, jealous love is willingly and freely offered to another individual. It cannot be manipulated, coerced, or purchased. If you are trying to win the affection of someone who has rejected you, stop acting like a fool and wasting your time and money. Draw close to the Lord and move on.

EXTINGUISHING THE INEXTINGUISHABLE FIRE

Breaking up stinks. It stinks because it hurts. It hurts because something is being ripped apart that was never intended to be ripped apart. Now if you are the one doing the ripping apart, it might not be so bad. But if the other person is ripping it apart, it really stinks. Why does it hurt so bad? Why won't the pain go away? Why can't you forget about that other person? The reason is right here in the Song of Songs. You started a fire. You fostered a permanent, death-like kind of love for another person, a jealous/zeal kind of love that was designed to be an inextinguishable fire. Now you are trying to extinguish what was never meant to be extinguished. You may not have had a physical relationship with that person, but you loved that person—you awakened love, and love is supposed to be as strong as death. Love is a flame, the very flame of the Lord. And now you are trying to put something out that was never designed to be put out. Don't awaken love!

Often when we talk to singles about the nature of love, someone ends up asking what everyone is thinking: "Well, I blew it. We broke up, and a fire still blazes in my soul. What do I do now?" You do something that is very difficult that only the Spirit of God can help you do. You extinguish the flames. We are going to give you four principles to help you extinguish the fire.

First, stop fueling the fire by speaking truth to yourself. We humans are very good at deceiving ourselves, particularly about something we earnestly desire. When a thought enters your mind that is not true, call it a lie and speak truth to yourself. When you think, "Maybe so-and-so does/will like me." That is a lie. Speak truth to yourself. Remind yourself of what that person *said,* and speak truth to yourself.

The second principle to help you extinguish a fire is to change your diet. We aren't talking about food here. Decrease your worldly consumption. You have more time available to you than you think you do. Unsubscribe from worldly media platforms and increase your consumption of the Bible. Don't just read God's Word every day; study it! When you would have watched a show or three, study God's Word instead. Study with a friend of the same gender. Memorize Psalm 1, meditate upon the Word of God, and be the blessed person.

Third, get out and be with real people. Setting up a Bible study with others is one way to do this. But do more than just study the Bible. Find people who need help, and be the hands and feet of Jesus to them. Talk to your pastor, parents, or godly mentors and pour your life into serving others. Certainly, working a job would be part of what we are talking about, but we are referring more to helping neighbors, widows, and struggling church members. Study James 2 and serve the modern day "widow and orphan" in your community; you know, the people who can never pay you back. While serving others, listen to good, biblical content that speaks truth to you. Finally, let your life be an example to others. Warn your friends about the folly of awakening love. Pray that the Lord, in His time, would bring someone else into your life whom you can love biblically. And if/when the Lord opens that door, don't awaken love this time. Respect the power of love and slow down!

FINDING LOVE IN THE RIGHT PLACES

We want to caution you strongly concerning dating. Dating has a high probability of awakening love. If you are not of marriageable age or if you are not in a spiritual or financial position to find a spouse, we suggest you do not date. Dating flirts with folly. When you date, you have a higher probability of hurting yourself or someone else. Dating encourages the awakening of love.

You may currently be in a relationship where the fire is blazing out of control. If you are in an "awakened" relationship, get someone involved who can help you assess the situation and provide guidance on taking the next step. These situations are too complicated and diverse for us to provide helpful counsel here. So, lean into the parents and spiritual leaders whom God has placed in your life; trust them and do whatever they advise.

For millennia, parents helped their children find a spouse by arranging their marriages. This model is still practiced by some Orthodox Jewish people and most of the non-Western world. The cultural setting of the Song of Songs arranged marriages as well. An arranged marriage did *not* leave a young person voiceless in the selection of his/her spouse. Song 8:5–14 seems to be written to shape the affections of the next generation. It teaches them what to desire in a spouse. This instruction would have been pointless if a young person's marriage was solely arranged by his/her parents. It would be unwise to consider this ancient method of finding a spouse backward and irrelevant, particularly considering the mess that dating has created. Consider what John Goldingay says concerning the familial focus of the ancient world and the individualistic culture of our day:

> In a Western context, we emphasize the individual more than the family or the community, and the idea that I should subordinate my attraction and my longing to the need of the community seems odd.
> That Western feeling lies behind our puzzlement at the idea of parents being involved in the arrangement of a marriage. This involvement need not mean that the parents made a decision that the boy or girl opposes, yet it worries us. It compromises the principle that's so important to us, that I and I alone make the key decisions in my life in light of what seems best for me and seems to me most likely to make me happy. But our affirmation of that principle doesn't seem to generate happiness for us. And it seems to produce fractured families and communities.[1]

Dating is a rather recent invention spawned out of the Industrial Revolution and the influx of workers into cities. Spatially disconnected from their parents, singles began spending time together without parental oversight. Dating is a new, "modern" invention, and not all things that are new are best.

You, however, will probably have to date to find a spouse. How can you do this without awakening love? First, regularly tell yourself that you do not love that person. Are you thinking, "*What*!?!"? As we discussed in chapter five, those three words, "I love you," awaken love. Do not stir up a fire in someone else's heart for yourself. Doing so is selfish and could hurt that person. Constantly tell yourself that you do not love that person. Your goal should be to *not* awaken love! The *selfish* single desires love and affection, so that person prematurely declares his/her

---

1   John Goldingay, *Old Testament Ethics: A Guided Tour* (Downers Grove, IL: InterVarsity Press, 2019), 138.

love. The *selfless* single genuinely does not want to hurt a brother/sister in the Lord and refuses to declare his/her "love." Prematurely awakening love hurts a brother/sister in the Lord.

> Prematurely awakening love hurts a brother/sister in the Lord.

Young lady, if your boyfriend (or boy who is a friend) tells you he loves you, tell him kindly that a young man is not allowed to declare his love for you until he can make a tangible commitment that supports that love. Many times, the men who profess love don't truly love the young woman they're with. They're really saying, "I lust you." Actually, a young man may think he loves her, but he doesn't really know what is going on himself. It may just seem like the right thing to say at the time. Or he could be a smooth, suave player who knows exactly what he is doing. The three words "I love you" have a powerful pull in your soul. He is flattering you and feeding your ego. Why do you think the Song of Songs wife admonishes *primarily* young ladies not to awaken love? Regularly listening to some young man tell you the lie that he loves you will not be good for you. And if he starts playing word games like saying, "I *really* like you," well, you know what you need to do. Walk away and don't look back.

In ancient days, a betrothal was as good as a marriage. Ending it required an actual divorce. Betrothal was a serious commitment to marriage. While a modern engagement does not correspond to a betrothal, it is close. Perhaps this commitment would be the time when a couple could declare their love and commitment to one another. Talk to your parents, mentors, and counselors and decide together when it would be wise to declare one's love to another.

If you have to date, we encourage you to have a disinterested interest in possible individuals. In other words, you are interested in that other person, but not too interested. Hold onto that interest loosely. It is usually easier to get into a relationship than to get out of one. Few singles have the courage and humility to get out of a bad relationship. We have seen it over and over again. Trust your divinely ordained authorities and mentors to help you through these situations. You should never be so interested in a person that if a parent, pastor, or mentor advised you to end a relationship, you would have trouble doing so.

> Few singles have the courage and humility
> to get out of a bad relationship.

James Sire recommends evaluating the validity of ideas in a similar way. When you have an idea, you want to test the idea to see if it is true.[2] If the idea is false, you possess the virtue (humility and courage) to admit it is false.[3] We encourage you to think the same way about relationships. Perhaps you will marry that person, but maybe you won't. You can be interested in that person but with a disinterested interest. Unfortunately, as exclusive relationships continue, the disinterested component gets silenced. Dating is dangerous. Be wise and remind yourself that you do not love this person and possess only a disinterested interest in him/her.

The more someone has awakened love, the greater the issues are that the person will have to unpack after marriage. The individual who is sexually experienced will bring that sexual experience into marriage.

---

2   **James W. Sire,** *Habits of the Mind: Intellectual Life as a Christian Calling* **(Downers Grove, IL: InterVarsity, 2000), 74–84.**

3   Ibid., 110–15

Before marriage, you and your significant other should make known to each other your previous intimate encounters (consensual and nonconsensual). Details are not needed, but each of you should know whether or not the other is a virgin. Sexual sin affects marital union, particularly for a woman. For a woman to enjoy intimacy according to the order of creation, she must trust her husband (Song 1:2–4; 8:6). Awakening love before marriage, then extinguishing what God designed to never be extinguished damages trust and often makes it more difficult for a wife to enjoy intimacy the way God designed it. Nobody likes to say what we have just said, because in our "equality" age, everyone wants everyone the same. God, however, made men and women different. The primary audience of the Song of Songs is virgin girls for a reason. Don't believe the world's lies, trust God, and do things His way. Young lady, you have the most to lose. You have a higher probability of contracting sexually transmitted diseases. You will have a more difficult time learning how to love after marriage. You could become pregnant. And you could end up like the many women who struggle with trust and intimacy because of premarital sex. Young man, you don't get a free pass. We could tell you some bad stories about how extramarital intimacy damaged the intimacy that God designed for men. The greater danger, however, is for women.

PROTECTED LOVE

SONG 8

⁸We have a little sister, but she has no breasts.
What should we do for our sister
in the day when she is spoken for?
⁹If she is a wall, we will build upon her a battlement of silver;
if she is a door, we will fortify her with cedar planks.

Christians live in a world where foolish people believe that all humans are inherently good. They claim that the world has corrupted and broken people. If we just let people mature and grow up outside the coercive structures of society, they say, everyone would be good. This reasoning is folly. The Bible consistently teaches that mankind is broken from birth (Ps 14:2–3); people are bad from the very beginning. They are born bad, and unless authorities guide and direct them to goodness, they will do bad things. Bad people victimize the most vulnerable in society, and women are more vulnerable than men.

Because women are more vulnerable and because wicked men have wicked desires, women need to be wise, and good men have a responsibility to protect them. Consider Song 8:8: "We have a little sister, but she has no breasts. What should we do for our sister in the day when she is spoken for?" The "sister" here is a sexually undeveloped little girl. The implied answer to the rhetorical question is that they should protect her. Young man, if you have a sister, you need to take seriously your responsibility to protect her. Dad can't always be there. Man up! This book is not a parenting book, but if God wills that you become a parent, remember Song 8:8. Don't be naïve in thinking that so-and-so is a "good guy (or boy!)" and leave him alone, particularly with your little girl. Wicked people do wicked things. Some little boys are capable of doing immeasurably wicked things. The family has the first and foremost responsibility to protect the vulnerable. Protect your little ones.

You, however, are probably not a "little one." The exhortation for protection continues in the next verse: "If she is a wall, we will build upon her a battlement of silver; if she is a door, we will fortify her with cedar planks" (Song 8:9). Protection from outside molesters is an *indirect* application of Song 8:8–9. The *direct* application concerns the siblings' role in conserving the little girl's purity. The metaphor "wall" refers to her desire for sexual purity. The metaphor "door" refers to proclivities, or inclinations, toward awakening love. In both instances the siblings help the girl retain her purity.

A close relative of ours started getting close to a young man whom we knew nothing about. We had a few conversations with her. Then we paid the $25 fee (or whatever it cost) to do a background check on him. Why shouldn't we! Who cares about $25? We had a responsibility to help her. Unfortunately, too often siblings do not desire to help, and/or they don't want help. Young people go it alone, cast prudence to the wind, and run headlong into danger.

The lesson from the Song is clear; love is not an "I've got this!" kind of thing. Love is difficult, and there is strength in numbers (Eccl 4:9–12). So don't go it alone! Protected love identifies the danger of love and proceeds with caution. Protected love has family that helps the family member retain his/her purity. If your family is out to lunch, then lean on mentors in the church to help you retain your purity in this perverse world. If you date, you should have a disinterested interest in a person all while turning to mentors who will keep you accountable for your actions. Remember what Goldingay said about dating? It is individualistic, but the Song teaches that finding a spouse should be communal. Involving others reduces the *probability* that things will go wrong. By decreasing risk, you are being wise.

> Involving others reduces the probability that things will go wrong. By decreasing risk, you are being wise.

The lie of this world is that your love life is simply yours. In truth, your love life is everybody's business. Well, maybe not everybody's, but everyone that is close to you. If you break up, where are you going to go? If you get pregnant or get someone pregnant, who is going to help you? If you marry a bum, who will help you walk through life? Listen to your parents, mentors, and counselors! God has placed them near you to help you retain your purity and marry wisely. And if you have messed up, go to your parents, church family, and/or mentors. They are in the best position to help you get back on the right path. Furthermore, if you are lost concerning the path forward in marriage, lean on these people, particularly the older, more experienced ones. They have wisdom and can guide you on the right path.

Angela and I want to emphasize this point a little more. So many young people say they want to remain pure until marriage, but they go it alone! The Song teaches that fools go it alone. Finding a spouse should be a "y'all" kind of thing that includes your parents and spiritual mentors. The female lover of the Song doesn't simply tell you, "Don't awaken love"; she gives you advice on how to keep love asleep. Have mentors (not peers) keep you accountable concerning the times when you and a young man/woman are together. Be intentional with the time you spend together, and make sure to account for all your time to your mentor. A lot more could be said here. Talk to your mentors and set up mutually agreed upon boundaries. This is the way that will *most likely* lead to success.

We find it ironic how in our female-empowered age that Christian women lack power or are helpless when it comes to finding a spouse. In the "old days," a daughter could initiate an interest through her father. Fathers, brothers, and spiritual mentors helped unmarried girls marry successfully. Young woman, we don't see anything in the Bible that says you cannot express an interest in a young man. But wisdom would recommend that you express interest through your father, brother, or spiritual mentor. The female lover of the Song is not a passive woman.

Sometimes a guy needs a kick in the pants. Your father, brother, or spiritual mentor may be the kick that a guy needs. Just as a caution, the Christian subculture may despise your assertive attitude. Be wise and fear the Lord, not man.

RESOLVED TO LOVE GOD'S WAY

SONG
8

¹⁰I am a wall, and my breasts are like towers.
Then I became in his eyes like one who finds peace.

The final exhortation to virgin young ladies seeks to fortify their resolve concerning purity. The woman of the Song asserts in Song 8:10, "I am a wall, and my breasts are like towers. Then I became in his eyes like one who finds peace." Notice that she has breasts, which represent her sexual maturity. This woman is ready for a sexual relationship. She uses the metaphor of a city (more about that later). She is saying she's a wall, not a door. She is an impenetrable wall; any man who seeks to enter her will be rejected. Not only is she a walled city, but she is also a city with towers for defense. Male suitors may seek her, but their pleas for entry are met with assertive resistance. Young lady, you need to cultivate this same spirit. Just as a conquering army employs various deceptive and coercive tactics to conquer a city, so also do wicked men. Be the Song of Songs female lover, and assertively resist their pleas for entry.

As we discussed in chapter ten, the Old Testament personified cities as women, including unconquered, or *virgin*, cities. For example, Isaiah 37:22 states, "She despises you, she ridicules you, the virgin daughter of Zion [the unconquered city of Zion, that is, Jerusalem]; she shakes her head behind your back, the daughter of Jerusalem." Jerusalem, personified as a virgin, mocks the invading king's attempt to conquer her. In Isaiah 47:1, Babylon is a virgin daughter, and similarly, in Isaiah

52:1, Zion is exhorted "Wear your beautiful garments! Jerusalem, the holy city! Because never again will the *uncircumcised* and unclean *come into you* again."

The Song picks up on this city personification and uses it to strengthen the female reader's resolve. Song 8:10 contains a terse statement consisting of only four nouns in the Hebrew: "I (אני), wall (חומה), and my breasts (ושדי), like towers (כמגדלות)." These four Hebrew nouns formulate a strong, forceful battle cry that should be every young woman's motto. Memorize the Hebrew and make it your battle cry! It is pronounced something like this: *ahnē hōmah; vĭshahdahy* (like El Shaddai) *kahmigdahlōt!* Towers contained archers that shot any invader who got too close. If an invader gets too close to her "city," the young woman doesn't hesitate to make him regret his decision. Her city doesn't belong to him. Her breasts are towers, meaning that she is a fortified city, and because her city is fortified, any man who attempts to gain entry will be met with forceful resistance. The king of Assyria attempted to conquer the daughter of Jerusalem using coercion, manipulation, flattery, and force. Wicked men use the same tactics to conquer the weak city. Young lady, may this be your battle cry: "I, wall, and my breasts, like towers!"

> If an invader gets too close to her "city," the young woman doesn't hesitate to make him regret his decision.

In the Song, however, one man does gain access to the city. He does not enter through strength of arms, coercion, deception, or manipulation. Nor does the city raise the battle cry in resistance to him. In fact, the city desirously invites this peaceful "invader" inside: "Then I became in his eyes like one who finds peace." The marriage covenant grants him peaceable admission into the city. Using this military metaphor, the covenant represents the treaty that the man made with the city (woman) that grants him entrance.

This entire section of the Song teaches singles the importance of sexual purity and gives wisdom concerning how to retain sexual purity in marriage. This wife is not a fort that totters at the flattery and enticement of suitors. Rather, she is a walled and fortified city, impervious to the affection of others, while being at peace with her husband, the one with whom she has covenanted.

CONCLUSION

Finding a spouse is not as complicated as the Christian subculture has made it out to be. Use wisdom (a low-risk decision), select a spouse, marry, and grow in wisdom together. Quit looking for a perfect "soulmate." Make a wise decision, and that person becomes your soulmate. Young lady, cultivate desire for a Song of Songs man, not a Solomon. Do not fall in love with anyone. Let love sleep by having a disinterested interest in several potential men. Then awaken love at the appropriate time. You are in control. Cultivate the secure, permanent, jealous, unquenchable, love that is freely given and freely received for the one whom your soul loves. Place yourself under the authority of your parents and let an older woman hold you accountable during your single years. This will increase the probability of success. Finally, be resolved in yourself. Remember that you are a fortified city and make any guy who gets too close regret it. Your attitude alone can repel many invaders. Be the Song of Songs female lover in singleness and marriage.

DISCUSSION QUESTIONS:

1. Discuss what kind of man a young woman should want to marry and what kind of woman a young man should want to marry.

2. Discuss the qualities of a low-risk, medium-risk, and a high-risk potential spouse.

3. What kinds of tips does the Song give young ladies when it comes to finding a husband?

4. When should love be awakened?

5. What does the seal in Song 8:6 represent?

6. What do the metaphors death, grave, and fire in Song 8:6–7 depict?

7. Why should you not awaken love prematurely?

8. Can love be bought? Why or why not?

9. Why is a breakup usually so hard/painful?

10. Can you awaken love even if you haven't been physical in your relationship?

11. How do you extinguish the flames if you have awakened love prematurely?

12. Discuss how a young person can date without awakening love.

13. Why is it dangerous to say "I love you" prematurely?

14. Discuss what an "uninterested interest" means/looks like.

15. Why is community a good idea when it comes to finding a spouse and sexual purity?

16. Discuss the metaphor of the woman being an unconquered city and of the one who is able to conquer the city.

BEGINNING LOVE CORRECTLY, PART 2
(8:11–14)

The woman in the Song of Songs is the woman that every man should want to marry. Who wouldn't want this woman? She is assertive, submissive, faithful, and sensuous, and she possesses a soulish love for her husband. She offers herself to her husband freely, without expectation or reward. She simply loves him and desires him. She offers her husband diverse sexual fruits and sexual rendezvous because she rejoices in his desire over her! But more important than her sex appeal, this woman truly loves her husband. She sacrifices for him, recognizes her role in raising his children (Song 8:5), and builds up her house, which is his house (Prov 31:10–31).

HELP! I WANT THIS WOMAN!

SONG
8

> ¹¹*Solomon had a vineyard in Baal Hamon;*
>   *he leased the vineyard to keepers;*
>   *a man would bring for its fruit a thousand silvers.*
> ¹²*My vineyard, which is mine, is before me.*
>   *The thousand to you, Solomon,*
>   *and two hundred to the keepers of its fruit.*

Solomon sought the Song of Songs lover, but he never found her (Eccl 7:28; Song 8:12). Remember in Song 8:10, the woman said, "I became in his eyes like one who finds *peace*." Remember that Solomon's name means "peace." Peace connects verse 10 to verse 11. Just as the harem girl in Song 3:6–11 is the direct opposite of the Song of Songs wife, so also is Solomon the antithesis to the male lover of the Song of

Songs. Solomon used himself and his harem girls as flat characters representing the natural inclinations of young men's and young women's hearts. These characters serve as types, the opposites of the lovers of the Song. The Song cultivates the affections of young women to desire to be the Song of Songs female lover instead of the harem girl. Similarly, the Song cultivates the affections of young men to desire to be the Song of Songs male lover instead of Solomon.

Young man, what are you looking for in a wife?

Young man, what are you looking for in a wife? The very first thing a young man sees in a woman is her outward appearance. How many times have you seen some pretty girl and thought, "I hope she is a Christian." Really! What is truly important to you in this situation? Remember that finding a spouse is a wisdom decision, right? I (Tim) am going to present a situation, and you be the judge. First, we have Plain Jane, whom you have known your entire life. She is a good girl, attends church faithfully, has a solid testimony, and serves regularly in various ministries at church. She is faithful. Then there is Bombshell Barbie. You don't know a lot about her, but everything you have seen excites every part of you! She works as a receptionist at the office, and every time you see her, she looks dazzling and has the most engaging personality. Now, you tell me, which woman is a higher risk as a marriage partner?

Let's up the ante! You and Bombshell Barbie go out on a few dates. She says she is a Christian. She seems like a good girl. Being beautiful isn't a sin, but still, what is driving you toward Bombshell Barbie? Which woman is a higher risk for matrimony?

You know Plain Jane. She is faithful. Are you looking for the right things in a woman?

Solomon valued the soft, supple, fragrant, nubile female body. Song 8:11 explains, "Solomon had a vineyard in Baal Hamon; he leased the vineyard to keepers; a man would bring for its fruit a thousand silvers." Solomon's vineyard was his harem, his thousand women, who presumably offered him a diverse and ideal intimate experience. Solomon's vineyard was located at a fictitious location, Baal Hamon. This name means "Master/Lord/Husband of many." Solomon had a harem at Husband of Many. This vineyard was the most beautiful vineyard around. Its fruit was expensive, costing one thousand silvers—a lot of money in the ancient world! Verse 12 says that the attendants cost another two hundred silvers. Remember the fruit and vineyard terminology throughout the Song of Songs? The fruit represents the sexual delights that the woman offers the husband (Song 7:13). When Solomon had sex with one of his women, he "ate" an expensive fruit. A rich king like Solomon would have been served only the best, whether it was the fruit on his dinner plate or the fruit in his bedroom chamber.

The story of Esther gives a small glimpse of what this "fruit" would have looked like. Esther went through six months of "oil of myrrh" (massage oil) treatments and six more months of perfume and ointments before she went to have one night with King Ahasuerus (Esth 2:12–13). After that night, she would go to the "second" house of the women, where she would stay unless the king called for her by name (Esth 2:14). Her time with the king was a "one and done" experience for the rest of her life unless she really made him happy. With so much riding on that one night, you can imagine how incentivized each woman would have been to create a special experience for the king.

When the Song of Songs was written, every reader would have been familiar with a kingly harem and how it worked. In Ecclesiastes 2:10

Solomon admits he did not restrain himself from anything he desired. His acquisition of whatever he wanted was not limited to things; it included women. Ecclesiastes 2:8 is not talking about musical instruments; it is talking about Solomon's harem. His male contemporaries would have coveted his wealth and his women. What man would not want to be in Solomon's position with multiple soft, supple, fragrant, beautiful, youthful women available to him whenever he wanted?

> **Something inside every man wants Solomon's harem.**

It doesn't take a long look around in our world to see that Solomons still exist today. Something inside every man wants Solomon's harem. Do you want his harem? What are you looking for in a woman? Maybe you want Bombshell Barbie because she is pretty? Are you willing to take the risk? You are just a poorer, inferior Solomon.

In his younger years, Solomon sought earnestly for wisdom; he wanted to live according to the order of creation. In many ways, he succeeded, but he failed in the area of women. Ecclesiastes 7:23–25 describes Solomon's earnest search for Lady Wisdom, the excellent wife. He earnestly searches for her, but he cannot find her. Instead, he finds someone else, Dame Folly: "But I found more bitter than death, the woman whose heart is snares and nets; her hands are bonds." If you go after a Bombshell Barbie, God may let you have your trophy wife. Just know that Solomon would have exchanged his thousand trophy wives for the Song of Songs female lover who would have freely loved him. Young man, you need to repent of your desire for a trophy wife. Even if you marry a beautiful, godly woman, she will never be a Song of Songs lover until you kill your desire for the trophy wife. The problem isn't with Plain Jane or a (godly) Bombshell Barbie; the problem is the desire of your heart. You and I know at least one man who did *not* want Solomon's harem—Solomon (Eccl 7:28).

> The problem isn't with Plain Jane or a (godly) Bombshell Barbie; the problem is the desire of your heart.

After it was too late, Solomon learned that he had cultivated the wrong kind of vineyard. He needed to have only one wife and to cultivate not only his wife's physical vineyard but also her spiritual vineyard. The physical pleasures of his wives' vineyard paled in comparison to the spiritual vineyard of the Song of Songs female lover. Solomon wanted the female lover of the Song, but she rejected him (Song 8:12). He wanted the wife who would be assertive, submissive, faithful, and sensuous and who would possess a soulish love for her husband. She would offer herself to her husband freely, without expectation or reward. She would simply love him and desire him. She would freely offer her husband diverse sexual fruits, set up sexual rendezvous, and rejoice in his desire over her. But Solomon chose one thousand female bodies and was rejected by the one woman he wrote about in the Song of Songs: "My vineyard, which is mine, is before me. The thousand to you, Solomon; and two hundred to the keepers of its fruit" (Song 8:12). Solomon explains his search for this woman in Ecclesiastes 7:28: "My soul still seeks, but I cannot find; one man out of a thousand I have found, but a woman among all of these, I have not found." Who can find the excellent wife (Prov 31:10)? Solomon sought her but found one thousand dame follies instead. Solomon never found the female lover of the Song of Songs because he was looking for the wrong woman and was cultivating the wrong vineyard.

Learning from his own experience, Solomon teaches his readers what *not* to look for in a woman. Do *not* make a decision based upon appearance. Remember Ruth? She was the excellent woman (Ruth 3:11). What did Ruth look like? What does the book of Ruth say about her appearance? Young man, marry a woman who fears the Lord. I don't care if she has the wrong hair color, is "big boned," has weak eyes, or laughs weirdly. Does she fear God? I don't care if she looks like an angel descended from heaven, leads the basketball team in scoring, has ten thousand social media followers, or just makes you feel good. Does she fear the Lord? "Charm is deceitful and beauty is passing; a woman who fears the Lord, she will be praised" (Prov 31:30). One thing matters; that is it. Does she fear God?

The woman who fears the Lord attends church faithfully. She does not make excuses but disciplines herself to prioritize her relationship with God and her love for others. She is a strong woman who builds up her house at personal sacrifice. She may have dirt under her fingernails from working outside or dried snot on her shirt from helping in the nursery. The woman who fears the Lord is a life-giver and a life-creator. She invests her physical, spiritual, and intellectual life into others. Just like the young man in Song 8:13, plead for her voice.

"KEEP" YOUR VINEYARD

Finding a woman who fears the Lord is only the beginning. After you marry her, you need to "keep" the vineyard. Forms of the verb *keeping* occur four times in the Song, twice in Song 1:6 and twice in Song 8:11–12. This word's use only at the beginning and end of the book seems intentional. In Song 1:6, the woman must attend to physical vineyards, so she has not been able to adorn the vineyard of her body. In Song 1:6, the focus is on the woman's physical beauty and the physical delight it brings her husband.

THE WORD *KEEPING* IN SONG 1 AND 8	
SONG 1:6	SONG 8:11–12

Do not look on me because I am black,
   because the sun gazed upon me.
The brothers of my mother
   were angry with me.
They made me *keeper* of the vineyards;
   my vineyard, which is mine,
   I have not *kept*.
	¹¹Solomon had a vineyard in Baal Hamon;
	   he leased the vineyard to *keepers*;
	   a man would bring for its fruit
	   a thousand silvers.
	¹²My vineyard, which is mine, is before me.
	   The thousand to you, Solomon;
	   and two hundred to the *keepers* of its fruit.

In Song 8:11–12, Solomon's vineyard is the best money can buy, but there is some irony here. His wives, his vineyard, not only do not "keep" (maintain, sustain, support) physical vineyards (like the woman in Song 1:6 does), but they *are* the vineyard, which is "kept," or tended, by others! Solomon paid others to "keep" his vineyard, but he never personally kept the vineyard himself.

So Solomon teaches in Song 2:15 and 8:12 that a husband, unlike Solomon himself, should not just cultivate a body, but should "keep," or cultivate/tend, his wife. Your future wife has a body, but she is first and foremost a person. The Song of Songs kind of wife requires personal cultivation from her husband (Song 2:15). Whomever you marry, she is *your* wife for life. She will sin against you, and you will sin against her. Through the cultivation of the vineyard, you will both grow in wisdom.

Young man, God's design embedded in creation places you in a position of authority over your wife. You should, therefore, physically and spiritually keep the vineyard. You are her head, and God will one day hold you accountable for the way in which you stewarded your headship. The most practical application of this truth involves physically serving your wife by putting her needs and desires above your own. In sum, love your wife as Jesus the Messiah loved the church and gave His life for her (Eph 5:25).

Serving your wife, however, does not mean that you give her whatever she desires. You are the head, and you should provide spiritual guidance in the relationship. Sometimes (rarely) that may mean you do not give her what she desires, just as sometimes God doesn't give His children what they want. This doesn't mean you order her around like she is your minion, but you aren't her puppet leader either. The biblical husband's leadership is driven by the fear of the Lord, not the fear of the wife. Women are relational, so a godly woman blossoms under the authority of a man who nurtures her spiritual health.

> The biblical husband's leadership is driven by the fear of the Lord, not the fear of the wife.

It is your responsibility to teach your wife (and children) the truths of God's Word. Consider Paul's exhortation in 1 Corinthians 14:35: "And if [your wives] want to learn something, let each one ask her own husband." The pastor should *focus* his instruction on the husband, and the husband should provide spiritual instruction to his wife. You, husband, are responsible for your wife's spiritual instruction. If she has a question, you are her first source of education. If you don't know, then you need to get an answer. Talk to your pastor; let him teach you. Then you teach her. Get off your lazy backside, learn, then teach your wife. You could even study together. A godly wife will love this! Studying together is literally "keeping" the vineyard. You are investing in your wife as a *person*, not just as a body. Because women are relational, it matters who nurtures your wife's spiritual health. If you abdicate this responsibility to the pastor, you are essentially paying your pastor to "keep" your vineyard. Furthermore, abdicating this responsibility can create a vulnerable situation for your wife and/or your pastor.

> You, husband, are responsible for your wife's
> spiritual instruction.

Wife, this also means you recognize that your husband is the *primary* one who should "keep" you. Certainly, you should receive instruction from your church's corporate gathering. And you should receive instruction from the older women in your church. But note that the older women are to "instruct the younger women to love their husbands" (Titus 2:4). Certainly, a woman can read and learn from other sources, but her *primary* teacher should be her husband. Your husband often may not have the answers. Encourage him to get the answers and to teach you.

The Song of Songs male lover does not pay others to take care of his vineyard. It is his responsibility. He puts aside his own desires (Song 2:8–14), seizes the jackals (Song 2:15), cultivates his wife's desire, and "keeps" her.

LET ME HEAR HER VOICE!

SONG 8

> [13]*The one who dwells in the gardens,*
>   *companions are listening for your voice.*
>   *Let me hear it!*
> [14]*Flee, my lover, and liken yourself to a gazelle or a young stag*
>   *on the mountains of spices.*

Just as Song 8:10 fortifies the resolve of young women to retain their purity until marriage, so does Song 8:13 cultivate young men's affections, not for the harem girl, but for the female Song of Songs lover. The word *companion* occurs only in Song 8:13 and 1:7. Back in Song 1:7, the female lover banters with the male lover, "Why should I be like one who veils herself alongside the flocks of your companions?" You may remember that companions are other single young men. In Song 8:13, they also *want* to hear the voice of the female lover of the Song of Songs. In other words, all the guys want this kind of girl. The Song is appealing to your affections, encouraging you, young man, to desire earnestly this kind of woman, not the harem girl. Look at the young man's response in Song 8:13: "Let me hear it!" The verb is an imperative conveying the earnestness of his desire to hear that woman's voice. This is the kind of girl you want! When harem girls clamor for your attention, let the Song of Songs woman's voice resonate in your ear.

The female lover speaks in Song 8:14 and exhorts the young man, "Flee, my lover, and liken yourself to a gazelle or a young stag on the mountains of spices." He hears her voice, but she oddly does not tell him to "come." Instead she says to "flee." The Hebrew word *flee* (ברח) is very similar to the Hebrew word *companion* (חבר). The alliteration in the Hebrew would not have been lost on the original audience. The woman entreats the man to flee his companions and come to her. Young man, when you hear the voice of a woman who fears the Lord, leave your buddies behind and snatch her before someone else does.

> Young man, when you hear the voice of a woman who fears the Lord, leave your buddies behind and snatch her before someone else does.

CONCLUSION

As we said at the end of chapter twelve, finding a spouse is not as complicated as the Christian subculture has made it out to be. Use wisdom (a low-risk decision), select a spouse, marry, and grow in wisdom together. Young man, desire the Song of Songs wife, not the harem girl. Solomon learned too late that he had valued the wrong things in a woman. Desire the woman who fears the Lord, not the soft, supple, fragrant, young body. Make a wise decision and marry a strong woman who fears the Lord. Then cultivate your wife yourself. Put aside your own desires, seize jackals, and "keep" your own wife. Earnestly desire to hear this woman's voice, not only when you are single but also after you marry. The Proverbs 31 woman isn't only found; she is "kept."

DISCUSSION QUESTIONS:

1. Explain the significance of "peace" in Song 8:10-11.

2. How does the Song cultivate the affections of young men?

3. Young men, explain what "looking for the right things" in a potential wife means.

4. What did Solomon consistently look for in women?

5. Why could Solomon never find Lady Wisdom?

6. What is the one thing in a woman that really matters?

7. How does Solomon teach a young man to "keep" his wife?

8. Discuss the practical implications of a husband who walks in the fear of the wife versus a husband who leads in the fear of the Lord.

9. Who is primarily responsible for the wife's spiritual health and why?

ARE THINGS DIFFERENT NOW?

The Song of Songs was written around three thousand years ago. A lot has changed. How much of the Song really applies today? All of it. God's revelation concerning relationships and sexuality hasn't changed at all. The New Testament has a slightly stronger emphasis on singleness, but that is it. This final chapter analyzes what the Bible teaches about singleness and gives you some concluding principles that can help you love successfully.

OLD TESTAMENT TEACHING ON SINGLENESS

The Old Testament assumed every young person would marry. The Old Testament man was expected to marry and have children. The Talmud (Jewish religious law) argued that the unmarried twenty-year-old man was living in sin and/or was cursed (*Qidd.* 29b). Ludwig Köhler comments, "It goes without saying that the Hebrew will marry, for that is the natural course of events. . . . It corresponds to the divine ordering of creation. . . . The Arabs still call the bachelor *azab*, 'forsaken, lonely.' The Old Testament has no word for this at all, so unusual is the idea. Nor is there known the woman who remains single. . . . Were there no unmarried people? We do not know."[1] Almost everybody in the ancient world married. Two categories existed, the married and the to-be-married.

---

1 Ludwig Köhler, *Hebrew Man* (trans. Peter R. Ackroyd; New York: Abingdon, 1953), 75–76.

God did, however, command Jeremiah the prophet not to marry, but this command was given during a specific time of judgment (Jer 16:1–4). God was about to judge the people of Judah for their sin and annihilate the population. God was essentially saying, "Hey, don't marry, because if you do, you will watch your wife and children die." Jeremiah was a unique exception. We also never read of Daniel's wife, likely because he was made a eunuch when he was taken into Babylonian captivity. Isaiah 56:4–5 encourages the eunuchs who are faithful to the Lord, "I will give an everlasting name to him which will not be cut off" (56:5). In the Old Testament, every man married and sought to have children because this was how a man's name would "not be cut off." But the Lord encouraged eunuchs, who could not have children, to be faithful to Him. The Lord would then see to it that their names were not cut off, although God did not say how He was going to do this. A eunuch simply had to believe.

Jesus, teaching during the Old Testament administration, described three kinds of eunuchs: (1) those born eunuchs, (2) those made eunuchs (e.g., Daniel), and (3) those who chose the life of a eunuch (Matt 19:12). According to R. T. France, this final group "represents those who have voluntarily chosen celibacy. Their choice is ascribed not to disinclination but to their perception of God's will for them. . . . And it is in obedience to that authority that they have been prepared to stand apart from the normal expectation of marriage and fatherhood."[2] While the vast majority of Old Testament individuals married, God called a few to lives of celibacy (the gift of singleness) to accomplish sacred and specific missions that God entrusted to them.

---

2   R. T. France, *The Gospel of Matthew* (NICNT; Grand Rapids: Eerdmans, 2007), 725.

NEW TESTAMENT TEACHING ON SINGLENESS

The New Testament begins with the gospels, which was the culture of the Old Testament—a culture where nearly everyone married. Jesus lived a celibate life in this culture, submitted to the will of the Father (Isa 50:4–11; Heb 5:8), and died a substitutionary death on our behalf (Isa 53). John the Baptist similarly appears to have never married and died a martyr's death. God entrusted John the Baptist, Jesus, and no doubt others with specific missions that were better accomplished by an unmarried individual.

The Apostle Paul, similarly, did not have a wife when he wrote 1 Corinthians 7 even though he had a right to one (1 Cor 9:5). He repeatedly encouraged his readers to remain as they were (1 Cor 7:8, 11, 20, 24, 40). Ancient Israel laid claim to a specific allotment of land that each father gave as an inheritance to his son. Because of the physical nature of this inheritance, the Old Testament emphasized physical offspring. Producing an heir who would acquire the family inheritance, however, was not a concern to the New Testament writers. While Isaiah 56:4–5 alluded to a spiritual offspring for eunuchs, the New Testament, with its deemphasis on physical land, more directly encouraged singleness for the Lord's sake (spiritual offspring). The writings of the unmarried Apostle Paul make this case.

Paul, Marriage, and the Order of Creation

The Apostle Paul's instruction concerning sex, however, does not contradict the instruction in the Old Testament. Some within the Corinthian church believed "It is good for a man not to touch a woman" (1 Cor 7:1). Paul then responded to their false theology of sex in 1 Corinthians 7:2: "On the contrary, because of sexual immorality, let each husband have his own wife, and let each woman have her own husband." Paul corrects their bad theology of sex (1 Cor 6:18–20) and continues teaching them a biblical sexual ethic in 1 Corinthians 7.

In 1 Corinthians 6:18–20, Paul explains *why* the Corinthians should not have sex with *prostitutes*. Two verses later he teaches "because of sexual immorality, let each husband have his own wife, and let each woman have her own husband" (1 Cor 7:2). Sexual immorality was a major issue in the Corinthian church and a reason why the Corinthians needed to marry and have sex with their own spouses.

The sexual ethic Paul continues to teach in 1 Corinthians 7 does not deviate from the Old Testament. Husbands and wives should serve one another sexually "so that Satan might not tempt you because of your lack of self-control" (1 Cor 7:5). Some in the church were teaching that believers should not have sex (1 Cor 7:1), which, according to Song 5:2–7, could contribute to immorality with prostitutes (1 Cor 6:18–20). Paul teaches that married couples should have regular sexual relations because of their lack of self-control. Just as the Song rebukes the wife for failing to have sex with her husband (Song 5:2–7), Paul in 1 Corinthians 7:1–7 teaches husbands and wives not to defraud one another.

Struggling with Purity? Then Marry

While this principle may seem logical, many "to be married" young men fail to connect their struggle with purity to marriage. Justin was a senior in college. He had a couple of girlfriends during his collegiate experience, but nothing ever came of those relationships. Reflecting upon his time in school and his failed relationships, Justin told me (Tim), "You know, I think I have the gift of singleness." I met with Justin privately and asked some more questions about his "gift of singleness." I asked him, "How are you doing with purity?" Justin confessed struggles with masturbation and a pornography addiction. He mentioned that he was doing better because of some accountability, but he was not completely free yet. I then told him directly, "You don't have the gift of singleness." Likewise, young man, if you struggle with masturbation, then you probably need to marry; you do not have the gift of singleness.

The apostle Paul encouraged "unmarried" Corinthians who struggle with self-control to marry. He wrote, "But I say to the unmarried and to the widows: It is good for them if they remain even as I am; but if they cannot exercise self-control, let them marry. For it is better to marry than to burn with passion" (1 Cor 7:8–9 NKJV). In this section, Paul gives specific details concerning a biblical sexual ethic. It is likely that the "unmarried" to whom Paul spoke were widowers. Paul regularly addresses men and women throughout 1 Corinthians 7, and widowers and widows fit that pattern. He tells them that if they cannot "exercise self-control," then "it is better to marry than to burn with passion." Paul's exhortation would apply to any unmarried person who struggles with self-control. You probably need to marry.

Joe had gone to church his entire life. He was a hard worker, accumulated a sizable savings account, and attended church sporadically. I met with Joe and asked him, "What about a wife?" He responded, "I can't get married." I asked him, "Why not?" He replied, "I just can't; I don't want to mess up some young lady's life." Several months later, Joe revealed that pornography had defeated him. He could not win the battle against porn, and he refused to bring a young woman into his moral mess. Joe was partly right; he needed to be free from pornography. A wife would not solve a man's moral mess, but she could help him have victory (Song 3:1–4; 1 Cor 7:2). And according to the Apostle Paul's instruction, Joe needs to marry.

Many Joes fill the seats of our churches. They need to marry! The apostle Paul says so. But before they marry, they need to be free from this dragon of pornography. We recommend reading *Finally Free* by Heath Lambert. It gives several practical guidelines that can liberate you from this enslaving dragon. The primary audience is men, but the principles Lambert communicates apply to men and women. A growing number of young women similarly struggle with pornography and sexual sin that will destroy the intimacy God designed for them and their husbands. The solution is the same. Confess your sin to an older/mature person of the same gender in your church, read *Finally Free* together, implement Lambert's grace strategies, be liberated by drawing close to the Lord, and then get married.

Pornography messes up a person's brain (male or female) so that in marriage, the person will likely struggle being intimate with his/her spouse without pornographic images in mind. Young ladies have asked me (Angela) if pornography is really that big of a deal, since after marriage, presumably, the young man can now have sex with his wife. Shouldn't that take care of the problem? The answer is usually no. Most young men are surprised to learn that after marriage they cannot have sex with their wives without thinking about pornographic images. I have explained, "He will be having sex with you, but he will be thinking about having sex with someone else." Eventually, these men become impotent—pornography and masturbation make them unable to have sex with their wives. Legions of men today are enslaved to pornography and can't even have sex with real women. Pornography's enslavement increasingly applies to women as well. Like men, many women cannot enjoy intimacy with a man because their minds and bodies have been rewired contrary to God's design. You don't want to be married to a person who is enslaved to pornography.

Joe humbled himself, confessed his sin, and pursued real accountability with me (Tim) and other older men in the church. He prioritized church attendance and his relationship with the Lord. Joe began gaining freedom from pornography, and the question became "When can I start looking for a wife." The answer to this question depends on the extent of the sexual sin. One young man needed significant sexual detox and waited two years. Trust the wisdom of your pastor and mentors concerning how long you should wait before seeking a spouse. A young person must be free from pornography for a season of time before pursuing a relationship. Get help, get free by drawing close to the Lord, then get married.

> A young person must be free from pornography for a season of time before pursuing a relationship.

Stay Unmarried Because of the "Present Distress"

The Apostle Paul later recommends that virgins remain as they are "because of the present distress" (1 Cor 7:26). He states, "I suppose therefore that this is good because of the present distress—that *it is* good for a man to remain as he is: Are you bound to a wife? Do not seek to be loosed. Are you loosed from a wife? Do not seek a wife. But even if you do marry, you have not sinned; and if a virgin marries, she has not sinned. Nevertheless such will have trouble in the flesh, but I would spare you" (1 Cor 7:26–28 NKJV). Just as the Lord told Jeremiah not to marry and have children because the Babylonians were going to annihilate nearly everyone, so also should unmarried singles reconsider marriage in light of present distresses. What, however, constitutes a present distress? Good question! If you live in a war zone, you should reconsider marrying because of the "present distress." Paul's "present distress," however, was not war. Gordon Fee captures the idea: "[Paul's] point would be: In light of the troubles we are already experiencing, who needs the additional burden of marriage as well."[3]

Many unmarried Christians remain unmarried for economic or political reasons. When I was in seminary, one semester was particularly challenging. I was unmarried at that time and interested in a young woman, but I quickly killed any thought of a relationship because my course load was much too difficult. One young man was a medical student who intentionally carved out several years of his life to devote to school. Forgoing marriage because of a "present distress" is simply a wisdom decision. It just might not be the "time" for you to marry. Some young people, however, never seem to be able to find the right time. They perpetually live in fear of some calamity around the corner. Lean on your parents, pastor, and mentors concerning whether your "present distress" should really prohibit you from pursuing a spouse.

Stay Unmarried and Please the Lord

Paul's primary argument in 1 Corinthians 7 is that the unmarried should remain unmarried so they can wholly concern themselves with the things of the Lord. Paul's teaching is not dissimilar from Isaiah 56:4–5 or Jesus' teaching in Matthew 19:12. Paul states, "But I want you to be without care. He who is unmarried cares for the things of the Lord—how he may please the Lord. But he who is married cares about the things of the world—how he may please his wife" (1 Cor 7:32–33 NKJV). Paul later explains that he wants the Corinthians to "serve the Lord without distraction." Paul's message is simple economics. You only have so many hours in a day; if you remain unmarried, you can devote more

---

3   Gordon D. Fee, *The First Epistle to the Corinthians* (rev. ed.; NICNT; Grand Rapids: Eerdmans, 2014), 364.

of those hours to pleasing the Lord instead of pleasing a spouse. Paul himself exemplified unencumbered service by laboring *night and day* in the ministry. One African young man acknowledged and clearly possessed the gift of singleness. He oversaw an orphanage, taught at a Bible college, assisted a church plant, and was working on his PhD. His choice was simple economics. He could not have done all those things if he had married.

Marriage is not eternal. Jesus taught that in the resurrection, nobody will be married—we will be "like angels in heaven" (Matt 22:30). In 1 Corinthians 7:7, Paul wrote, "Now I wish that all men were even like myself. But each one has his own gift from God, one has this, and another has that." Jesus, John the Baptist, and Paul had a special gift from God that was connected to the mission to which God had called them. We encourage you to consider a life of celibacy in unencumbered devotion to the Lord (1 Cor 7:32). By being unencumbered with the cares of this world, you will be able to focus on eternal concerns. Most people, however, have a different gift, a different calling of God—a calling to be married. And just as Paul says, if you want to marry, go ahead and marry (1 Cor 7:28).

Paul's instruction concerning singleness is not that complex. If God has given you this gift, embrace it, and use your freedom for God's glory. If you struggle with purity, you do not have the gift of singleness and you need to marry. Or, you may be focusing on a specific task (e.g., school) and plan to marry later. Trust the wisdom of your parents, pastors, and mentors, and then marry. Young man, you may need to stop drinking the cultural water and quit using the excuse of the "gift of singleness" to indulge in your own selfish lifestyle. Confess your sin, draw close to the Lord, and seek a spouse.

LOVING SUCCESSFULLY

Most Christians need to marry; it is the order of creation. Song of Songs teaches readers wisdom concerning how they can love successfully. As this book comes to an end, we want to leave you with a few concluding wisdom principles.

Oaths

As Angela and I wrote this book, we were torn about whether we should recommend that our readers swear an oath not to awaken love. Many within the purity culture from our generation made a mockery of pledges by encouraging the swearing of imprecise and ill-conceived (emotional) vows. As a result, the Christian subculture today despises and mocks pledges. The adjuration refrain in Song 2:7, 3:5, and 8:4, however, encourages the reader to *take an oath* not to awaken love. Those who despise purity oaths need to contend with Song of Song's specific admonition to take an oath. The problem is that Western culture has forgotten the significance of a vow.

If you are interested in taking a purity oath, consider its significance and the terms to which you bind yourself. God does not take delight in fools who promise things that they cannot deliver (Eccl 5:1–7). Do not make an emotional decision! Ecclesiastes 5:5 states, "It is better that you do not vow, than that you vow and not repay." Oaths are significant, binding arrangements. So don't take an oath . . . unless you truly plan to fulfill it.

Some contend that a believer today should no longer take an oath because in Matthew 5:33–37 Jesus said not to take oaths. But Jesus was not teaching the people to not take oaths; He was teaching them to always tell the truth, whether they swore an oath or not. In Matthew 23:16,

Jesus rebuked the hypocrites who said, "Whoever swears by the temple; it is nothing; but whoever swears by the gold of the temple is bound by the oath." Jesus corrected this broken culture in Matthew 5:33–37 and taught that a person's *yes* should be *yes* and his/her *no* should be *no*, whether that person swore an oath or not. Similarly, the Christian should be a person who always speaks the truth, whether he/she swears an oath or not.

When Jesus was placed under oath at His trial and the high priest said, "I put you under oath by the living God" (in a Greek construction very similar to the Hebrew oath construction of Song 2:7, 3:5, and 8:4), Jesus responded, "You have said it." Jesus stood mute, but when the high priest put Him under oath, He responded. In Matthew 5:33–37, Jesus taught that a person should *always* speak the truth, not only when that person crosses his/her heart and hopes to die.

Nevertheless, because our culture has lost the significance of oath taking and keeping, we hesitate to encourage readers to take purity oaths. Our culture needs to recapture the principles of truth, honesty, and oath keeping. Medieval knights and maidens, for example, understood the significance of oath taking; they would swear "troth," which was a solemn agreement of pledged faithfulness. In "The Franklin's Tale," one of Geoffrey Chaucer's *Canterbury Tales*, Dorigen swore troth to her husband, the knight Arveragus and, later, to the deceptive squire Aurelius. Dorigen found herself in a dilemma, being forced to break troth with one of these men. Taking the situation seriously and despairing for what she had done, she contemplated death rather than breaking her troth. When a Medieval person swore troth, that person kept it. If you decide to take an oath, you need to fulfill it.

Oaths should not be entered into rashly either. If you think you should swear an oath, wait a few days, and consider it again before you put yourself under oath. Consider the words from Ecclesiastes 5:2: "Do not be rash with your mouth and do not let your heart say something quickly before God." Do not swear an oath when you are on an emotional high. The purity movement of our generation erred when its leaders compelled oaths after emotional concerts or speaking engagements. Spend a few days considering the practical implications of taking an oath, and only swear an oath if you fully intend to take practical steps to ensure that you keep it.

Awakening Love

Whether you decide to take an oath or not, you need to purpose to let love remain sleeping. We are often asked, "What does that mean?" We have explained it numerous times, but many don't seem to understand the ramifications and consequences. The Christian subculture has been so affected by worldly media and romance novels (including secular ones) that the Song's definition of love often doesn't even register until after they have already messed up or find themselves disillusioned in marriage. We will share four guidelines that can help you at least not awaken love as much. These guidelines are an oversimplification! The Song of Songs as a whole defines what it means to awaken love. Nevertheless, here are four guidelines to help you, we hope, start walking on the correct path.

First, if you are in a stage of life when it would be unwise (or impossible) to marry (e.g., you are still in high school), remain single and learn how to shut down love. Do not be a victim to your emotions or feelings. You can intentionally cultivate love, and you can also intentionally shut it down. Have a lot of friends and have fun. When feelings for a specific person arise within you, speak truth to yourself and shut them down. Create distance between yourself and that person. Submit to your parents' and mentors' counsel concerning how much you should contact each other, even through electronic media. It is not the time for love. Learning to kill those feelings now can help you avoid an unbiblical relationship or deliver you from a bad relationship in the future.

Second, establish healthy physical boundaries for your relationships in advance. Statistics reveal that almost all Christian youth kiss before marriage. The purity movement of our generation failed to equip young people with the tools necessary to fulfill their purity oaths. Kissing awakens love, so let your first kiss be at the altar. (If you are nervous about kissing your lover for the first time in front of a bunch of people, fine—practice a little the *day* before.) As the Song of Songs teaches, oral union prepares a couple for sexual union. Purpose not to transgress your physical boundaries, and get accountability from your parents, pastor, and godly mentors.

Third, establish a community who can hold you accountable and guide you through your dating years. Your love life *should* affect others; bring those closest to you into the conversation now. Your parents should be part of that conversation. We recognize that your parents may not be spiritually qualified to guide you. If that's the case, become a member of a church that preaches the Bible, place yourself under the authority of that church, and seek godly mentors who can hold you accountable and give you wisdom during this time of your life.

Finally, be resolved. The Christian life is not something that you can "try." You have to go all in and walk by faith. You can't try God's instruction concerning sexuality either. Don't even entertain physical thoughts or desires for your boyfriend/girlfriend. Discipline your mind to shut those thoughts down. Just as you build muscle at the gym, you will need to train your affections to resist desires for physical and emotional affection. You can follow the first three guidelines flawlessly but still fail. If you *want* to have sex, you will likely find a way. The world's allurements and enticements are tasty, "Stolen waters are sweet, and food eaten in secret is pleasant" (Prov 9:17). Guys like Solomon are alluring, and those harem girls are enticing. But listen to the advice of the king who had everything he ever wanted but was rejected by the one he truly desired. Resolve yourself not to *try* God's way but to *commit* to it.

STOP WAITING FOR LOVE

The time for you to marry may be now. Go get married. It isn't as complicated as you think. If you're a guy, get a job (or two); save money for a ring; talk to your pastor, parent, or godly mentor; and marry a good girl who fears the Lord. Yes, this is an oversimplification, but you need to make a move.

Alex and Hannah had attended church together for five years. They had a group of friends that regularly fellowshipped together and served in various ministries at church. Hannah was interested in Alex, but he never seemed to make a move. Then one day when Hannah's parents were in town, Alex met with Hannah's father and asked for her hand in marriage. Hannah's dad remarked, "You haven't even dated my daughter!" Alex replied, "I've seen her serve others and minister in church for the last five years. I know she is a woman who fears the Lord, and I'd like to marry her." They married six months later. Alex and Hannah's story is certainly unique, but it exemplifies a young man's resolve to not awaken love until the correct time. When he was ready for marriage, he made his move and married the girl. He was convinced that the best way to determine if a young woman feared the Lord would be through her interactions in the local church. We need a few more Alex's in this world.

Max was a faithful young man, had a solid job, and was ready to marry. I met with him over lunch and asked him if he had his eye on someone. He said he had pursued a couple of girls, but they had both turned him down. He wasn't a fan of dating, and the young ladies in whom he had expressed interest did not reciprocate. If you, like Max, try what Alex tried, you may get rejected. I advised Max, "You may just have to date." If you're a guy and you get turned down, ask someone else. Don't compromise your morals; only ask girls who fear the Lord. But if you get rejected, ask another girl who fears the Lord. Finding a spouse is a wisdom decision, and if one girl rejects you, don't pine away after her, ask her girlfriend.

Enlist your parents, pastor, or godly mentors to help you find a spouse. Kim was in her mid-20s and still single. She wanted to marry, but no guys were pursuing her. She talked to a couple godly mentors at church and informed them of her desire to marry. She told them, "If you know of a godly young man, I would be happy to go out on a date and get to know him." Matt, similarly, was ready to marry. He talked to a couple of godly mentors at church and asked if they could recommend a young woman. A year later, Matt and Kim were married.

Many unmarried Christians have this false idea that God will personally arrange the most spontaneous and impossible encounter that will bring them together with their future spouse. God does not usually work that way. Usually, God works through the authorities whom He has sovereignly placed over a young person to guide and direct him/her on the correct path. If you refuse to ask the authorities in your life or submit to them, you may struggle finding a spouse. Involve the authorities God has placed over you, listen to them, and get married.

The assertive nature of the Song of Songs wife has caused us to encourage young women to take a more active role in finding a husband. We don't see anything in the Bible that should discourage you from initiating appropriate interest in a young man. The scenario in Ruth 3 was definitely not "normal," but Naomi (the "parent") instructed Ruth to take the initiative and propose to Boaz! Wow! And she is the model Proverbs 31 woman (Prov 12:4; 31:10; Ruth 3:11)! In our culture, you would likely have greater success speaking through your parents or a godly mentor who can function as a liaison between you and a young man. They can find out for you if the interest is mutual. If it isn't, then ask them to inquire about another young man. Some guys today really just need a kick in the pants to go after a girl. You can be that kick.

Whatever situation you find yourself in, stop waiting for love. Write your own story. Ours was bumpy. We wish several things had gone differently. God, however, is the God who loves to create beauty from ashes. He has done that for us, and we know that He can do it for you too. If you are of marriageable age, make finding a spouse a priority. Get your own life in order, get plugged into a local church, and get married.

DISCUSSION QUESTIONS:

1. What was the Old Testament's assumption for marriage and singleness?

2. Who are some unique biblical examples of living single?

3. Why should a single person consider a life of celibacy?

4. Why was marriage such a big deal in the context of 1 Corinthians 6 and 7?

5. Discuss the connection between the struggle with sexual self-control and marrying.

6. Why is pornography so destructive to a person's mind?

7. Discuss the importance and wisdom of gaining and sustaining victory over pornography before pursuing a relationship.

8. What are some legitimate and illegitimate "present distresses" that might keep someone from pursuing marriage?

9. Discuss the significance of oath taking. Why should someone take an oath? Why shouldn't he/she take an oath?

10. Explain Jesus' instruction concerning oaths in Matthew 5.

11. What are the four guidelines to help keep love sleeping until the appropriate time?

12. Discuss some practical ways a person can train his/her affections toward purity.

APPENDIX: THE SONG OF SONGS

Students and Bible study attendees requested Tim's translation from the Hebrew text of the Song of Songs. For this reason, we have included it below. We encourage you to consult multiple translations when studying the Song of Songs. Our favorite translations are the NKJV and ESV, but Tim agreed with the NJPS (New Jewish Publication Society) translation frequently while translating the Song of Songs. We hope Tim's translation below can help you study the Song of Songs for yourself.

¹The Song of Songs, which is Solomon's

Stanza 1

Wife

²Let him kiss me with the kisses of his mouth,
 for your caresses are better than wine.
³The scent of your oils is good;
 oil poured forth is your name,
  therefore virgins love you.
⁴Draw me after you, let us run!
 The king has brought me into his chambers.
  Let us be glad and rejoice in you!
  Let us exult in your caresses more than wine.
Rightly do they love you.

Stanza 2

Wife

⁵I am black and lovely, daughters of Jerusalem;
 like the tents of Kedar, like the curtains of Solomon.
⁶Do not look on me because I am black,
 because the sun gazed upon me.
The brothers of my mother were angry with me.
They made me keeper of the vineyards;
 my vineyard which is mine I have not kept.

[7]*Tell me, one whom my soul loves,*
where do you graze;
where you gather at noon?
Because why should I be like one who veils herself
alongside the flocks of your companions?

Husband

[8]*If you do not know, O most beautiful among women,*
follow the tracks of the flock,
and feed your little lambs by the tents of the shepherds.
[9]*I have likened you, my sweetheart,*
to my mare among the chariots of Pharaoh.
[10] *Your cheeks are lovely with jewels;*
your neck with necklaces.
[11]*Let us make ornaments of gold for you,*
with studs of silver.

Wife

[12]*While the king was around his table,*
my spikenard gave off its scent.
[13]*A sachet of myrrh is my lover to me;*
he spends the night between my breasts.
[14]*A cluster of henna blossoms is my lover to me,*
in the vineyards of En Gedi.

Husband

[1:15]*Look at you! Beautiful, my sweetheart.*
Look at you! Beautiful, your eyes are doves.

Wife

[16]*Look at you! Handsome! Surely, pleasant.*
Surely, our couch is green.
[17]*The beams of our houses are cedar; our rafter is firs.*

Wife

[2:1]*I am a meadow flower of Sharon,*
a lily of the valleys.
[2]*Like a lily among the thorns,*
so is my sweetheart among the daughters.
[3]*Like an apple tree among the trees of the forest,*
so is my lover among the sons;
in his shade I desired passionately,
and his fruit is sweet to my palate.
[4]*He brought me to the house of wine,*
and his banner over me is love.

⁵*Sustain me with raisin cakes;*
refresh me with apples,
because I am lovesick.
⁶*His left arm is under my head,*
and his right arm embraces me.
⁷*I put you under oath, O daughters of Jerusalem,*
by the gazelles or by the does of the field;
do not stir up; do not even awaken love,
until it pleases.

Stanza 3

Wife

⁸*The voice of my lover. Look! He comes!*
Leaping upon the mountains; skipping upon the hills.
⁹*My lover is like a gazelle or a young stag.*
Behold, he is standing behind our wall;
looking from the window;
gazing through the lattice.
¹⁰*My lover answered and said to me,*
"Raise yourself, my sweetheart,
my beautiful, and take yourself.
¹¹*Indeed, look! The winter has passed;*
the rain has passed, and it is gone.
¹²*The blossoms have appeared in the land;*
the time of singing has come,
and the sound of the turtledove is heard in our land.
¹³*The fig tree has ripened its figs,*
and the vines have blossomed;
they give a scent.
Raise yourself, my sweetheart,
my beautiful, and take yourself!"

Husband

¹⁴*My dove in the clefts of the rock, in the secret place of the cliff;*
show me your face; let me hear your voice;
for your voice is pleasant, and your appearance is lovely.

Wife

¹⁵*Catch us the jackals,*
the little jackals that ruin vineyards,
for our vineyard is in bloom.
¹⁶*My lover is mine, and I am his;*
the one who grazes among the lilies.
¹⁷*Until the day breathes its last and the shadows flee away;*
Turn! Liken yourself, my lover, to a gazelle or a young stag
upon the divided mountains.

Wife

³:¹*Upon my bed in the night,*
I sought the one whom my soul loves;
I sought him, but I did not find him.
²*I will rise now, and I will go about the city,*
in the streets and in the open squares.
I sought the one whom my soul loves;
I sought him, but I did not find him.
³*The watchmen found me, the ones who go around the city.*
"Have you seen the one whom my soul loves?"
⁴*Shortly after I passed by them,*
then I found the one whom my soul loves;
I seized him, and I would not release him
until I brought him to the house of my mother,
to the bedroom of the one who conceived me.

Stanza 4

Wife

⁶*Who is this coming up from the wilderness?*
Like pillars of smoke, a fragrant cloud of myrrh and frankincense
with all the merchant's fragrant powders.
⁷*Look! It is Solomon's couch!*
Sixty valiant men surround it, from the warriors of Israel.
⁸*All of them hold swords, being well-trained in war;*
each man has his sword on his thigh,
because of terror in the night.
⁹*King Solomon made for himself a palanquin*
from the wood of Lebanon.
¹⁰*Its pillars were made of silver, its back of gold,*
its seat of purple, its interior is inlaid with love
by the daughters of Jerusalem.
¹¹*Go out, daughters of Zion, and see King Solomon*
with the crown which his mother crowned him
on the day of his wedding
and on the day of the gladness of his heart

Husband

⁴:¹*Look at you, beautiful! My sweetheart!*
Look at you, beautiful! Your eyes are doves.
²*Your teeth are like a flock of shorn sheep,*
which have come up from the washing;
every one of them bears twins,
and there is not one missing.

³Like a strand of scarlet are your lips,
and your mouth is lovely;
like a slice of a pomegranate
is your open mouth behind your veil.
⁴Your neck is like a tower of David, built for an armory,
on which hang a thousand shields,
all of the shields of mighty men.
⁵Your two breasts are like two fawns;
twins of a gazelle,
who graze among the lilies.
⁶Until the day breathes, and the shadows flee away,
I will go, myself,
to the mountain of myrrh and to the hill of frankincense.
⁷All of you is beautiful, my sweetheart;
and there is no blemish in you.

Husband

⁸Come with me from Lebanon, spouse, with me from Lebanon;
descend from the top of Amana,
from the top of Senir and Hermon,
from the lairs of the lions,
from the mountains of the leopards.
⁹You have captivated my heart, my sister, spouse;
you have captivated my heart with one of your eyes,
with one link of your necklace.
¹⁰How beautiful are your caresses, my sister, spouse;
how much better than wine are your caresses,
and the scent of your perfumes
are better than all spices.
¹¹Your lips drip honeycomb, spouse;
honey and milk are under your tongue,
and the scent of your garments
are like the scent of frankincense.
¹²A garden enclosed, my sister, spouse;
a spring bolted shut, a sealed fountain.
¹³Your plants are a garden of pomegranates
with pleasant fruits, henna with nard.
¹⁴Spikenard and saffron, calamus and cinnamon,
with all the trees of frankincense,
myrrh and aromatic aloes, with all the best spices.
¹⁵A fountain of gardens, a well of living waters,
and streams from Lebanon.

Wife

¹⁶*Awake, north wind! And come, south wind!*
Blow upon my garden; let its spices flow.
May my lover come into his garden,
    and may he eat its pleasant fruits.

Husband

⁵:¹*I have come into my garden, my sister, spouse;*
I have gathered my myrrh with my spice;
I have eaten my honeycomb with my honey;
I have drunk my wine with my milk.

The Lord

Eat, friends; drink and be drunk, lovers!

Stanza 5

Wife

²*I was sleeping, but my heart stirred,*
 the sound of my lover, knocking,
 "Open for me, my sister, my sweetheart,
   my dove, my perfect one;
 because my head is filled with dew,
   my locks with the droplets of the night.
³*I have taken off my tunic; how can I put it on?*
 I have washed my feet; how can I defile them?
⁴*My lover sent his hand from the hole,*
 and my feelings roared concerning him.
⁵*I, myself, arose to open for my lover;*
 my hands dripped myrrh,
 my fingers with myrrh passing over,
   on the handles of the lock.
⁶*I, myself, opened for my lover,*
 but my lover had gone and turned away;
   my soul despaired when he departed;
 I sought him, but I could not find him;
 I called for him, but he did not answer.
⁷*The guards found me, the ones who go about in the city;*
 they struck me; they bruised me;
 they took away my veil from upon me,
   the ones who guard the wall.
⁸*I charge you, daughters of Jerusalem, if you find my lover;*
 what should you tell him? I am sick with love.

Daughters of Jerusalem

[9]How is your lover better than another lover,
   most beautiful among women?
How is your lover better than another lover,
   that you should charge us?

Wife

[10]My lover is dazzling and ruddy, standing out from a crowd.
[11]His head is fine gold; his hair is curly, dark as a raven.
[12]His eyes are like doves by streams of water,
   bathed with milk and fitly set.
[13]His cheeks are like a garden bed of spices,
      growing forth scents;
   his lips are lilies, dripping liquid myrrh.
[14]His hands are rods of gold, fitly set with Tarshish stones;
   his abdomen is carved ivory, inlaid with sapphires.
[15]His legs are pillars of marble,
      established on bases of fine gold.
   His appearance is like Lebanon, chosen like the cedars.
[16]His palate is sweet, and all of him is desirable.
   This is my lover, and this is my friend,
      daughters of Jerusalem.

Daughters of Jerusalem

[6:1]Where has your lover gone, most beautiful among women?
   Where has your lover turned, then we will seek him with you?

Wife

[2]My lover went down to his garden, to the garden bed of spices,
   to graze among the gardens, and to gather lilies.
[3]I am my lover's, and my lover is mine,
   the one who grazes among the lillies.

Stanza 6

Husband

[4]You are beautiful, my sweetheart, like Tirzah;
   lovely like Jerusalem, terrifying like banners.
[5]Turn your eyes away from me,
   because they have made me defiant;
   your hair is like a flock of goats, which move down Gilead.
[6]Your teeth are like a flock of ewe lambs,
   which have come up from the washing;
      all of them are bearing twins,
      and there are none missing among them.

7*Like a slice of a pomegranate is your open mouth*
behind your veil.
8*Sixty are they—queens, and eighty concubines,*
and virgins—innumerable.
9*She is unique—my dove, my perfect one;*
she is unique to her mother,
she is the pure one to the one who bore her;
the daughters saw her and blessed her;
queens and concubines, and they praised her.
10*Who is this? The one who looks down like the dawn,*
beautiful like the moon, pure like the sun,
terrifying like banners.

Husband

11 *To the garden of nuts I went down,*
to see the vegetation of the valley,
to see if the vines have sprouted,
if the pomegranates have bloomed.

Wife

12 *I did not know what happened;*
my soul put me in the chariots of my noble people.

Husband

13 *Return! Return! Shulamite!*
Return! Return! So that we may look at you.

Wife

What would you see in the Shulamite,
like the dance of the two camps?

Husband

7:1*How beautiful are your feet in sandals, princely daughter;*
the curves of your thighs are like jewels,
the work of a master craftsman.
2*Your navel is a round bowl, may it never lack spiced wine;*
your belly is a heap of wheat, hedged about with lillies.
3*Your two breasts are like two fawns, twins of a gazelle.*
4*Your neck is like an ivory tower;*
your eyes like pools in Heshbon,
by the gate of Bath Rabbim;
your nose is like the tower of Lebanon,
looking toward Damascus.

⁵Your head upon you is like Carmel,
*   and the hair of your head is like purple;*
*   a king is captivated by your locks.*
⁶How beautiful! How pleasant! O love, with your pleasures!
⁷This! Your stature is like a palm tree,
*   and your breasts, clusters of grapes.*
⁸I say, let me ascend the palm tree, taking hold of its branches.
*   Now, let your breasts be like the clusters of the vine,*
*   and the scent of your breath like apples.*
⁹And your palate like the best wine.

Wife

Flowing to my lover smoothly,
*   gliding between the lips of sleepers.*
¹⁰I am my lover's; and over me is his desire.

Wife

¹¹Come, my lover, let us go out to the field;
*   let us spend the night in the villages!*
¹²Let us rise early to the vineyards;
*   let us see if the vine has sprouted,*
*   the buds of the vine have opened,*
*   the pomegranates have bloomed;*
*   then/there I will give you my love.*
¹³The mandrakes give a scent,
*   and over our doors are all choice fruits.*
*   New fruits! Also, old ones!*
*   I have stored up for you, my lover.*
⁸:¹If only you were like a brother to me,
*   one who sucked upon the breasts of my mother;*
I would find you outside; I would kiss you!
*   They would not despise me.*
²I would lead you; I would bring you,
*   to the house of my mother; she taught me.*
I would make you drink from the spiced wine;
*   from the sweet wine of my pomegranate.*
³His left hand is under my head,
*   and his right hand embraces me.*
⁴I put you under oath, O daughters of Jerusalem;
*   why would you stir up, why would you even awaken love,*
*   until it pleases.*

Stanza 7

Wife

⁵Who is this coming up from the wilderness,
  leaning upon her lover?
Under the apple tree I awakened you;
  there your mother conceived you;
  there she conceived and gave birth to you.

Wife

⁶Set me as a seal upon your heart, as a seal upon your arm;
  because love is as strong as death;
  jealousy is hard like the grave;
              its flames are flames of fire, the flame of the Lord.
⁷Many waters are not able to extinguish love,
  and rivers cannot flood over it.
If a man would give all the wealth of his house for love,
  they would despise him for it.

Others

⁸We have a little sister, but she has no breasts.
  What should we do for our sister
              in the day when she is spoken for?
⁹If she is a wall, we will build upon her a battlement of silver;
  if she is a door, we will fortify her with cedar planks.

Woman

¹⁰I am a wall, and my breasts are like towers.
  Then I became in his eyes like one who finds peace.

Wife

¹¹Solomon had a vineyard in Baal Hamon;
  he leased the vineyard to keepers;
              a man would bring for its fruit a thousand silvers.
¹²My vineyard, which is mine, is before me.
  The thousand to you, Solomon,
              and two hundred to the keepers of its fruit.

Man

¹³The one who dwells in the gardens,
  companions are listening for your voice.
              Let me hear it!

Wife

¹⁴Flee, my lover, and liken yourself to a gazelle or a young stag
  on the mountains of spices.

SCRIPTURE INDEX

Genesis
1:31 57
2:18 . . . . 141, 145
2:24 . . . . 101, 141
2:25 189
3:7 50
3:16 . . . . 172, 183,
  185–86, 200
4:7 186
12:11 61
12:14 61
18:25 61
27:26 88
29:17 61
31:28 88
39:6 62
39:7 129
41:4 62
41:18 62

Exodus
15 91–92
32 92

Leviticus
11–15 65
15:19–24 158
21:16–21 62
22 62

Numbers
1:52 175
2:2 175

2:10 104
2:17 104
2:18 175
2:25 . . . . 104, 175
5 210

Deuteronomy
5–6 205
5:6–21 22
6:4 219
6:4–5 35
6:5 85–86
6:6–9 18
7:3–4 80
22:13–30 22
24:1–5 22
25:5–10 53
25:5–12 22

Judges
14:2 80
15:4 113
19 128

Ruth
2 . . . . 73, 103
2:18 66
3:3–5 73
3:11 . . . . 232, 254
4:1 54
4:5 53
4:6 53

1 Kings

1:3 39
1:3–4. 62
11:1–3. 41
11:3 174
11:9–25 41

1 Samuel

16:12 . . . . 62, 66
17:42. . . . . 62, 66
25:3 62

2 Samuel

6:14–26 92
13:1 62
14:25. 62
14:33. 88

Nehemiah

4:3 113

Esther

2:12–13 229
2:14. 229

Job

28 205

Psalms

1 . . . . 86, 213
2:12. 88
14:2–3 219
42:1. 85–86
51. 35
63:10. 113
139:2. 23

Proverbs

1–2 205
1:6 16
1:7 24
1:8 . . . . 18, 30
1:10 30
1:15 30
1:20–33 205
1:31 119
2 205
2:1 30
2:5 143
2:16–20 20
3:1 30
3:11–12. 205
3:11 30
3:21. 30
5 134
5–7 126–27
5:1–20. 20
5:6 150
5:18–23 162
5:19 . . . . 127, 162
5:19–20 133
5:20 . . . . 127, 162, 190
5:21. 164
6:20–35. 20
6:25 150
6:26 127
7 . . . . 89, 127–28, 191
7:4 162
7:5 162
7:5–27. . . . . 20, 161
7:8 128
7:9 128
7:10. 128
7:11 128

7:12. 128
7:13. . . . . 89, 99, 128,
   132
7:15. . . . . 128, 191
7:17. 128
7:18. 191
7:21. 99
7:22–23 128
7:26 128
8:22–24. 47
9:13–18 20
9:17. 252
10:4 48
12:4. 254
14:1 190
18:22 145
31. . . . . 127–28, 131,
   181, 196, 237, 254
31:10 . . . . 71, 231, 254
31:10–17 71
31:10–31 . . . . 43, 227
31:16 71
31:16–17 71
31:30. . . . . 64, 232

Ecclesiastes

2:1–11. 43
2:8 . . . . 42, 230
2:10. . . . . 42, 229
2:24 42
2:24–25. 65
2:24–26. 43
3:10–15 48
3:11 57
3:13. . . . . 18, 42
4:9–12. 220
6:12. 48
5:2 250

5:1–7 248
5:5 248
5:19 42
7:20 22
7:23–25 230
7:28 . . . . 131, 227, 231
7:29 43
8:17. 48
9:9 42
10:8–10 204
10:11 204
11:5–6 48
11:7–12:7. 64
11:9 106
11:9–10. 106
12:13 . . . . 48, 106

Song of Solomon

1:1. 40–41
1:1–2:7. 26
1:2 . . . . 32, 33, 49,
   51, 89, 130, 189, 195
1:2–4. . . . . 24, 32–33,
   39, 218
1:3 . . . . 17, 37–38,
   47, 51, 168, 203, 206
1:4 . . . . 32, 37, 54,
   89
1:5 . . . . 17, 30, 37,
   40–42, 60, 104
1:5–6. . . . . 39, 67, 118
1:5–11. . . . . 25, 69, 72
1:5–2:7 . . . . 97, 102, 104,
   107, 130, 137
1:6 . . . . 31, 43,
   67–68, 232–33
1:7 . . . . 68, 105, 195,
   235

1:7–8. . . . . 37, 39

1:8–9. 68

1:9 . . . . 39, 69, 74

1:10–11 72

1:11 70

1:12 37

1:12–14. . . . . 39, 98, 101, 118

1:12—2:6 . . . . 26, 98

1:13–14. . . . . 34, 41, 130

1:13 99

1:14 . . . . 99–100, 182

1:15 100

1:15–16. 101

1:16 130

1:16–17. 100

1:17 . . . . 100–101, 103

2:1 103

2:1–2. 105

2:1–6. 102

2:3 . . . . 103, 130, 187

2:3–5 98

2:4 . . . . 103, 183–85, 187

2:4–5 103

2:5 39

2:6 98

2:7 . . . . 10, 11, 17, 20, 30, 37, 81, 84, 86–87, 90, 104, 109, 248–49

2:8 . . . . 111, 120, 130, 196

2:8–9 . . . . 37, 110

2:8–13. 111–112

2:8–14. . . . . 114, 118, 235

2:8–15. 38

2:8–17. . . . . 16, 109–110, 125–26, 135

2:8—3:5 . . . . 26, 110–11, 125, 135, 137

2:9 130

2:9–14. 111

2:10–13 . . . . 109, 112

2:10. . . . . 112, 130

2:13. . . . . 109, 112

2:14. 112

2:15. . . . . 42, 109, 113–14, 118, 135, 138, 173, 187, 233, 235

2:16–17 120

2:17. . . . . 37, 120, 130, 135

3:1 . . . . 128, 130, 135

3:1–3. 128

3:1–4. . . . . 26, 39, 127–30, 134–35, 159, 161, 171, 243

3:2 128

3:4 . . . . 31, 128, 132, 135

3:3 . . . . 132, 159

3:4 . . . . 132, 135

3:5 . . . . 10, 11, 17, 20, 30, 37, 81, 84, 86–87, 90, 248–49

3:6 . . . . 179, 207

3:6–11 . . . . 36, 144–46, 179, 208–9, 227

3:6—5:1 . . . . 26, 130, 141, 143, 148, 155

3:7 40–41

3:7–8 . . . . 180, 207

3:7–10 42

3:9 40–41

3:9–10 . . . . 180, 207

3:10. . . . . 37, 146, 180

3:11 . . . . 31, 40–43, 146–47, 180, 197, 208

4 . . . . 162, 184, 197–98

4:1 196

4:1–5. 197

4:1–7. . . . . 39, 64, 129, 148–50, 173

4:3 66

4:5 151

4:6 197

4:7 . . . . 62, 149

4:8 . . . . 152, 176

4:8–11 152

4:9 . . . . 74, 153, 173–74, 176

4:9–11 152

4:10 . . . . 39, 153

4:11 153

4:12. 153

4:12–5:1 . . . . 39, 153, 182

4:16 154

5 163–64

5:1 . . . . 21, 38, 39, 82, 154, 172, 193

5:2 . . . . 158, 171–73, 196, 200

5:2–3 . . . . 172, 176, 190

5:2–5 38

5:2–7 . . . . 161–62, 172–73, 242

5:2–8 158

5:2–6:3 . . . . 26, 157

5:2–7:10 . . . . 27, 185

5:2–8:3 . . . . 171, 186, 190

5:3 . . . . 27, 158–60, 166–67, 186

5:4 163–65

5:4–6 161

5:5–6 173

5:6 . . . . 161, 173

5:7 159–60

5:8 . . . . 17, 37, 165

5:8–16. 165

5:9–16. 172

5:9 37

5:10 . . . . 66, 166

5:10–16 . . . . 38, 168, 180

5:11–15. 166

5:12. 39

5:16 . . . . 17, 37, 39, 90, 166, 168

6 175

6:1 . . . . 37, 167–68

6:2 . . . . 39, 182

6:4 . . . . 172, 175, 183

6:4–7 . . . . 173, 184

6:4–9 39

6:4–10. . . . . 104, 172–74, 178–79

6:4–13. 183

6:4–7:10 . . . . 173, 178

6:5 . . . . 173–74, 176–77

6:8 209

6:8–9 180

6:8–10. . . . . 173, 177, 179–80, 184, 196, 209

6:9 . . . . 31, 172

6:9–10. 172

6:10 . . . . 39, 60, 175, 179–80, 183, 209

6:11. 182

6:11–12. 173

6:11–13. 182

6:12. 182–83

6:13. . . . . 39, 183

7 . . . . 186, 195, 198

7:1 91
7:1–6. . . . . 39, 65, 129, 183–84
7:1–7. 197
7:1–9. 91
7:2 65
7:8 . . . . 184, 197
7:9 90
7:9–10. 39
7:10. . . . . 183–84, 186–87, 189
7:11–13 . . . . 39, 129, 189, 191–92, 197
7:11–8:3 . . . . 27, 186, 189
7:11–8:5 179
7:12. 189
7:13. . . . . 192, 229
8 . . . . 198, 209
8:1 . . . . 89, 198
8:1–2. . . . . 31, 151, 195, 197–98
8:1–3. 198
8:2 . . . . 18, 50, 89, 190, 195, 198–99, 208
8:4. . . . . 10, 11, 17, 20, 30, 37, 81, 84, 86–87, 90, 200, 209, 248–49
8:5 . . . . 31, 105, 145, 179–80, 190, 195, 207–9, 227
8:5–6 38
8:5–10. . . . . 207, 209
8:5–14. . . . . 27, 203, 207, 214
8:6 218
8:6–7 . . . . 84, 107, 209
8:7 212
8:8 219
8:8–9 218–19

8:8–10. 40
8:9 . . . . 40, 219
8:10 . . . . 39, 40, 104, 175, 183–85, 187, 222, 227, 235
8:10–12 39
8:11. . . . . 42–43, 227, 229
8:11–12. . . . . 36, 40–41, 119, 227, 232–33
8:11–14. 31
8:12. . . . . 41–43, 227, 229, 231, 233
8:13. . . . . 31, 203, 235–36
8:13–14 . . . . 36, 235
8:14 . . . . 37, 41, 129, 236

Isaiah

6:5 23
7:14. 17
13:9. 22
13:11–12 22
37:22. . . . . 175, 184, 222
40:13–14 23
40:26–28. 23
40:27–31 61
40:28 61
42:5 23
42:13. 210
47:1. . . . . 175, 184, 223
50:4–11 . . . . 126, 135, 205, 241
52:1. . . . . 175, 223
52:1–2. 184
53 241
56:4–5 . . . . 240–41, 246
56:5 240

59:17 210
60 . . . . 57, 75

Jeremiah
16:1–4 240
31:13 92

Lamentations
5:18 113

Ezekiel
8:3 210
13:4 113
23:2–3 93

Habakkuk
1:7 175

Zechariah
14:9 210

Matthew
5:27–28 35
5:33–37 248–49
14:6 92
18:21–35 . . . . 116, 118
19:1–12 22
19:4–6 178
19:10 141
19:12 . . . . 240, 246
22:30 247
22:37–38 114
22:37–40 35
23:16 248
25:1–13 145

Mark
6:22 92
12:31 84

John
3:36 . . . . 23, 116
9:2–3 62

Romans
3:23 121
3:24–25 23
5:1 115
8:1–11 23
12:1 23
12:2 32
12:1–2 27
13:12–14 35
16:16 88

1 Corinthians
2:14 24
6:18–20 242
7 . . . . 163, 241–43, 246
7:1 241–42
7:1–7 242
7:2 241–43
7:2–5 158
7:5 . . . . 163, 242
7:7 . . . . 22, 247
7:8 241
7:8–9 243
7:11 241
7:20 241
7:24 241
7:26 245
7:26–28 245
7:28 247
7:32 247
7:32–33 246
7:32–35 . . . . 18, 22
7:40 241

9:5 241
13. 84
14:35. 234
16:20. 88

2 Corinthians
6:14 117
10:5 32
13:12 88

Galatians
3:26–28. 186
5:16 36
6:7 119

Ephesians
5:22–23. 186
5:25 . . . . 53, 206, 233
5:28–33. 33

Colossians
3:2 12
3:5 . . . . 12, 50
3:5–6 88
3:5–15. 90
3:12. 12

1 Thessalonians
5:26 88

1 Timothy
4:8. 167
5:2 87

2 Timothy
3:16–17 31
3:17. 33

Titus
2 . . . . 181, 196
2:3–4 199
2:4 . . . . 30, 235

Hebrews
5:8 241
13:4. 82

James
1:2–8. 205
1:13–15. 35
2 214
2:19. 210
4:1–10 88
4:4. 24

1 Peter
3:3–4 58
3:15. 135

1 John
1:9 35
4:19 163
5:3 85

www.ingramcontent.com/pod-product-compliance
Lightning Source LLC
Chambersburg PA
CBHW021713120626
46545CB00004B/1539